Giovanni Gentile and the State of Contemporary Constructivism

A Study of Actual Idealist Moral Theory

James Wakefield

imprint-academic.com

Copyright © James Wakefield, 2015

The moral rights of the authors have been asserted.
No part of this publication may be reproduced in any form
without permission, except for the quotation of brief passages
in criticism and discussion.

Published in the UK by
Imprint Academic, PO Box 200, Exeter EX5 5YX, UK

Distributed in the USA by
Ingram Book Company,
One Ingram Blvd., La Vergne, TN 37086, USA

ISBN 9781845407643

A CIP catalogue record for this book is available from the
British Library and US Library of Congress

Contents

Acknowledgements and List of Diagrams	vi
Summary	viii
Chapter 1. Introduction	1
1. Defining 'constructivism'	2
2. Introducing Giovanni Gentile	11
2i. The death of the author	14
2ii. Gentile criticism since his assassination	17
3. A new approach to Gentile	22
4. The argument in outline	25

Part I. Components of Actual Idealism

Chapter 2. The Pure Act of Construction	29
1. On method	29
2. Toward *pensiero pensante*, or 'the thought that thinks itself'	34
2i. The Cogito Justification	37
2ii. The Logical Priority Justification	39
3. The abstract/concrete division	40
4. Truth in the method of immanence	43
4i. The will and truth	44
4ii. The Gentilian will: being and Being There	46
4iii. The value of truth and its construction	50
5. Coherence and construction	52
6. Actual idealism's positivity and the unknown	58
7. Conclusion	62
Chapter 3. The Priority of the *Socius*	63
1. Actual idealism and the person	64
1i. The Solipsist Objection	64
1ii. The Conditionality Objection	67
1iii. Persons and personalism	69
2. Socialising the pure act	71
2i. The internal society and the conscience	73
2ii. The internal dialogue	75

3. Constructing the universal will	78
3i. Internality and indeterminacy	80
3ii. A schematic for the socius	82
4. Politicising the internal society	84
4i. Internal and external dialogues	85
4ii. The state and the universal will	87
5. Conclusion	90
Chapter 4. The Total Ethical State	92
1. Gentile on the state in *Diritto* and *Introduzione*	93
2. Gentile on Hegel's ethical state	96
3. Gentile's mature state	104
4. 'The real shipwreck of actualism': some standard objections	108
5. The ethical state of mind	114
6. Conclusion	115

Part II. Gentilean Constructivism in Moral Theory

Chapter 5. Gentile contra Kant on Practical Reason	119
1. Reason in actual idealism	120
1i. The internal dialogue re-visited	123
1ii. Universality and objectivity	125
1iii. The heart of reason	128
1iv. The IDP in outline	130
2. Kant's categorical imperative	131
3. The Universal Law Formula	134
3i. O'Neill on universality	137
3ii. A Gentilean reply to Kant and O'Neill	140
4. The Kingdom of Ends Formula	142
5. The Autonomy Formula	144
5i. Kant on autonomy	145
5ii. Korsgaard's account of Kantian autonomy	147
5iii. Gentile on autonomy (and autarchy)	149
6. Re-constructing Gentilean moral theory	153
7. Conclusion	155

Chapter 6. The Construction of Value in Gentilean Education	158
1. Autonomy, indeterminacy and 'determined subjectivity'	159
2. Gentile's phenomenology of education	162
3. Education and the state	166
4. Three objections to Gentilean education	172
4i. The Falsity Objection	173
4ii. The Manipulation Objection	176
4iii. The Coercion Objection	179
5. Replies to the Objections	181
6. Re-appraising Gentilean education	185
6i. Gentilean education and political theory	185
6ii. Gentilean education and the IDP	188
7. Conclusion	189
Chapter 7. Dialogical Constructivism and the Idea of Agreement	191
1. Justifying dialogue	192
2. Internalism and the real world	197
2i. Triangulation and objectivity	199
2ii. Two principles for the IDP	202
3. Agreement and the IDP	204
3i. Hypothetical agreements and constructivism	206
3ii. Verification and the IDP	209
3iii. Falsification and the IDP	211
4. Inter-personal applications of the IDP	213
4i. 'Stacking' and objectivity	213
4ii. Persons and principles	217
5. Conclusion	223

Part III. Giovanni Gentile and the State of Contemporary Constructivism

Chapter 8. Conclusion	229
1. Overview of conclusions	230
2. Actual idealism assessed	234
3. Constructivism writ large	236
4. Final remarks	238
Bibliography and Appendix	241
Index	254

Acknowledgements

This book began life as a PhD thesis. It was researched and written between October 2010 and July 2013 under the supervision of Prof. Bruce Haddock and Dr. Peri Roberts at the School of European Languages, Translation and Politics at Cardiff University, and was successfully defended in a viva examination in September 2013. Aside from some additions to the introduction and conclusion, some superficial alterations to the formatting and the addition of a subtitle, the published book is substantially the same as the thesis manuscript.

Throughout my years as a research student I was conscious of how lucky I was to be able to undertake this unusual project and spend several years thinking, reading and writing about challenging ideas. I am grateful to the many people who supported me on that long road. For brevity's sake, I shall thank just a few in particular: Bruce, for his unwavering enthusiasm, valuable advice and genuine liberalism; Peri, for his useful suggestions, searching questions and coffeehouse diagrams, which steered me toward a constructivism that was Gentilean but not strictly Gentile's; the Arts and Humanities Research Council, which kept me fed and watered, suited and booted throughout; James Connelly, Peter Sutch and David Boucher, who made up the panel at my viva examination; Jenny Hulin, chiefly for tolerating my endless questions, though also for helping out in a hundred ways besides; and my parents, who, whether or not they remember, actually suggested all of this in the first place. Their kindness, indulgence and toleration were invaluable to me while this book was being written. To those others who listened to, read or commented upon my ideas as they grew into the thesis: please accept my sincerest thanks for your advice and your patience.

Still more thanks are in order. When I began this research project I could not yet read Italian. Now this obstacle has been overcome, and throughout the book I have used my own translations of quotations from Gentile while acknowledging my debts to other translators where appropriate. When quoting sources in other languages, such as Descartes' French, I have submitted unabashedly to the expertise of others. For helping me achieve the monumental task of learning a little Italian, I should thank especially Angelo Silvestri, Marco Catizone and all at Dilit International House, Matteo

Fabbretti, Fabio Vighi, Giuseppe Vatalaro, Mark Donovan, Paul Furlong, the Coppa family in Rome and, once again, Bruce Haddock. Any and all errors in the translations I have presented are, of course, my own.

For allowing me access to some of the resources used in writing this book, I should like to acknowledge the assistance of the staff at Cardiff University's Arts and Humanities Library, La Biblioteca Nazionale Centrale di Roma, the Main Library at the University of Birmingham, and the Information Commons at the University of Sheffield. Others at Edinburgh University Library, the British Library and Oxford University's Bodleian Library provided resources through inter-library loans. For their valuable roles in helping me identify and track down resources, I am grateful to Alessandro Amato, Lucy Andrew, Tom Barker, Michael Baxter, David Boucher, Daniela Coli, Brian P. Copenhaver, Rebecca Copenhaver, Elise Rietveld, Richard Gale, Sarah Gallimore, Graeme Garrard, Bruce Haddock (again!), Greg Ireland, Kevin Jones, James Lenman, Richard North, Davide Orsi, Antonio Giovanni Pesce, Mary Raschella, Peri Roberts, Sabine Schulz, Richard Shorten, Peter Sutch, Hade Turkmen, Jean Wakefield, Michael Wakefield and Howard Williams. To some of these people I owe debts of thanks that are now several years overdue. I can only hope that, if any of them come to read this, they will excuse my tardiness in giving them proper acknowledgement.

J.R.M. Wakefield
Friday 31 January 2014

List of Diagrams

Number	Title	Page
1	Non-constructed moral authority	124
2	Minimal dialogical construction	126
3	The IDP in outline	130
4	'Stacking' IDPs	215

Summary

This book presents Giovanni Gentile's actual idealism as a radical constructivist doctrine for use in moral philosophy. The first half describes the moral theory that Gentile explicitly identifies with actual idealism, according to which all thinking, rather than an exclusive domain of 'practical reason', has a moral character. It is argued that after Gentile's turn to Fascism in the early 1920s, his moral theory is increasingly conflated with his political doctrine. This entails several major changes that cannot be squared with the central tenets of the theory. The second half of the book develops a more plausible account of Gentilean moral constructivism based on the pre-Fascist idea of reasoning as an internal dialogue. Comparisons and contrasts are drawn with contemporary constructivist doctrines, as well as theories employing dialogical conceptions of reason. The internal dialogue is presented as a device enabling the thinking subject to make objective judgements about real-world problems despite the impossibility of her occupying a fully objective standpoint. Thus actual idealist moral theory is offered as an example of constructivism at its most radical, inviting advocates of less radical varieties to re-assess the foundations on which their theories are built.

Chapter 1
Introduction

This book represents an attempt to bring together two topics whose commonalities have, for a variety of reasons, remained unexplored until now. The first of these topics is the moral theory of Giovanni Gentile (1875-1944), the Sicilian philosopher who devised the doctrine of 'actual idealism'. The second is 'constructivism', a family of theories concerned with the relationship between knowledge and truth. Most of the modern-day philosophers discussed in this book, and especially those who explicitly identify themselves as constructivists, present their theories in the analytic style typical of contemporary Anglophone philosophy. By this I mean that they are narrowly concerned with establishing clear arguments and not, as authors working in the 'continental' tradition are sometimes supposed to be, with hermeneutics, history and holistic evaluations of great (or not-so-great) minds. I mean to present actual idealism as a thoroughgoing constructivist doctrine whose moral theory is plausibly grounded in the phenomenological experience of actual thinking. The Gentilean constructivism developed herein offers an account of how practical reasoning is to proceed, and this, while distinctive, shares several of its main features with the more radical varieties of Kantian constructivism put forward in recent decades.

There is already a large body of literature about constructivism, as well as a smaller, though still considerable, body of literature about Gentile. At least one existing book deals specifically with Gentile's conception of thinking as the act by which reality is constructed, a theme that recurs prominently throughout his works.[1] To date, however, the two relevant groups of specialists — intellectual historians interested in Gentile and philosophers interested in constructivism as a distinctive class of moral theories — have continued to plough their respective fields without paying attention to developments in the other. None of the major English-speaking constructivists refer to Gentile, and none of the Gentile specialists have applied actual idealism to the questions

---

[1] Hervé A. Cavallera (1994) *Immagine e costruzione del reale nel pensiero di Giovanni Gentile*, Rome: Fondazione Ugo Spirito.

that the constructivists have set themselves. Nor has there been a systematic analytic study of actual idealist moral theory. The present book should be considered an attempt to bridge these hitherto separate areas of study. The project may be deemed a success if it can be shown that each has something to offer the other.

1. Defining 'constructivism'

The central thesis of this book is divided into two parts. Part I explains and criticises the tenets of actual idealism. In doing so it shows how Gentile makes sense of practical reasoning and enduring moral commitments without surrendering the theory's basis in a single subject's act of thinking. It also suggests some modifications to make the theory self-consistent. Part II engages directly with contemporary constructivism, showing how a corrected version of Gentile's theory is able to resolve some of the problems that recent theorists have encountered. Since in the English-speaking world constructivism is far better known than actual idealism, and since my approach owes more to contemporary analytic normative theory than to the continental style of Gentile's usual interpreters, it seems appropriate now to defer any further discussion of actual idealism until after it is clear what constructivism is and what problems there might be with it. With those established, we can consider which of these problems Gentile's theory can help us address.

It is remarkably difficult to extrapolate from the particular examples of constructivism, or of theories classified as such by their authors and subsequent commentators, a fully generic, clear-cut and widely accepted definition of the term, specifying precisely what qualifies for inclusion in this class of theories. To complicate matters further, the term has come into use relatively recently, at least in connection with moral and political philosophy, but is regularly applied to earlier authors who are alleged to have affirmed its principles without knowing the word. The question of who among these honorary constructivists properly belongs to the group is open for debate, and the cases for and against the inclusion of any given candidate depends, of course, on how the term is defined. Faced with such a motley collection of examples, the term cannot specify much more than a family resemblance between a group of more or less closely aligned theories. Nonetheless, there are some features common to all the major varieties of 'practical constructivism'. In the 1970s and 1980s, these were elaborated in a series of pioneering articles and lectures, the centrepiece of which was 'Kantian Constructivism in Moral Theory', in which John Rawls attempted to clarify the purpose and workings of his own doctrine, especially the account of 'justice as fairness' described in *A Theory of*

Justice. His use of the term 'constructivism' is deeply rooted in his interpretation of Kant, although he notes in passing that 'there are other forms of constructivism' as well.[2] Subsequent authors have had to work to identify the defining features of constructivism, unpacking a general and more widely applicable definition from the particular features of Rawls's version.[3] To extend our familial analogy, Rawls might be thought of as the common ancestor of the contemporary English-speaking constructivists. These theorists trace their intellectual inheritance to a variety of earlier sources (Kant, Hume, Vico), but it is Rawls who established the existing tradition. He writes:

> [T]he idea [of constructivism] is to formulate a procedural representation in which, as far as possible, all the relevant criteria of correct reason [...] are exhibited and open to view. [... J]udgements are valid and sound if they result from going through the correct procedure correctly and rely only on true premises.[4]

All constructivist theories in ethics are opposed to what Christine Korsgaard calls 'substantive moral realism', or the view that there is a moral standard that obtains independently of us, as though, to borrow James Lenman's vivid example, it consisted of a set of precepts 'written on the sky'.[5] If there were such moral facts in the same way that there are facts about empirical objects, the correctness of the procedure (and of the way in which we go through it, as Rawls says) would not be what determined whether judgements were sound. Rather, they would be sound, and to that extent correct, when they matched the moral

---

[2] John Rawls (1980) 'Kantian Constructivism in Moral Theory', *Journal of Philosophy*, 77 (9), pp. 515–572 [515].

[3] Most self-identifying constructivists have used the Kantian template chosen by Rawls, but a major alternative has arisen in the form of 'Humean constructivism', based, as the name suggests, on the moral theory of David Hume, for whom the subject's 'passions', rather than an objective moral sense, represented the ultimate source of reasons. Prominent Humean constructivists include Sharon Street, Valerie Tiberius, James Lenman, Dale Dorsey and arguably Harry Frankfurt, although he never uses the term himself. See Lenman and Shemmer's introduction to (2012) *Constructivism in Practical Philosophy*, Oxford: Oxford University Press [4].

[4] John Rawls (2000) 'Moral Constructivism', in Barbara Herman (ed.) *Lectures on the History of Moral Philosophy*, Cambridge, MA: Harvard University Press, pp. 235–252 [238–239].

[5] James Lenman (2013) 'Ethics Without Errors', *Ratio*, 26 (4), pp. 391–409 [395]. The same example is used to illustrate what 'a simple-minded moral realist' might believe in (1999) 'Michael Smith and the Daleks: Reason, Morality and Contingency', *Utilitas*, 11 (2), pp. 164–177 [176–177].

facts.[6] This opposition to moral facts aligns constructivism with anti-realism, which is the view that there is not, or we cannot know whether there is, an independent reality about which correct judgements can be made. Nonetheless constructivism differs from relativism, the position to which realism is most obviously opposed, by its insistence that *moral questions have correct answers*. The correctness of these answers is conferred by the procedure. As such, the status of this judgement (as well as moral reality itself, or whatever domain of reality is in question) is constructed, not discovered.[7]

This claim need not apply to the whole of reality. It might be that the empirical world exists independently of our knowledge of it, for example, but some kind of procedure is needed to bring about (and not merely to ascertain) the correctness of normative judgements, or even, as is the case in Rawls's theory, of the subset of normative judgements concerning justice. Regarding the status of judgements that have not resulted from such a procedure, we have two options. One is to say that such judgements cannot be valid and sound: in other words, they are *incorrect*. The other option is to say that we *cannot know* whether they are sound, valid and correct. This response, as Miriam Ronzoni has urged, amounts to agnosticism about their correctness.[8] Whichever option is chosen, or if it is decided that both amount to the same thing, the constructivist position is distinguished from other anti-realist views — including radical scepticism, according to which all moral claims might be false — by the belief that judgements which bear scrutiny from within the procedure are *objectively* correct, and not the arbitrary

---

[6] Rawls (1980) writes that the constructivist procedure 'replaces the search for moral truth interpreted as fixed by a prior and independent order of objects and relations, whether natural or divine, an order apart and distinct from how we conceive of ourselves' [519].

[7] Onora O'Neill calls constructivism 'a third, distinctive possibility' that exists 'in the space between realist and relativist accounts of ethics'. See O'Neill (1989) *Constructions of Reason: Explorations of Kant's Practical Philosophy*, Cambridge: Cambridge University Press [206]. Carla Bagnoli, in a seminal article, writes that 'The question is not: how does value get attached to the world? The question is, rather, how the agent establishes normative relations with her surroundings and acquires moral reasons. And this is also the correct way to reconsider how Sisyphus could restore meaning and value to his life. [...T]he metaphor of construction helps us to frame these questions correctly.' See Bagnoli (2002) 'Moral Constructivism: A Phenomenological Argument', *Topoi*, 21, pp. 125–138 [131].

[8] Miriam Ronzoni (2010) 'Constructivism and Practical Reason: On Intersubjectivity, Abstraction, and Judgment', *Journal of Moral Philosophy*, 7, pp. 74–107 [78–79].

opinions of subjects who could just as well have thought otherwise.⁹ Their status is rooted in 'the practical point of view' that a correctly formulated procedure is intended to model.¹⁰ This grants appropriately constructed judgements inter-subjective validity. Ronzoni writes:

> Constructivism rests on a conception of reason that embraces two fundamental claims: (1) the idea that it is rational (or reasonable) to acknowledge the unavailability of a compellingly objective moral truth; and (2) the idea that practical reason is necessarily inter-subjective. [...These claims are reconcilable, since] the inter-subjective nature of reasons provides constructive tools to generate authoritative normative principles.¹¹

The establishment of 'objective' reasons, as opposed to unaccountable and 'subjective' ones, is crucial to the constructivist view that moral judgements can be correct (or incorrect) without the need for a domain of independent 'moral facts', defined, perhaps, by God, goblins or, less fancifully, the internal structure of the human brain. One objection to constructivism is that, in order to identify the right procedure or 'constructive tools', which consistently produce the correct results, the aspiring constructivist must appeal to something that is not constructed—reason or intuition, for example. Hence the 'correct' conclusions are indistinguishable from 'moral facts' of the kind that realists presuppose. Such objections motivate Ronzoni's view that claims of objectivity are to be justified by reference to some kind of inter-subjective evaluation. The source of truth and good reasons is not a freestanding, fully objective reality, but some aggregate, however conceived, of potentially revisable claims made by other subjects. (Broadly similar views have been supported by radical constructivists such as Onora O'Neill and Christine Korsgaard.) The fine details of how suitably inter-subjective reasons are to be conceived of are deeply contested, and it is to this debate that the present book contributes.

---

⁹ This conforms to Sharon Street's view: 'Constructivist views in ethics understand the correctness or incorrectness of some (specified) set of normative judgements as a question of whether those judgements withstand some (specified) procedure of scrutiny from the standpoint of some (specified) set of further normative judgements.' See Street (2008) 'Constructivism about Reasons', in Russ Shafer-Landau (ed.) *Oxford Studies in Metaethics* (Volume 3), Oxford: Oxford University Press, pp. 207–246 [208] (emphasis removed).

¹⁰ Street notes that this concern with the proper configuration of 'the practical point of view' is shared by Kantian and Humean constructivism alike. See her (2012) 'Coming to Terms with Contingency', in James Lenman and Yonatan Shemmer (eds.) *Constructivism in Practical Philosophy*, Oxford: Oxford University Press, pp. 40–59 [41].

¹¹ Ronzoni (2010) [77–78].

Let us see how all of this might be applied in practice. As the most influential and best-known constructivist, John Rawls serves as a convenient reference point as we set out. His theory has been discussed at great length elsewhere, and my interpretation is neither original nor radical. Nonetheless, this brief examination will enable us to discern which features of constructivism I will address in the remainder of the book, even when Rawls is confined to the margins.

Rawls famously sought an answer to the question of what principles define justice. He assumed that persons' beliefs about personal morality are too closely bound up in their various 'comprehensive doctrines', or their beliefs about what a good life entails, to be judged objectively. Justice, as 'the first virtue of social institutions', is identified with fairness, and concerns the distribution of benefits and burdens across a society of persons with different comprehensive conceptions. Rawls assumes that persons will disagree about what counts as a fair distribution, even if they initially agree to the equation of fairness and justice. Their ability to choose principles of justice will be impeded by their personal interests and moral convictions, with the result that no widely accepted principles will ever be reached. It may be that no two people, taken as they are, will choose the same principles.

Rawls's solution to this problem takes the form of a two-stage constructivist procedure for choosing principles of justice. The first stage outlines a hypothetical choice situation framed by the concept of a 'veil of ignorance', which prevents the chooser from knowing her personal characteristics, such as wealth, social status, age, health, gender and religion, although she knows that people will vary, sometimes greatly, in each of these respects. Thus she is prevented, in the choice of principles, from exercising bias on her own behalf; the veil effectively keeps her from knowing which of the diverse citizens she is, so she must assume that she could turn out to be anyone in the society when the veil is lifted.[12] Rawls believes that under these conditions, the chooser would be rationally motivated to secure the most extensive liberties and provisions to mitigate the effects of bad luck in the initial lottery of birth: her opportunities to achieve her goals could be neither permissibly guaranteed nor restricted by her position in an arbitrary social hierarchy, for example. Inequality would be permitted so long as it benefitted the worst-off members of society, justifying the increased height of the ceiling, as it were, by raising the floor.

---

[12] Rawls (1980): the participants in the procedure 'are represented solely as moral persons and not as persons advantaged or disadvantaged by the contingencies of their social position, the distribution of natural abilities, or by luck and historical accident over the course of their lives' [529].

At the first stage of the procedure, it does not matter whether there is one chooser or many. The artificial constraints imposed upon the chooser(s) mean that each is interchangeable with any other. All are granted the same carefully restricted knowledge and full rationality, but deprived of the personal characteristics (preferences beyond the generic desire to live a good life, relations to other people) that would prompt them to select different principles. Their common anonymity means that none has any bargaining advantage over any other, so it is equally rational for each person to select the same principles. For the second stage of the procedure, by contrast, the veil of ignorance is removed. The chooser knows who she is, what her 'comprehensive doctrine' entails, and so on. She is in a pluralist society alongside other people whose equivalent personal characteristics are known and in play. The principles of justice selected in the first stage already govern the society's institutions. At this second stage, members of society must work to establish 'general and wide reflective equilibrium' through a test of 'how well the view as a whole meshes with and articulates our more firm considered convictions […] after due examination, once all adjustments and revisions that seem compelling have been made'.[13] Here the principles derived at the first stage are exposed to the considered judgements of the persons subject to them—regarded not strictly as 'citizens in a well-ordered society', but as unadorned folk ('you and me'), with full arrays of opinions, beliefs, hopes and fears[14]— weighing both sides (that is: the principles and the judgements) until the two overlap. This amounts to a test of whether the first-stage principles or conception of justice '[match] more accurately than other views our considered convictions', and by extension a test of persons' abilities to devise ways of living together that, despite their different convictions, are both widely acceptable and compatible with general principles drawn from the abstract first-stage procedure. There is no guarantee that they will succeed. If the coherence test for reflective equilibrium scotches the proposed principles of justice, the search must start again, based upon different grounding assumptions.[15]

The central motifs of constructivism can be seen in the foregoing summary of Rawls's theory. One such motif, which I have noted already, is its *anti-realism*. The principles of justice are not already in the world, waiting for us to discover them. Rather, they are created or con-

---

[13] Rawls (1980) [534].
[14] Rawls (1980) [533].
[15] Rawls (1980) [368].

structed as we theorise them.¹⁶ It may be that Rawls's principles are different from those that anyone held prior to the development of his theory. Nevertheless, it is by reference to persons' prior beliefs about the world (or about justice) that the resultant principles are kept from becoming wholly arbitrary. As such they are drawn from but not identical with the raw materials we use to construct them.¹⁷ Another motif is that the conclusions are licensed by means of a constructive *procedure*. We may draw a distinction here between *epistemological constructivism*, which is the general view that some or all features of reality are created in the process by which we come to know them; and *procedural constructivism*, a subdivision of epistemological constructivism according to which the parts of reality that are 'constructed' are considered to have objective truth status, or at least truth status that elevates them above mere subjective opinion, to the extent that they conform to an appropriately designed procedure. The metaphor of construction is not the same as one of inventing a world (or a set of principles) and then deciding, no less capriciously, to regard this as authoritative. Rawls's aim to design principles of justice applicable to people in conditions of broad social pluralism makes clear why he places such conspicuously artificial conceptions of the person and the 'practical standpoint' or 'deliberative perspective' at the heart of the theory: it is assumed that there will be intractable disagreement if people are left to choose principles of justice without the help of a procedure based on such regulating assumptions.¹⁸

Even before the publication of 'Kantian Constructivism in Moral Theory', Rawls was criticised for helping himself, at the first stage of the procedure, to a conception of the person as rational and reasonable.

---

16   Larry Krasnoff notes that the idea that 'ethical truths are made, not found' emerged strongly from Rawls's work *after* Ronald Dworkin drew attention to it in his review of *A Theory of Justice*. See Krasnoff (1999) 'How Kantian is Constructivism?', *Kant-Studien*, 90, pp. 385-498 [389].

17   I have alluded already (see footnote #5, this chapter) to Lenman's thought experiment for illustrating just this point: 'Suppose you believed there were sentences written on the sky that said, *Don't kill, Don't steal*, etc. Then you might think the prohibition of these things drew its authority from the presence of these sentences. But you'd be wrong. After all, suppose we discovered there were sentences written in the sky that said [...] *Do kill, Do steal*, etc. [W]ould we then think it was OK or indeed desirable to do these things[?] No, we would (at least if we had any sense) think, how odd, there appear to be some rather obnoxious and stupid sentences written in the sky and we would take no further notice of them.' See Lenman (2013) [395].

18   Thomas E. Hill uses the phrase 'deliberative perspective' in e.g. (2008) 'Moral Construction as a Task: Sources and Limits', *Social Philosophy and Policy*, 25 (1), pp. 214-236.

This conception dictates which principles will and will not be chosen, and, by extension, which are to be considered appropriate or 'morally justified' material for discussion at the second stage. The qualities Rawls assigns to persons at the first stage are not justified or 'constructed' within the procedure itself. Rather, they are postulated in order to make subsequent constructions possible. Thus Rawls indirectly excludes a range of conceptions of justice already affirmed by real people, rather than artificial conceptions selected by their unreal representatives.[19] First-stage principles will never be licensed if the people on whose behalf they are selected do not agree that rationality and reasonableness are more fundamental to justice than, say, adherence to a specified set of precepts that are *not* products of a constructive procedure. While Rawls makes plain that he is interested in devising a theory of justice for people in liberal, democratic societies, or at least for people whose conceptions of the good life are broadly compatible with such a system,[20] this is no consolation for anyone whose beliefs are, by Rawls's lights, 'unreasonable' but nevertheless sincere.

In short, the problem with Rawlsian constructivism, or at least the problem most germane to the theory developed in this book, is that the design of the procedure, and especially the conception of the person at its heart, appears to include a number of unconstructed features. Since the features postulated at the beginning effectively determine what principles may and will be selected at the end, the entire procedure has a regrettable air of quasi-realism; the dice are loaded in favour of preconceived liberal principles of justice, which may satisfy those of us who are inclined toward liberalism already, but not those who dispute the starting premises. Rawls is able to reach such clear-cut liberal-democratic conclusions precisely because half the work is already done by the time the constructive process begins. Other authors have volunteered constructivist theories more capacious than his, placing morality (rather than only justice) and reason itself within the scope of construction. Some have even claimed to describe constructivist theories that run, in Korsgaard's useful phrase, 'all the way down', conceiving of thinking as a constructive activity and knowledge itself as something

---

[19] Krasnoff (1999) [387].
[20] This point is stressed in *Political Liberalism,* in which Rawls distinguishes between 'reasonable' doctrines, whose holders are prepared to subject them to criticism and re-evaluation after trying to regard them from other persons' points of view; and 'unreasonable' doctrines, which are straightforwardly dogmatic principles that are not made available for negotiation or discussion. See, for example, Rawls (1993) *Political Liberalism,* New York: Columbia University Press [xvi–xvii].

that is constructed.[21] Most of these theorists, including Korsgaard, have furnished their more thoroughgoing constructivist theories using the same Kantian sources as Rawls, drawing out features that are not adequately stressed in his theory. But this shared basis in Kant's philosophy may also skew the procedure in favour of certain versions of morality whose justifications lie outside the procedure itself. It is also notable that several Kantian constructivists do not see any need to endorse a constructivist account of anything but practical reason. They are, in other words, only constructivists about certain things. Constructivism is presented as a response to the unavailability of fully objective moral facts, but it does not, or need not, extend to the philosophy of mind, (non-moral) epistemology and so forth.

The inclusion of any unconstructed features in the design of the procedure and its corollaries is bound to be controversial. However, if we were to exclude *all* unconstructed features, we would face a new problem: the process of construction could never get started, since there would be no material with which to work.[22] We would therefore be deprived of any means by which to discipline our moral judgements. Constructivists have typically responded to this problem by including in their theories only those unconstructed features (assumptions) necessary to make the procedure reach firm conclusions, while at the same time satisfying anyone concerned about weighing the procedure in favour of pre-determined conclusions reached only through a biased selection of features at the outset. By designing the theory along these lines, the potential for controversy is lessened, but not eliminated. It is not obvious which features rightly belong in this minimal, though ideally still impartial, set of features. Kantian constructivists have tended to base theirs on postulates of Kant's moral theory, such as freedom and equality, though very often elaborating or otherwise adapting these to make them clearer or more consistent, either with each other or with other elements of the doctrine to which they are latterly added. I

---

21 Christine M. Korsgaard uses this phrase in (2003) 'Realism and Constructivism in Twentieth-Century Moral Philosophy', *Philosophy in America at the Turn of the Century* (APA Centennial Supplement to Journal of Philosophical Research), pp. 99–122. She maintains that Kant's constructivism does run 'all the way down', and so does hers [117–118]. Rawls 'treats the problems of practical philosophy as problems that are practical all the way down', but he stops short of full constructivism [112].

22 I must stress that this claim is controversial. Plainly 'all-the-way-down' Kantian constructivists *do not* think that the postulates of their theories should be regarded as unconstructed features. What matters for me is that, if Gentile is correct, even these basic postulates exceed the necessary minimum.

have noted already that some of these theorists regard themselves as constructivists 'all the way down', which implies that they do not consider their Kantian postulates to constitute unconstructed features, or, at least, that they provide a minimal *necessary foundation* for any possible constructivist doctrine, and as such may be legitimately included in it. Gentile, for reasons that will soon become clear, thinks that even Kant assumes too much, and that realist residues can be found throughout his theory (and, as a result, those of today's Kantian constructivists). Actual idealism is presented as a more rigorous alternative to Kant's doctrine, which is in some ways closely aligned to it, though reaching its conclusions — some similar, others strikingly different — via a different path.

The challenge for us, then, is to develop a constructivist moral theory that does not make any controversial concessions to realism; or, if this proves impossible, to develop a theory that makes the fewest or least controversial of such concessions. A successful theory will be rooted in a phenomenologically accurate account of the person, which is to say, an account that embraces the facts about how each of us actually experiences the world and the process of making judgements about it. This is to be distinguished from any theory that idealises this experience to the degree that it no longer reflects phenomenological reality. Recalling the objection to Rawls's constructivism, the problem with an idealised procedure is that it produces results applicable only to correspondingly idealised persons in counterfactual circumstances. Since the persons and circumstances about which we usually ask moral questions are not ideal, our theory must accommodate a wider range of configurations of beliefs, reasons and circumstances than do the existing constructivist theories that specify or limit these in advance. It may yet be that certain configurations must be excluded in order for the theory to work at all. The limits of our theory's inclusiveness are bound to be somewhat controversial and arbitrary, but we can at least aim to accommodate as many plausible configurations as possible. Our policy of non-idealisation necessitates a trade-off in the specificity of the procedure's conclusions with regard to what is true and what we ought to do.

2. Introducing Giovanni Gentile

The model for the constructivist theory developed in this book is Giovanni Gentile's actual idealism. This doctrine was developed in the first half of the twentieth century in an attempt to do away with the presuppositions and baseless speculation that Gentile believed to have run through the history of western philosophy up to that point. At the doctrine's heart is the claim that reality is created in the course of the act of thinking. He writes that

> there is no *theory* or contemplation of reality that is not at the same time action and, as such, the creation of reality. In fact, there is no cognitive act that does not have a value, or rather, that is not judged, *precisely insofar as it is a cognitive act*, according to whether it conforms exactly to its own law, so that it may be recognised or not as what it ought to be. [...] Were we not the authors of our ideas—that is, if our ideas were not our pure actions—they would not be *ours*, we would not be able to judge them, and they would have no value: they would be neither true nor false.[23]

Actual idealism is manifestly an uncompromising form of epistemological constructivism, according to which *the act of thinking entails the construction of reality*. Nothing can be real unless it is thus constructed. Gentile believes that his radical position is *the only tenable alternative* to the 'absurdity' of transcendence, which he considers a presupposition of any form of realism. In what follows, I present actual idealism as a thoroughgoing constructivist doctrine comprising sophisticated conceptions of the person and society, truth and reason, and the way all of these are joined in moral enterprise. Gentilean constructivism is different from those described by Kant or any other post-Kantian philosopher, and grounded on metaphysical foundations that, beneath recondite technical vocabulary, are both familiar and credible. The purity of Gentile's constructivism—his unwillingness to make *any* concession to realism—gives rise to one of the chief difficulties that actual idealism must face. If there is nothing we can know or say without thinking, and to think is to construct a world, it follows that *everything* is constructed. Some critics have thought that this means actual idealism is reducible to solipsism or Protagoreanism, according to which truth and reality are just whatever the thinking subject happens to think they are. Objective standards appear to be ruled out. This is a problem that any tenable Gentilean theory must solve, and much of the present book is concerned with showing how this is possible. The solution takes the form of a procedure that is not fully elaborated in any of his works, but is, I argue, implicitly supported by the actual idealist conception of thinking. Once the mechanics of this procedure have been laid bare, we may legitimately promote Gentile's epistemological constructivism to the class of procedural constructivist theories.

Given that Gentile is so transparently a constructivist, it may appear strange—if only to readers unfamiliar with his biography—that he has

---

[23] Giovanni Gentile (2003) *Teoria generale dello spirito come atto puro*, Florence: Le Lettere [36]; Carr translation [33] (Gentile's emphasis).

been ignored by all of the major theorists working on constructivist theory today. Now is the time to face an inconvenient truth. Gentile is most often remembered for his contributions to the Italian Fascist regime, first as Minister of Public Instruction, later as a Senator and head of the Institute of Fascist Culture, and in general as one of the Party's most vocal and erudite spokesmen. He remained loyal to the regime between 1923, when he officially joined the Party, and 1944, when he was assassinated.[24] His reputation as a serious philosopher was undone by the popular perception of him as nothing more than 'the philosopher of Fascism'. This affiliation has, perhaps understandably, excluded him from the canon of serious moral philosophers. I argue that this moral theory is worthy of rehabilitation even if the political theory extending from it is not. To show this I must separate Gentile's ethics from his work (and, more pressingly, his enduring reputation) as 'the philosopher of Fascism'. There is a healthy flow of work on that topic already. A systematic treatment of actual idealism's implications for contemporary moral constructivism is noticeably absent from the secondary literature. In correcting this paucity I mean to present a Gentilean theory that shares its major aims with the better-known versions of constructivism in recent Anglo-American philosophy. In order to meet the high standards for analytic moral philosophy, this Gentilean doctrine must be shown to be both workable and well poised to counter the chief objections to those theories.

It might be thought that to defend a Gentilean moral theory — a theory modelled on the work of a card-carrying Fascist — is to defend Fascism, if only indirectly. However, for the purposes of this book I have no real interest in Gentile's personality, motives and allegiances, nor in the moral problems that go with his complicity, at first active and later passive, in a political experiment that began and ended in violence. I treat his work as a series of *arguments*, and aim at the rational re-construction of his ideas, assembling a composite doctrine from those that are persuasive and rejecting those that are faulty. By operating at this carefully maintained level of abstraction I mean to keep the discussion firmly within the realm of moral philosophy and divorced as cleanly as possible from the soul-searching intellectual biographies that have dominated the literature elsewhere. That Gentile

---

[24] When Gentile served as education minister in the Fascist government of 1922, he initially did so as a Nationalist and Liberal. He applied for membership in the PNF in May 1923, albeit while describing himself in his letter of application as 'liberal by deep and firm conviction'. The letter is reprinted in Giuseppe Calandra (1987) *Gentile e il fascismo,* Bari: Laterza [8]. See also Gregor (2001) *Giovanni Gentile: Philosopher of Fascism,* New Brunswick, NJ: Transaction [2].

was a Fascist is an undeniable fact about him. But this does not make all of his ideas *Fascist ideas*. To reject a theory unseen because we do not approve of its author is *argumentum ad hominem*, and in what follows I mean to show that actual idealist moral theory is largely comprehensible irrespective of the dubious political context from which it arose.

Part of this book's originality is in its attempt to treat actual idealist moral theory strictly as philosophy, not as a window onto its author, an era or some larger concept like modernity or Italian culture. Although I often mention Gentile's name, for the most part this can be understood as shorthand for 'someone accepting the central tenets of actual idealism'; the fact that he happened to express them is not essential to the theory I ultimately support. I refer to the historical figure only where this is necessary to understand why particular arguments are made in quite the ways they are—why, in other words, Gentile sometimes deviates from the sober logic of his theory to reach unexpected conclusions. My approach would be orthodox in analytic moral philosophy, but it is uncharacteristic of the existing literature on Gentile and actual idealism.[25] To understand previous authors' unwillingness to distinguish theory from theorist, it is worth briefly setting aside the details of Gentile's philosophy while we consider the circumstances of his death.

2i. The death of the author

On 15 April 1944, Gentile was assassinated outside the gates of his villa on the outskirts of Florence. The city was then in the short-lived Italian Social ('Salò') Republic, formed in 1943 after the Kingdom of Italy's surrender to the invading Allies. The Republic comprised only the northernmost parts of the country, and stood as the last bastion of the *Partito Nazionale Fascista* (PNF; National Fascist Party), supported by German resources and personnel in anticipation of the Allied advance. Between 1922 and 1943 the PNF had been the dominant force in Italian politics, suppressing opposition and trying to realise its stated goal of *totalitarianism*, whereby the state and its citizens share a unified identity and will. By April 1944, its powers were severely depleted. Mussolini himself, as well as prominent loyalists like Gentile, had moved north to receive the protection of the Nazis. The Republic was politically vola-

---

[25] Martin Heidegger's famously brief summary of Aristotle's biography is instructive here: 'He was born on such-and-such a date, he worked, and he died.' I do not go quite so far as Heidegger in setting the theorist outside theory's ambit of inquiry, but with him I agree that biography, however interesting it may be, is not philosophy. See Heidegger (2002) *Gesamtausgabe II, Vorlesungen 1919–1944. Band 8: Grundbegriffe der aristotelischen Philosophie*, Frankfurt am Main: Vittorio Klostermann [5]. (Thanks to Sabine Schulz for her advice regarding this translation in December 2012.)

tile, with the on-going struggle between pro- and anti-Fascist groups spilling into something approaching a civil war, and frequent tit-for-tat killings of activists on both sides.

Gentile was well known as a member of the Party. His political influence had been greatest in the 1920s, when he had established his place as the PNF's foremost theorist, responsible for both the *Manifesto degli intellettuali fascisti* (Manifesto of the Fascist Intellectuals) and the *Origini e dottrina del fascismo* (Origins and Doctrine of Fascism). As an ideologue and spokesman, he promoted some of the Party's most controversial policies and ideas. Among these were the concept of totalitarianism, which he gave its first positive theory, and the claim that Fascist violence was an expression of the ideology's irreducibly moral nature. Thereafter his opponents dubbed him 'the philosopher of the blackjack' (*il filosofo del manganello*), after the favoured weapon of Fascist Blackshirts (*squadristi*). Although his political influence dwindled through the 1930s,[26] and in his public role he advocated tolerance and clemency toward anti-Fascist activists, he remained an indelible symbol of the *ancien régime*.[27] In his final weeks he had received death threats in which he was identified (accurately) as an 'exponent of neo-fascism', symbolically (and more dubiously) responsible for the deaths of five anti-Fascists in March of that year.[28] On 15 April, a small group[29]

---

[26] Herbert Schneider notes that, by 1928, Gentile was no longer a minister, but his 'disciples' were 'the most conspicuous and [...] distinguished group of [F]ascist thinkers [...] both in their numbers and in philosophic erudition'. See Schneider (1968) *Making the Fascist State*, New York: Howard Fertig (originally 1928) [344]. Although Gentile ghost-wrote the official *Doctrine of Fascism* under Mussolini's name in 1933, his direct political influence had peaked in the early–mid 1920s, before he was, as Harry Redner puts it, 'kicked upstairs to the honorific, but powerless, post as a Fascist senior dignitary' — as president of the *Istituto Fascista di Cultura* (Fascist Institute of Culture), in which position he remained from 1925–37 — where he remained 'irked that in the world of practical politics he counted for so little'. Redner (1997) *Malign Masters: Gentile, Heidegger, Lukács, Wittgenstein,* Basingstoke: Macmillan [5–6]. H.S. Harris likewise confirms that 'after 1929 it was no longer possible for [Gentile] to nourish any illusion that he was a power in the land'. Harris (1960) *The Social Philosophy of Giovanni Gentile*, Urbana, IL: University of Illinois Press [198].

[27] Daniela Coli (2004) *Giovanni Gentile: la filosofia come educazione nazionale,* Bologna: Mulino [18].

[28] Coli (2004) [23–4].

[29] Most reports refer to five assassins, but Gabriele Turi puts the figure at four. However, it may be that he discounts Bruno Fanciullacci, often described as the principal assassin. See Gabriele Turi (1998a) *Giovanni Gentile: una biografia,* Milan: Giunto [522].

of Communist partisans posed as students[30] and waited outside his villa. Seeing his car approaching, they called for the driver to halt, and after identifying the passenger as 'Prof. Gentile' — they did not know him by sight — they shot him where he sat before mounting bicycles and fleeing the scene. Gentile's chauffeur drove him to a hospital in Florence, but by the time they arrived, the philosopher was dead.[31]

That brief and violent episode is the only part of Gentile's life that I shall recount in any detail. I include it because of its neat illustration of how closely opponents of Fascism associated Gentile with the ideology he had helped to devise and promote, even when his involvement in political decisions was minimal. The biographer Sergio Romano reports that the assassins boasted of having killed 'not a man, but his ideas'.[32] As the regime's best-known theoretician, to kill him was, in a sense, to strike a blow against it. Such grand gestures are rarely without unintended consequences, however, and along with the Gentilean vision of Fascism, the assassins did serious harm to the subsequent reception of his ideas about epistemology, mind, logic, history and ethics. I assume that this was not a major motivation for the act. If in actual idealist metaphysics there is anything to warrant the author's murder, it has eluded me. But Gentile's death and the events that followed — the Allied victory in Europe, the co-ordinated effort to prevent the future resurgence of Fascist and Fascist-like powers, and both condemnation of and bewilderment at the ways in which such regimes were able to gain and hold power at all — meant that he was soon left

---

[30] Among the architects of the assassination was Teresa Mattei, a former student of Gentile. Mattei later reported that various reasons were offered that Gentile 'had to die', including revenge for the death of Mattei's brother, Gianfranco, who, as a 'great intellectual,' warranted the death of someone like Gentile. See Antonio Carioti (2004) 'Sanguinetti venne a dirmi che Gentile doveva morire', *Corriere della sera*, 6 August 2004, p. 29, [Online] http://archiviostorico.corriere.it/2004/agosto/06/Sanguinetti_venne_dirmi_che_Gentile_co_9_040806079.shtml [accessed 08/01/2012].

[31] The basic details of the assassination and its consequences are included in several studies, including Gabriele Turi (1998a) [522-3]; Daniela Coli (2004) [20-4]; Sergio Romano (1984) *Giovanni Gentile: la filosofia al potere*, Milan: Bompiani [299-300]; Giano Accame (2004) 'Gentile e la morte', in Roberto Chiarini (ed.) *Stato etico e manganello: Giovanni Gentile a sessant'anni dalla morte*, Venice: Marsilio, pp. 51-62 [56-8]. For a reasonably detailed account in English, see Mario M. Rossi (1950) '*Genesi e struttura della società*, by Giovanni Gentile' (review), *Journal of Philosophy*, 47 (8), pp. 217-22 [218]. Note that Rossi puts the assassination on 17 April, two days later than the overwhelming majority of others.

[32] Romano (1984) [299].

behind in the murky period from which people worldwide, not least philosophers, meant to distance themselves.

2ii. Gentile criticism since his assassination

I contend that unless actual idealism's Fascist connections are set aside, we cannot hope to judge the theory *as moral philosophy*, rather than as an historical artefact. In this respect my approach is unusual; Gentile's political associations loom large in the existing secondary literature on actual idealism. This is especially apparent in what little such work is available in English.[33] Given that his philosophy is usually categorised as a species of Hegelianism, which non-Marxist Anglophone authors have tended to view with suspicion, it is hardly surprising that he has remained somewhat obscure. His consistent support for Fascist totalitarianism exacerbates this tendency, since this affiliation remains, for better or worse, his most distinguishing feature. Marxists like Herbert Marcuse use Gentile as an example of Hegelianism gone badly wrong, and, by extension, as a standard for their contrasting readings of the same source materials. Practically no one since the Second World War has wanted to be seen to endorse Fascism, not even tacitly by omitting to denigrate it roundly when the opportunity arises.[34] Among the simplest ways to display one's anti-Fascist credentials is to deny that its exponents said anything worthwhile whatsoever, even about topics seemingly unrelated to politics. Thus it is easy to consign whole thinkers to the dustbin of history without the need for close engagement with works that are presumably insincere, ideologically warped and thoroughly distasteful.[35]

---

[33] Consider this clutch of recent titles: Thomas Clayton (2009) 'Introducing Giovanni Gentile, "the Philosopher of Fascism"', *Educational Philosophy and Theory*, 41 (6), pp. 640–60; M.E. Moss (2004) *Mussolini's Fascist Philosopher: Giovanni Gentile Reconsidered*, New York: Peter Lang; A. James Gregor (2001) *Giovanni Gentile: Philosopher of Fascism*, New Brunswick, NJ: Transaction. If nothing else, these show just how unshakeable the '...of Fascism' epithet has proven to be.

[34] I say 'practically' because there are some theorists, like A. James Gregor, who argue that Fascism has been misunderstood; and others who, for a variety of reasons, identify themselves with what they take to be Fascist ideology.

[35] Gabriele Turi writes of how Gentile's Fascist associations 'long relegated [him], historiographically, to the status of a figure known to have been loyal to Mussolini and the Italian Social Republic to the bitter end and hence unworthy of further investigation'. See Turi (1998b) 'Giovanni Gentile: Oblivion, Remembrance, and Criticism', *Journal of Modern History*, 70 (4), pp. 913–33 (translated by Lydia P. Cochrane) [913].

The failure of the Anglophone secondary literature to portray Gentile convincingly is partly due to his unattractive political connections, which give all but those already interested in Fascism a good reason to avoid him, but also to the limited availability of his major works in English. These are Carr's useful but in some respects misleading translation of the *Teoria generale dello spirito come atto puro*, Bigongiari's of *La riforma dell'educazione*, Gullace's of *La filosofia dell'arte*, and Harris's of *Genesi e struttura della società*.[36] Since *Educazione* is addressed to schoolteachers, not philosophers, and *Arte* chiefly concerns aesthetics,[37] readers without access to Italian find themselves caught between *Atto puro*'s ostensibly apolitical metaphysics and the hurried, erratic argumentation of *Genesi*, with only a handful of philosophically unsound political works by which to estimate the connections between them.[38] They find themselves dismissing the later work as a baffling corruption of the earlier one, or else relying excessively on what a small number of commentators have said about Gentile's output in the nearly three decades between the two.[39]

In 1960, H.S. Harris published his influential study *The Social Philosophy of Giovanni Gentile*, alongside an English translation of Gentile's

---

[36] Note that to save words, after the first citation of any of Gentile's works I employ abbreviations when referring to them. See appendix for details.

[37] It is important to note that *Arte* does include some chapters (especially *Parta prima*, chapter 4) on sentiment, which, as Harris notes, plays a role in Gentile's moral philosophy. See Harris (1960) [234–5]. However, to my moral inquiry they add nothing that is not covered as well in *Introduzione* [38–67]. *Arte* is largely ignored in the present book.

[38] For the purposes of this book, it is particularly notable that the *dialogo interno* does not appear in *Atto puro* (1916), but it does in *Diritto* (also 1916) and the *Logica* (1917–22). This, coupled with Gentile's exaggerated claims about the novelty of the dialogue as presented in *Genesi* (see 'Avvertenza', no page number), gives non-Italian readers the false impression that he suddenly turned to moral theory in the last months of his life.

[39] Harry Redner is a particularly good example of such a theorist. He reads Gentile almost entirely through *Atto puro* and *Genesi*, which he identifies as his 'primary' and 'secondary masterwork[s]'. He writes that 'it is hard to see how real action could emerge from [*Atto puro*] at all' [47]. *Genesi*, he argues, takes the former's 'double-think' and 'willing suspension of disbelief' [26] and 'adjust[s] itself to the Fascist reality' in which it had since developed [quotation 55–6; see also 97–8]. But in presenting these arguments he makes no real reference to works before and between the two, with occasional (and often misinformed) claims recycled from H.S. Harris. One example is Redner's claim that Gentile only developed 'a more original conception of language' in 1921's *Prologemena to the Study of the Child* [73–4]. This is false, and suggests that Redner is unfamiliar with Gentile's *Sommario*, written before the First World War.

last work, *Genesi e struttura della società*. Harris presented the former as 'a rescue operation, or an essay in salvage'.[40] Several of the books' reviewers were puzzled at the thought that Gentile's political or moral philosophy was worthy of attention, except, perhaps, as a cautionary example of how widely held ideals (liberty, democracy, order) might be abused. Fascism represented something to be avoided. Then, as today, the term retained an unusually poisonous taint, connoting unprincipled pragmatism, intolerance, brutality, indoctrination and worse besides.[41] We may be forgiven for thinking that anyone turning to a Fascist for ethical insights must have mischievous intentions or else is shopping in the wrong store. Since Gentile never dedicated a whole book to ethics, anyone seeking an actual idealist moral theory must disentangle it from works on metaphysics, the philosophy of mind, and law.[42] To insulate actual idealist ethics from the surrounding system is bound to prompt Gentile's most orthodox Gentilean interpreters to cry foul on grounds of vicious abstractionism. He did not treat ethics as a discrete discipline, runs the objection, so to present his works in this way is illegitimate. As I have said, my intention in this book is to side-step that

---

[40] Harris (1960) [viii]. The importance of this book to the survival of Gentile studies, especially in English, cannot easily be overstated. Rik Peters notes that it is thanks to this book, plus Harris's translation of Gentile's last work, *Genesi e struttura della società* (Genesis and Structure of Society), 'that Gentile's name is not forgotten [...] and his name is not simply associated with Fascism'. See Peters (1998b) 'Talking to Ourselves or Talking to Others: H.S. Harris on Gentile's Transcendental Dialogue', *Clio*, 27 (4), pp. 501-14 [501]. A year earlier Harry Redner noted that Gentile's philosophy was 'almost forgotten outside Italy', adding that this 'ha[d] much to do with the collapse of Fascism after the Second World War and with Gentile's untimely death at the same time'. See Redner (1997) [15].

[41] Several scholars have made similar observations. Roger Griffin rightly notes that the transformation of the party identification 'Fascist' into the 'pejorative' term 'fascist' was cemented by the popular view of the Second World War as a 'show-down between "fascist" and "anti-fascist" forces'. Since then the term has been 'passed on to post-war generations as an emotionally charged word of condemnation for any political regime or action perceived as oppressive, authoritarian or elitist'. Stanley Payne speaks of it is 'one of the most frequently invoked political pejoratives', while Andrew Vincent calls it 'a hackneyed term of political abuse' that 'conjur[es] horrifying visions of pogrom and unprecedented European destruction'. See Griffin (1993) *The Nature of Fascism*, Abingdon: Routledge (originally 1991) [1-2]; Payne (1995) *A History of Fascism, 1914-1945*, Abingdon: Routledge [3-4]; and Vincent (1995) *Modern Political Ideologies*, Malden: Wiley-Blackwell (second edition; originally 1992) [142].

[42] Harris (1960) [63]. In 1913, Gentile promised his readers that he would write an *Etica* at some point in the future, but no such work appeared.

objection by presenting a theory that is, at most, Gentilean in spirit. It is not an account of what he thought about ethics, but of a moral theory he could plausibly have supported.

Italian scholars have faced a different set of problems. They could not ignore Gentile altogether, since for a time he undoubtedly played a prominent role in Italian politics and culture. However, while his role as an historic public figure kept him from becoming obscure, any serious post-War discussion of his philosophy was engulfed in the lively controversy over his PNF affiliations and his role in Italian public and intellectual life, which, of course, directly affected the post-War intellectual culture in which these controversies thrived.[43] Some authors refused to treat him as a philosopher at all,[44] and it is telling that, at the end of the 1980s, Augusto Del Noce claimed it was only then possible to discuss Gentile's idealism with an appropriate degree of 'serenity', as opposed to the kind of 'polemical virulence' that had until then characterised the debate over its relationship with Fascism.[45] Even so, most of Gentile's works had been re-published several times between his assassination and Del Noce's remark,[46] and there had been a steady

---

[43] Daniela Coli lists some of the charges directed at Gentile. He was called a 'most vulgar traitor', a 'political bandit', a 'racketeer' and a 'corruptor of the whole of Italian intellectual life'. See Coli (2006) 'La concezione politica di Giovanni Gentile', in *Logoi*, Castelvetrano: Edizioni Mazzotta, pp. 37–57 [37].

[44] Reviewing Harris's translation of Gentile's *Genesi*, Dante Germino writes that 'a philosophical system is not automatically discredited (although one's suspicions about it are likely to be aroused) because its author happened to have committed himself, on the basis of that same philosophy, body and soul to a totalitarian political regime' [585]. He concludes that *Genesi* is 'the crowning work of a man who is unlikely to be accorded a place in the first rank of philosophers' [587]. See Germino (1961) '*The Social Philosophy of Giovanni Gentile*, by H.S. Harris; and *Genesis and Structure of Society*, by Giovanni Gentile, translated by H.S. Harris' (review), *Journal of Philosophy*, 23 (3), pp. 584–7. Ronald Gross likewise affirms that it is as a result of Gentile's associations with 'a completely cynical disregard of programs and political promises in favour of an activist, inspirational, purely charismatic style of leadership' that Italian scholars had, until 1961, 'understandably avoided him', culminating in a 'tide of indifference' [222]. Gross (1961) '*The Social Philosophy of Giovanni Gentile*, by H.S. Harris; and *Genesis and Structure of Society*, by Giovanni Gentile, translated by H.S. Harris' (review), *Annals of the American Academy of Political and Social Science*, 336, pp. 222–3.

[45] Augusto Del Noce (1990) *Giovanni Gentile: per una interpretazione filosofica della storia contemporanea*, Bologna: Il Mulino [7–16, but esp. 16].

[46] Del Noce died in late 1989, shortly before the publication of his book in 1990. I recognise that the book, much of which consisted of essays originally published in the 1960s, was not the only cause of the resurgence of serious Gentile scholarship. Strange though it may sound, the change may also owe

trickle of secondary texts, including two major biographies[47] and many articles. Del Noce succeeded in spurring his peers into a more productive mode, and the last two decades have seen the publication of another major biography,[48] several more highly regarded studies,[49] a number of collections of essays to mark the fiftieth and sixtieth anniversaries of Gentile's death[50] and further articles in journals and specialist periodicals.

Italian authors have now recognised the absurdity of discounting a theorist's entire body of work in protest against part of it,[51] and it is now more than a decade since Gabriele Turi called for '[a]n attempt to return to a strictly philosophical Gentile'. This, he claimed, would be 'a legitimate operation, justified by the need to break with rigid interpretive criteria that froze Gentile into the reductive pose of the "philosopher of fascism"'.[52] Turi's call has been answered to an extent, with an increasing number of studies acknowledging the need to engage with Gentile as a major philosopher and not just as the philosopher of Fascism.[53] But even these studies are shackled by the distinctly Continental style in which their authors trade. As an interesting figure in the history of Italian philosophy and politics, Gentile *himself* is never allowed to fall from view. There is a tendency for the Italians to expound on Gentile's contribution *as a whole*, or to chart his development by noting greater or lesser resemblances to other canonical texts over a succession of publications. Big questions are routinely asked:

---

something to the collapse of the USSR and the subsequent change in the tenor of the Italian debate over Fascism and anti-Fascism. Still, we cannot firmly establish cause and effect with respect to such large-scale paradigm shifts, so this cannot be much more than a conjecture.

[47] Manlio Di Lalla (1975) *Vita di Giovanni Gentile,* Florence: Sansoni; and Romano (1982).
[48] Gabriele Turi (1998a) *Giovanni Gentile,* Milan: Giunto.
[49] Chief among which is Gennaro Sasso (1998) *Le due Italie di Giovanni Gentile,* Bologna: Mulino.
[50] An example includes Roberto Chiarini (ed.) (2004) *Stato etico e manganello: Giovanni Gentile a sessant'anni dalla morte,* Venice: Marsilio.
[51] Riccardo Pedrizzi argues that Gentile's 'ostracism' is particularly absurd given how we conventionally treat Plato and Aristotle, despite their influence on, respectively, 'the tyranny of Syracuse' and Alexander the Great. See Riccardo Pedrizzi (ed.) (2006) *Giovanni Gentile: il filosofo della nazione,* Rome: Pantheon [7–8].
[52] Turi (1998b) [915–16]
[53] Alessandra Tarquini probably exaggerates when she claims that '[Italian] studies on the role Gentile played in fascism are few and represent but a fraction of the by now very large body of literature devoted to Gentile's philosophy.' Tarquini (2005) 'The Anti-Gentilians During the Fascist Regime', *Journal of Contemporary History,* 40, pp. 637–62 [639n].

was actual idealism really the philosophy of Fascism, or was it co-opted and distorted to fit the Party line? Where does it fit into the grand Italian intellectual tradition? How best to characterise Gentile's relations to Hegel, Kant, Marx, Croce and Mussolini? Thus the Italians have created a complex, multi-faceted picture of the man, his works and his place in history. Missing from this picture is a persuasive account of why his ideas are worthy of attention *irrespective of the cultural and historical circumstances from which they arose*, and, by extension, why theorists with no special interest in the man himself should trouble themselves to bring his philosophy, unusually laden with baggage both in its political connections and its rarefied style, in from the cold.

3. A new approach to Gentile

Quite apart from his historical significance, Gentile is an unlikely candidate for analytic treatment. His approach to philosophy is, or at least seems to be, thoroughly metaphysical; he takes as his starting point the 'pure act' of thinking and on that builds an elaborate system from which nothing is excluded, giving the doctrine an 'omnibus character' that defies attempts to address any part in isolation.[54] Ethics, epistemology, religion, history and aesthetics are all bound up in this self-supporting system, which relies on unconventional and notoriously abstruse idealist metaphysics. Thus key steps in Gentile's arguments are obscured by esoteric allusions to Italian history and literature, and presented in arcane terms like 'Spirit', 'the universal subject' and 'thought that thinks itself'. Reviewing Harris's translation of *Genesi* in 1962, H.P. Rickman wrote that

---

[54] A. James Gregor (1977) 'Giovanni Gentile, contemporary analytic philosophy, and the concept of political obligation', in Simonetta Betti, Franca Rovigatti and Gianni Eugenio Viola (eds.) *Enciclopedia 76–77: il pensiero di Giovanni Gentile* (Volume 1), Florence: Istituto della Enciclopedia Italiana, pp. 445–55. Gregor begins his article thus: 'Perhaps the most formidable difficulty with which Anglo-American philosophers have had to deal, when considering the thought of Giovanni Gentile, is its omnibus character. In attempting to come to grips with any aspect of [actual idealism], one finds oneself inevitably drawn into a complex conceptual web. When dealing with Gentile's thought, it is all but impossible to devote oneself to a single conceptual issue to the exclusion of indeterminate number of others' [445]. He adds that 'It is impossible to predict the subsequent course of Anglo-American philosophy, but it is clear that it can no longer simply dismiss systems of thought such as [Gentile's] on the grounds that they are more preachment than analysis or more metaphysical than scientific' [447].

Gentile's terminology and mode of argument are unfamiliar and uncongenial to our own climate of thought. If we are to be convinced of the importance of his speculations [...] a more radical translation from his jargon and a more drastic confrontation with our own philosophic presuppositions would have to be attempted.[55]

Half a century on, that challenge remains unmet. I do not here propose to translate any of Gentile's *works* into English, but instead to translate a selection of his ideas into an idiom better suited to the 'climate of thought' in today's Anglo-American philosophy. To discuss all the corollaries of actual idealism would require a book far larger than this. I propose to analyse only those parts of Gentile's extensive system needed to make sense of his moral theory. These include his conception of the subject and the epistemological principles connected to it. In Gentile's works these provide a prelude to his more elaborate political theory, but I shall argue that his preferred conception of politics is not well supported by the moral arguments used to reach it. At that point I desert his stated position and try to construct the theory his earlier assumptions would have led him to develop if he had more rigorously followed the logic of his own system. To defend a Gentilean moral theory that is both internally coherent and plausibly relevant to the problems of today, I must counter the claim that metaphysics is not philosophy at all, but instead tantalising but unsound speculation that muddies the waters philosophy is, at its best, uniquely suited to clearing.[56] There is a real risk that once philosophers take their speculations farther than their arguments permit, they will find themselves (to borrow a line) 'got into fairy land',[57] trading in fictions and metaphors beyond the reach of analysis or meaningful criticism. In place of those assumptions I try to develop one important part of his moral theory, the internal dialogue, as a model for constructivist practical reasoning.

---

[55] H.P. Rickman (1962) '*Genesis and Structure of Society* by Giovanni Gentile and H.S. Harris; *The Social Philosophy of Giovanni Gentile* by H. S. Harris' (review), *International Review of Education*, 8 (3/4), p. 498 [498].

[56] This claim is famously expressed by A.J. Ayer (1971) *Language, Truth and Logic*, London: Penguin. On [49] Ayer does not cite Hegel by name, but instead selects a passage from Bradley's *Appearance and Reality*, and on [67-9] he argues that metaphysics, unlike philosophy, 'does not constitute a branch of knowledge'. Herbert Marcuse includes a similar claim about Gentile, claiming that his version of Hegelianism 'cannot be treated on a philosophic level'. See Marcuse (1955) *Reason and Revolution: Hegel and the Rise of Social Theory*, London: Routledge & Kegan Paul (second edition; originally 1941) [404].

[57] David Hume (2003) *An Enquiry Concerning Human Understanding*, Oxford: Oxford University Press [72; §57].

Since I have no qualms about abandoning Gentile's stated positions where I find his justifications lacking, this is not quite a study in the history of ideas as conventionally understood, with theories faithfully described, compared with antecedents and successors, and mined for insights into the historical periods from which they emerged. It is instead an analytic study in the *history of philosophy*, which aims at 'rational reconstruction' of its subject's ideas, always with one foot firmly in the present.[58]

Let me make clear exactly what I mean to achieve. My general aim is

i. ...to discover not what Gentile's philosophy meant for him and his contemporaries, but what it could mean for us.

Beyond this first, general aim, I have two further aims, one more ambitious than the other. Either can be achieved independently, but because I try to ground my Gentilean moral theory on the strongest basis that actual idealism can provide, it would be best for me if both tasks were achieved in tandem. These aims are

ii. ...to describe a kind of moral constructivism that stands as an alternative to the dominant Kantian variety; and

iii. ...to rehabilitate Gentile as a major moral and political philosopher whose ideas can be fruitfully applied to contemporary analytic normative theory.

The constructivist theory mentioned in (ii) will be *Gentilean* in the sense that it draws on and articulates elements of Gentile's philosophy, but is not simply an exposition of them. The resultant theory is not strictly Gentile's, and should not be taken as a true and accurate exegesis of his views as presented in any one of his works. Instead it is an amalgamation of the best ideas described in several, or an interpretation of one composite view that can reasonably be attributed to him. Above all I aim to render actual idealism *clearly*. Strict loyalty to Gentile's works is secondary to this. Problematic or superfluous parts of his theory are sympathetically adapted or jettisoned. In this way I emulate the method adopted by Derek Parfit and John Rawls when interpreting Kant.[59] The relation between my 'Gentilean constructivism' and Gentile's writings is one of resemblance rather than identity.

---

[58] For a valuable discussion of the difference between these approaches, see the preface to Bernard Williams (1978) *Descartes: The Project of Pure Enquiry*, Harmondsworth: Pelican [9–10].

[59] Cf. John Rawls (1980) 'Kantian Constructivism in Moral Theory', *Journal of Philosophy*, 77 (9), pp. 515–72 [517]. Rawls' phrase is in fact 'analogy rather

It might be thought that there is a tension between aims (i) and (iii). To the extent that the resultant theory is Gentilean but not Gentile's, runs this objection, we have no grounds to say that he has been rehabilitated; all the credit belongs to a different theory that happens to resemble his in some limited respect.[60] I do not accept this view. The controversial features of Gentile's case bring the issue of rehabilitation to the fore in ways that philosophers without such baggage would not. Even if I succeed in developing a persuasive Gentilean moral theory, the man himself will not be exonerated. His personal record is not the topic of this book. That I leave for historians to judge. My interest is in moral philosophy, and that, as a discipline concerned exclusively with ideas, is not well suited to overall assessments of personalities or political careers. We may admire or abhor the people we write about, but the worst criticism philosophy permits us to make of them is that they were *mistaken*. What matters for my purposes is that actual idealism can be made to stand on its own feet, which is to say, that it can be shown to be plausible and self-consistent. Actual idealism is not to be equated with Gentile's ideas *simpliciter*. Instead it represents a body of ideas rooted in the conception of reality as the product of the act of thinking. It was this that Gentile so vividly described, and for this, if anything, that he deserves credit. Plainly he made some philosophical mistakes and poor political decisions. It is a matter of historical record that his support for Fascism had disastrous consequences for him and many others in Italy and elsewhere. But these mistakes must not be allowed to obscure what was right and original about his theory. I will not ask the reader to forgive him for what he did or failed to do in his political career. I ask only that we show him, the philosopher, a little charity.

4. The argument in outline

This book has eight chapters, of which this introduction is the first. Chapters 2, 3 and 4, which constitute Part I, are mainly expository. There my main aim is to make sense of Gentile's distinctive position and specialist terminology, and to provide the basis for the constructive project carried out in Part II. To this end, Chapter 1 focuses on his conceptions of the relation between thinking and reality and the account of the person, or rather, the thinking subject, as a self-creating act of thinking, to which this gives rise. Chapter 2 refines this conception of the person by explaining how Gentile accounts for the relationship

---

than identity'. See also Derek Parfit w/Samuel Scheffler (ed.) (2010) *On What Matters* (Volume 1), Oxford: Oxford University Press [17 and 300].

[60] I am grateful to James Connelly for bringing this objection to my attention in September 2013.

between the thinking subject and other people. This move separates Gentile's position from solipsism, in which the subject cannot be bound by any moral responsibilities, and out-and-out subjectivism, in which truth is simply a matter of what the subject happens to believe. By the end of this chapter it is still unclear how the subject should settle the question of what she ought to do. Chapter 3 goes on to show how Gentile answers this question by means of the state. I argue that this move is largely illegitimate, since it relies upon a poorly defined concept (the 'transcendental state') that may or may not resemble any actual political institution. The ascription of unrestricted and unconditional moral authority to the political state, or even to a single, specified person, is wholly incompatible with the tenets of actual idealism, and is in fact a realist claim of exactly the kind Gentile meant to avoid.

In Chapters 5, 6 and 7, which constitute Part II, I set about developing a more plausible and self-consistent Gentilean moral theory. At the heart of this theory is the 'internal dialogue', and over the course of these chapters I will aim to promote this from an ambiguous metaphor to a full-blown constructivist procedure. Chapter 5 compares Gentile's theory of practical reason with Kant's and those of his latter-day followers, showing how they share a commitment to the idea that persons are free and equal, but construe this demand in different ways. Chapter 6 addresses Gentile's theory of education, showing how he thinks it is possible for a subject to be at once free and bound by substantive moral commitments. This chapter provides a clearer and more convincing indication of the proper role of the political state in Gentilean moral theory. Chapter 7 further refines this dialogical procedure to show how it might be applied by a single subject reasoning in isolation, or by several different people attempting to provide reasons applicable to all of them. Thus this chapter will give some indication of how Gentilean constructivism might be applied to questions of political justification.

Chapter 8 is the conclusion, which consists of a brief survey of the preceding chapters followed by an evaluation of actual idealism's plausibility as a distinctive and workable constructivist moral theory.

Note that, from this point forward, the generically conceived thinking subject will be called S. This is first and foremost a word-saving measure, since it enables me to avoid frequent repetition of phrases such as 'the thinking subject', 'the thinker' and 'the subject implicit in the act of thinking'. Another advantage of using S as a technical term is that it avoids some of the difficulties arising from Gentile's rather unusual account of precisely what the thinking subject is. More will be said about this topic in Chapter 2.

Part I

Components of Actual Idealism

Chapter 2

The Pure Act of Construction

In this chapter I lay out the main components of Gentile's account of thinking as the act by which reality is constructed. This will give us the beginnings of a conception of the person and a theory of knowledge. To save words, I draw regular comparisons with Descartes' and Kant's better-known theories. Thus I intend to establish the main tenets of actual idealism in a maximally efficient and accessible way.

To begin (sub-heading #1), I describe Gentile's distinctive 'method of immanence', showing what led him to adopt it and why it so deeply affects the development of his theory. Next (#2) I show how Gentile describes his radical conception of *pensiero pensante,* or 'thought thinking', before offering two justifications for it. I then (#3) describe some of the difficulties to which this conception gives rise, before explaining how Gentile addresses them using the distinction between abstract and concrete *logoi*. Next (#4) I describe Gentile's theories of truth and knowledge, showing how his demanding method forces him to discard conventional conceptions of truth, and rely instead on one grounded on the act of thinking. Following this (#5) I discuss Gentile's conception of the will and its role in assigning truth claims their *value*, which in subsequent chapters we will see play a central role in actual idealist moral theory. At the last sub-heading (#6) I discuss the *positivity* of Gentile's theory, showing how his conception of the act of thinking stands as a challenge to scepticism.

1. On method

Actual idealism constitutes an attempt to describe reality in phenomenological terms without relying upon unjustified presuppositions or descending into mysticism. If it is to be useful for us as a model of practical constructivism *that we have reason to choose over other theories*, it must supply, at the very least, a criterion of truth and a conception of the subject (or person, which may or may not amount to the same thing). As a phenomenological theory, actual idealism's conceptions of truth and the person are closely related. Without the first we cannot hope for it to yield conclusive answers to any questions we might ask. Without the second the moral theory has nothing with which to work.

To begin, let us examine the method by which Gentile means to distinguish truth from falsity and reality from unreality. To identify a method that is rigorously defensible, he surveys a series of previous thinkers' theories in search of untenable assumptions. Where he finds any, he discards the theory as speculative or unsound. It would be a mistake to infer from this that he is a sceptic. He is certainly highly demanding of the philosophers with whom he engages, but his aim is not only to expose error. He means instead to clear the ground for his own positive inquiry, noting whatever parts of his predecessors' works he *does* consider rigorously defensible, and retaining them for his own theory. This marks a clear distinction between his project and those of, say, Nietzsche or the existentialists, who are similarly preoccupied with finding complacent assumptions, but little concerned with correcting them.[1]

Gentile considers the problem of transcendence to be the heart of epistemology. His account of and solution to it are most clearly set out in his essays 'Il metodo dell'immanenza' (The Method of Immanence) and 'L'atto del pensare come atto puro' (The Act of Thinking as Pure Act), and further elaborated in his *Sistema di logica* (System of Logic).[2] To illustrate the problem, he describes two kinds of *logos* in ancient Greek thought. The term 'logos' is notoriously ambiguous,[3] but in Gentile's usage it can be understood to mean 'conceptions of the relation between truth, reality and knowledge'. As such it bears directly upon the method by which the correct answers to questions are identi-

---

[1] I accept that this is maybe a little unfair on Nietzsche, who does offer a kind of moral theory. He does not offer much to those of us who are not *übermenschen*, though. Gentile means to describe the necessary universal structure of moral thinking, not the story of its emergence.

[2] Different terminology is used in each of these works. As its name suggests, 'Metodo' refers to method; *Logica* refers to the logos. For brevity's sake I run the two accounts together.

[3] This is put particularly well by Roger Holmes (1937b) *The Idealism of Giovanni Gentile,* New York: Macmillan: Gentile 'use[s ...] a concept which, in modern philosophy, has so fallen into disuse that when unqualified it is open to serious misinterpretation. [...] [T]he Logos fulfil[s] the function of that in relation to which thinking is ultimately either true or false. It is the norm of thinking. In such a sense, removed strictly from rational or theological considerations, Gentile uses the concept' [34].

fied.[4] The first of the ancient Greek *logoi* is Heraclitus's 'objective logos', which is 'a pre-condition of any knowledge' of it. It is entirely free-standing, god-given, and independent of S. The second is the 'subjective logos', which Plato discusses (but does not entirely endorse) in his dialogue *Cratylus*. Under the subjective logos, a given claim's truth-value depends upon whether it corresponds with some outer criterion of truth.[5]

Gentile claims that it is impossible to make sense of either logos without the other. The objective Heraclitean version is unknowable without S's intervention, whereas the Platonic version requires a Heraclitean counterpart to make sense of any truth claim. Plato famously supplies a permanent edifice of truth with his 'world of forms', from which all concepts and names are derived. This means that when two critics disagree in their judgements about which of two artworks is more beautiful, for example, *one of them is right.* By invoking the form of beauty, they are trying to square their claims with a real and permanent object. As such their claims can be objectively true and are distinct from subjective opinions. Since the question of the artworks' beauty does not have more than one correct answer, a critic can believe sincerely *and mistakenly* that he has correctly identified which of the artworks is more beautiful. If this were not the case, and every claim S could make about an external world were nothing more than a claim about her opinions,[6] there would be no possibility of falsity or error, nor any place for a meaningful account of truth.

Plato's method is the dialectic, or the process of question and answer by which the correctness of a judgement is ascertained. In each of his dialogues he identifies a core set of uncontroversial beliefs that all participants share, before testing successive answers to whatever question is under examination — what justice entails, for example — and discarding those that contradict the starting beliefs. Thus Plato means to

---

[4] Note that Gentile's use of the word 'logic' is unusual. In contrast to its familiar definition as 'the inquiry which has for its object the principles of correct reasoning', Gentile uses it interchangeably with 'logos', denoting not only an inquiry but a whole conception of reality, truth and knowledge. See Mautner (2005) [357].

[5] *Logica 1* [46–7]. Gentile here refers us to Plato's *Cratylus*, in which Socrates and Hermogenes discuss the latter's belief that names have no necessary relation to their objects. Plato (1921) *Plato in Twelve Volumes* (Volume 12), Cambridge, MA: Harvard University Press (translated by Harold N. Fowler) [§385b].

[6] In moral philosophy, such a view might be *emotivism*. In epistemology, we might associate that view with Protagoreanism, or the doctrine according to which 'man is the measure of all things'.

discover the answer corresponding most closely to the 'form' of the object in question. Gentile objects that Plato assumes that the unchanging world of forms contains an answer to any question dialectically addressed. But the world of forms is transcendent; it is by definition removed from the world of possible experience. Its existence can only be a presupposition. (Plato famously hints that the forms can be understood by wise philosophers like himself, but he neglects to explain how he can be certain that they exist at all.) Objects of experience — which, in the language of a later time, we might call *phenomena* — can have at most partial resemblances to these forms. Since our experiences rely on objects of experience, Plato posits a truth to which S has no access, and about which she cannot make intelligible claims. Thus he falls into contradiction, and S remains estranged from the reality against which the truth-value of her claims is to be tested.[7]

This brings Gentile to a familiar problem of philosophy. If there is an objective reality, how can we account for S's knowledge of it? If there is no objective reality, does all truth collapse into opinion? This must be solved without falling into mysticism, whereby unverifiable claims are made about vaguely defined objects *and yet held to be true*.[8] However tempting it may be to invoke ideas like absolute Perfection (with a capital 'P') when accounting for those 'tracts of experience connected with man's most intense and fruitful willing, loving and conceiving',[9] without a clear idea of what these ideas mean we cannot hope to make sense of them. There is no way that we can talk about them in terms of truth and falsity; they are necessarily unknown and unknowable. To root a theory of truth in such mystical abstractions is to include in our theory something that we are unable to account for, if only because of 'the inadequacy of speech'.[10] This is effectively to give up on philosophy and embrace wishful thinking. The mystical features

---

[7] See Gentile's essay 'Il metodo dell'immanenza', in *Hegeliana*, Florence: Le Lettere, pp. 196–232 (this essay originally 1912) [198–202].

[8] Evelyn Underhill puts the matter thus: 'For Gentile, mysticism requires "the annihilation of the subject before an unknown transcendent Object." And here again, the mystic would answer that "unknown" is the last word which he could truthfully apply to the "Mighty Beauty" he has seen.' Evelyn Underhill, R.G. Collingwood and W.R. Inge (1923) 'Can the New Idealism Dispense with Mysticism?', *Proceedings of the Aristotelian Society, Supplementary Volumes* 3, pp. 148–84 [150–1].

[9] Underhill (1923) [156].

[10] Underhill (1923) [153]. It is worth noting that Underhill, an established writer on mysticism, seems to have been lured into a misunderstanding of Gentile by his use of the quasi-religious term 'spirit'. This term is a problem, but the systematic character of his work clearly distinguishes it from the kinds of mystical humbug with which Underhill wants to identify it.

act as a presupposed backdrop to all subsequent inquiry, and S is deprived of the ability to make meaningful judgements about them.[11]

Gentile notes that, until the modern period, in the Christian world there prevailed a conception of truth based on a combination of Aristotelian naïve realism and religious faith. That is: the empirical world exists because God deigns that it should exist, while God himself, along with the supernatural planes of heaven and hell, is beyond human comprehension. He has a plan, but keeps it mysterious; He is perfect, but His creations are not; He knows the whole truth, but He reveals it only in parts. This view hinges on the idea of a transcendent reality, manifest in God, who represents a complete and objective truth that He has freely created. Human knowledge is at best an imperfect reflection of that creation. Thus the Scholastic account is vulnerable to the criticisms directed at Plato: with the invocation of S's faith in the existence of God, who possesses all the special qualities attributed to Him—omnipotence, omniscience, infallibility and perfection—the question of *knowledge* becomes redundant. S's thought has no bearing on the truth; there exists an 'absolute spirit' in God, and human thought either corresponds with that spirit or not. The best that fallible persons can do is to endorse codified Church doctrine, to love God and 'forget [them]selves', assuming that the truth will be revealed to them.[12] Thus the truth transcends S, who passively waits for this presumed God to reveal its proper contents.

Christian philosophy's real advance, Gentile thinks, was in its placement of truth inside the subject. St Augustine's claim that 'truth resides inside man' (*in interiore homine habitat veritas*)[13] follows from St Paul's

---

[11] For the equation of the logos and 'thinkability', see *Atto puro* [66-7]; Carr translation [65-67].

[12] Giovanni Gentile (1963) *I problemi della scolastica e il pensiero italiano*, Florence: Sansoni [39-42]. Note that in these pages Gentile refers especially to the way in which Bonaventure's 'Platonic spiritualism' gets around the problems of the Greek conceptions of knowledge and the world, in which the subject was a mere 'spectator'. The more Aristotelian Scholastics encountered the same problem as the Greeks (i.e. the presupposition of a real world). See also 'Metodo' in *Hegeliana* [210-13].

[13] This comes from Augustine's *De Vera Religione* [chapter 39, §72]. Gentile gives this reference in *Sommario 1* [3n]. The whole passage runs '*Noli foras ire, in teipsum redi; in interiore homine habitat veritas.*' This has been translated in various ways, including this from Charles Taylor: 'Do not go outward; return within yourself. *In the inward man dwells truth.*' The last sentence corresponds to the one Gentile quotes in Latin. Given actual idealism's unusual conception of S, I can afford to translate more literally. See Taylor (1989) *Sources of the Self: The Making of Modern Identity*, Cambridge: Cambridge University Press [129] (emphasis added).

claim that, because he (Paul) has faith in God, Christ 'liveth in [him]'.[14] Since Christ is 'the way, the truth and the life',[15] S, who has faith in God, will find the truth inside herself, for that is where Christ (and, by extension, truth) resides. In this way S is reconciled with the object of her investigations. Yet the problem of transcendence remains: although in a sense the Scholastics situate truth on the plane of immanence, they leave the real substance of reality (God) substantially beyond S's grasp. God's plan is perfect and unchanging, but it is unclear how S can conclusively uncover any part of its content. The truth that is said to be inside man is trapped there. Knowledge relies on revelation, and revelation relies on the intervention of God, who can never be known in His entirety.

2. Toward *pensiero pensante*, or 'the thought that thinks itself'

The major step forward from this pre-modern position occurs with Descartes' 'moment of subjectivity and certainty',[16] achieved in his *Meditations* and later developed in his *Discourse on Method* and *Principles of Philosophy*. Following the 'general demolition of [his] opinions' in his first *Meditation*,[17] Descartes offers *cogito ergo sum* (I think; therefore, I exist) as a firm and certain principle on which he can reconstruct his knowledge. Having established *his* existence, he can manage his ideas with impunity and set about confirming or disconfirming other truth claims as they occur to him. While the full sense of the *cogito* has been questioned, it remains very difficult to deny this initial claim without dismissing all of ontology as a non-starter.

Gentile is broadly in favour of Descartes' aim to establish a subjective basis for *certain truths*. The *cogito* marks a significant step forward from earlier philosophical systems that had conceived of thought as an 'object of mere speculation, antecedent to the philosopher's act of thinking [*pensiero in atto del filosofo*]'. He writes:

> Certainty is the Cartesian philosophical problem, resolved with the *cogito ego sum*, which is [...] the construction of a concept of the real [that remained] unknown in all of ancient philosophy. It conceives of being as something that thought continually realises [in the process of] realising itself. [It is] reality as self-knowledge [...] the same thought that searches

---

[14] Galatians 2: 20 (King James version).
[15] John 14: 6 (King James version).
[16] 'Metodo', in *Hegeliana* [215].
[17] René Descartes w/John Cottingham, Robert Stoothoff and Dugald Murdoch (eds., trans.) (1984) *The Philosophical Writings of Descartes* (Volume 2), Cambridge: Cambridge University Press [11].

for being, and, in searching, realises it. So it is not intellect, a spectator on its reality; but rather will, creator of that which is real.[18]

The significance of Descartes' cogito is not in its inference, the 'ergo sum', understood as the plucking of a fact from the obscurity of previously unknown truths, but the 'cogito' — I think — itself. Gentile insists that, on any tenable account of knowledge, the act of thinking that one exists is effectively to make oneself exist by fiat. The act of thinking *creates* what is true and real. Of course, it is also possible to think (express) statements that one does not recognise to be true. The key difference between true and untrue propositions, then, is that only the former are affirmed through an act of will. Hence Gentile's remark about the role of the will as the creator of the real: S thinks that she exists and recognises (wills) this claim to be true, so 'realising' herself as part of reality. In this way she is re-cast as the creator rather than passive receptacle or recipient of knowledge. This is something that earlier philosophers had failed to do. S is no longer estranged from the object of knowledge, relegated to a secondary plane of reality beneath a complete, transcendent and mysterious 'Truth', but unified with it in the act of thinking.

Gentile thinks that the act of thinking, rather than thought, a thinker or a prior reality as object of thought, is basic to any investigation of truth and reality. Since the act of thinking entails the creation of reality, it makes no sense to refer to a reality outside, prior to or conditioning the act. To ascertain the existence of even a thinker, conceived as something separate from the thought the thinker purportedly thinks, we require an act of thinking, i.e. 'I think that I am a thinker.' Gentile reasons that, given its necessity for and absolute priority over any claims about truth and reality, the act of thinking is the only possible 'pure act', creating and conditioning itself without deferring to any prior act or fact. He uses several terms to capture this counter-intuitive concept. These include *autoctisi*, a Greek term meaning 'self-creation', inherited from Bertrando Spaventa;[19] 'creative self-consciousness', which is reasonably self-explanatory, and captures the idea that reality, including the empirical self, is a product of consciousness, rather than consciousness a product of it;[20] *autonoema* ('the autogenetic act of the

---

[18] *Logica 1* [33–4].
[19] M.E. Moss (2004) [8]; also Harris in Gentile (1960) *Genesis and Structure of Society*, Chicago: University of Illinois Press [73n]. Note that Harris elsewhere translates this as 'self-constitution'. See his (1960) *Social Philosophy of Giovanni Gentile* [35].
[20] *Genesi* [43]: '*autocoscienza creatrice.*'

intelligence');[21] and *causa sui* ('[that which is] its own cause'), which comes from Spinoza.[22] Perhaps the most important, though, is *pensiero pensante* (literally 'thought thinking'),[23] or 'thought which actuates and thinks itself'.[24] This grammatically awkward formulation is intended to distinguish between thought understood as an object (which is *pensiero pensato*, or 'thought [already] thought') and as an act. The act always occurs in the present, or rather, it is timeless, since it is only through that act of thinking that one can possibly comprehend time, space and the relation of events and physical objects that make sense of them. Hence thinking is always *attuale* (actual), which in Italian carries the double meaning of 'current; of the present time', and 'of or pertaining to an act'. *Pensiero pensante* is the crux of Gentile's system, which he calls *idealismo attuale* (actual idealism).[25]

It is tempting to dismiss *pensiero pensante* as the result of a major category error whereby an abstract noun (namely *pensiero*, thought) is granted agential qualities independent of any thinker. If successful, this objection will prove fatal to actual idealism, showing it to rest on a confused notion no less nonsensical than 'twitching kicks the ball' or 'literacy forgets'. Before advancing any further, it is worth countering this objection by re-stating Gentile's meaning in more familiar language. I see two ways by which Gentile reaches his conception of *pensiero pensante*. The first I call the *Cogito Justification*, since it involves a variation on Descartes' cogito inference. The second, which I call the *Logical Priority Justification*, involves showing that thinking is the only

---

[21] *Logica 2* [75]; also cited Holmes (1937a) [90].

[22] *Atto puro* [188]; Benedict de Spinoza w/Edwin Curley (trans.) (1996) *Ethics*, Oxford: Oxford University Press [4; Part 1, Proposition 7].

[23] Since English uses 'thought' in a variety of senses, it is worth offering a brief summary of the relevant word forms in Italian. *Pensiero* (plural: *pensieri*) is equivalent to the abstract noun 'thought', as in 'I was lost in thought' or 'a thought occurs to me'. *Pensare* is the infinitive form of the verb 'to think', and can be used to express 'thinking' as an active alternative to 'thought' (hence *'l'atto del pensare'*: the act of thinking). *Pensante* is the present participle ('wait a moment; I'm thinking'). *Pensato* (*pensati* when attached to a plural noun) is the past participle.

[24] *Atto puro* [105]: '...*atto reale del pensiero, che si attua e si pensa.*' For this translation I have following the wording of the Carr translation [108]. Gentile raises the same point in 'Pensare', in *Hegeliana* [195]: 'The thesis does not make the synthesis possible, but, on the contrary, the synthesis makes the thesis possible, creating it with its antithesis, or rather, creating itself. And so the pure act is *autoctisi*.'

[25] Note that Gentile freely interchanges this term with the alternative *attualismo* (actualism). Secondary authors also use both, but in general I favour the two-word version so as to avoid confusion with any of several unrelated doctrines also named 'actualism'.

possible *pure act*, and must be adequately accounted for in any tenable theory of knowledge. For that I will draw comparisons with Immanuel Kant's idea of the 'I think'.

2i. The Cogito Justification

First, then, let us turn to the *Cogito Justification*. While Gentile admires Descartes' broad project of accounting for the subjectivity of experience, he identifies transcendent residues in the Cartesian method of achieving certainty. One such fault is found in Descartes' understanding of what the cogito properly implies. If 'I think' requires that 'I am', what can we say with equal certainty about S — what form does the 'I' take? The cogito does not by itself prove the existence of an external material reality or any physical matter, such as S's body, within it. Descartes' answer is to posit the existence of a mind, or soul, or pure self, existing ontologically separate from, if not entirely independent of, the body. The self is 'a thing that thinks'; not a material object, but one capable of effecting changes to the material world. This kind of dualism leads to the old problems of pre-modern philosophy. S is simultaneously posited in and cut adrift from the reality she might conceivably know, but, as we have seen, Gentile's attempt to solve this problem by conceiving of reality (including the self) as secondary to the act of thinking leaves him open to the accusation that he has made a category error.

Gentile objects that there is nothing in the cogito to suggest the existence of a separate entity beyond or prior to the act of thinking. But to reduce the cogito to the simpler assertion that *there is thinking* is problematic, since it seems to erase the subject entirely. There is no room in the claim 'there is an act of thinking', nor Ayer's 'there is a thought now', for us to insert a recognisable subject except as a presupposition; and without that, we cannot very well account for the apparent continuity of experience, the passage of time, or the sequence of and relations between thoughts.[26] Gentile observes that we can think about thoughts that we have thought previously, so it seems that there is a need to account for some kind of continuity of consciousness. From here he reasons that if the self-evident truth of our thinking is to be cashed out without groundless presuppositions, and without adding anything new to our initial belief that 'there is an act of thinking', we are forced to characterise S as an act of thinking that thinks itself.

This idea is not entirely original to Gentile. Something very similar occurred to Thomas Hobbes in his Objections to Descartes' *Meditations*.

---

[26] Ayer (1971) [62–3]. I am grateful to Tom Bunce for bringing the continuity objection to my attention in November 2011.

He complains that if Descartes sets aside the concept of a material body in order to ensure that his conception of the ego 'does not depend on things of whose existence [he is] as yet unaware',[27] he lets verbs go unmoored from their nouns, resulting in awkward concepts such as 'jumping without a jumper' or 'thinking without a thinker'. This kind of double-talk is reminiscent of the scholastic philosophy of the medieval period, which is to say, 'obscure, improper and quite unworthy of M. Descartes' usual clarity'. Descartes' reply is instructive. He writes: 'I do not deny that *I, who am thinking, am distinct from my thought* [...] I simply mean that all [...] modes of thinking inhere in me.' Thought is part of him, but he himself is not thought.[28]

We can see here that Descartes' concept of the subject is different from Gentile's. Descartes straddles the old (transcendent) and new (immanent) concepts of reality, acknowledging the special status of the thinking subject as an active participant in the creation of the real, but still defining it in terms comprehensible within the old tradition. The Cartesian pure ego is a thing that thinks, but on Gentile's account, Descartes cannot hope to know anything about that thing without first thinking about and thereby creating it in thought. To treat the pure ego's existence as a given is to part ways with epistemology, replacing knowledge with presupposition.

The outcome of the Cogito Justification is principally a negative one. It shows that Descartes' argument rests on false claims about entailment and necessity. That is: that there is thinking neither entails nor requires as a condition the existence of a thinker. We can be certain that there is thinking without assuming the prior existence of a thinker, but not the reverse; we cannot know that a thinker exists without first thinking about it. This goes some way to dispelling the idea that Gentile's theory rests on a category error, for unlike Descartes and many idealist philosophers, Gentile need not treat thought as a *thing* or *substance*. It is instead an activity, and references to it as a noun are abstract and metaphorical. We might say that in Gentile's system there is no 'ghost in the machine', with a world of thought somehow transcending yet by mysterious means influencing the world of 'real'

---

[27] In the Second Meditation, Descartes writes that 'if the "I" is understood strictly as we have been taking it, then it is quite certain that knowledge of it does not depend on things of whose existence I am as yet unaware.' See Descartes w/Cottingham et al. (eds.) (Vol. 2) [18–19; 27 in standard pagination].

[28] Second and Third Objections, in Cottingham et al. (1984) (Vol. 2) [122–5; 172–7 in standard pagination] (emphasis added). Note that I do not capitalise 'scholastic' because Hobbes refers to 'the scholastic way of talking' [125; 177 in std. pag.].

material things.[29] When thought is conceived as an act, or *pensiero pensante,* the division between ghost and machine disappears.

2ii. The Logical Priority Justification

As I have said, the Cogito Justification explains Gentile's abandonment of conventional conceptions of the subject as a 'thing that thinks', but seems unable to offer a strong positive conception in its place. To attain that we can re-construct the case in a different way, examining Gentile's reasons for choosing *pensiero pensante* as the basic feature of his theory rather than Kant's 'I think', as described in the first *Critique.* Gentile calls this Kant's 'great discovery', adding that it gave philosophy 'a new horizon'.[30] The Prussian philosopher writes:

> It must be possible for the *I think* to accompany all my representations: for otherwise something would be represented in me that could not be thought at all, and that is equivalent to saying that the representation would be impossible, or at least would be nothing to me.[31]

The main idea here is that it is inconceivable that S should know anything without thinking it. To say 'it is true that I exist' implies (entails) 'I think it is true that I exist'. The former 'truncated' claim 'is not a judgement we can make' without presupposing the extra features present in the latter.[32] So understood, thinking is not an action like breathing, jumping or speaking. For it to be true (or untrue) that I am breathing, you are jumping or we are speaking, I must *think* we are performing these actions. Without that 'I think', breathing, jumping or speaking would be, let us say, *ontologically indeterminate.* Absent from my thoughts, they would not exist, and claims about them would not even be false. It is necessarily 'I' that thinks, since only one 'I' can be subject to any given subjective experience. I cannot think your thoughts, for if I tried to do so, they would become my thoughts. The exercise would be wholly self-defeating. It is possible to think without jumping, but not to jump (or, at least, to know that one is jumping, and, by extension, for the action to be *real*) without thinking. The act of jumping is known, created, as the object of thought. The same cannot be said of the act of thinking without tautology. The act of thinking is unique in this respect: it is the only act that possesses this universal character.

---

[29] The 'ghost in the machine' myth is well articulated by Ryle (1990) [13–25].
[30] *Logica 2* [40]; for more relevant material, see also *Sommario 1* [76–8].
[31] Immanuel Kant w/Norman Kemp Smith (1929) *Critique of Pure Reason,* London: Palgrave Macmillan [152–3; §16, B131–2 in std. pag.].
[32] *Atto puro* [94–6]; in the direct quotation I have followed Carr's translation [97].

This is not the end of the Logical Priority Justification. Before concluding, it is worth underlining one point: while Gentile is closer to Kant than to Descartes, he does not reject Cartesian dualism only to adopt Kantianism wholesale. He breaks with Kant not only over the 'I think', but also over Kant's general aim of describing *pure reason*. This requires him to separate knowledge from its object, referring to a 'pure faculty of knowledge', including 'pure reason, pure intellect, or pure sensibility', in order to make objective *a priori* judgements possible.[33] The problem here is that in conceiving of reason, intellect and sensibility in their 'pure' forms, Kant employs an 'absurd' and faulty conception of each of the faculties described. Gentile insists that there is no knowledge without an object; there is no thinking over and above thinking *something*. Kant can draw up his table of judgements, for example, only by abstracting from actual thinking about actual problems. Likewise the 'I think', which Kant—with Gentile's support—takes to be a necessary predicate of any possible judgement, is not detachable from the judgement in which it is situated. The 'I' of 'I think' is all of a piece with the act of thinking, and meaningless without it.

The Logical Priority Justification can be summarised as follows. Every possible judgement must include the predicate 'I think'. This is true of judgements about the 'I', or individual, contained in that phrase. The act of thinking is therefore logically prior to its subject. 'I think' cannot be reduced to several separate elements—the 'I', a thought and (perhaps) that thought's object—without resorting to absurd abstraction. Thinking, then, must be conceived in its 'actuality', with all these components in place: that is, as S's act of thinking about an object. Thought in its actuality cannot be other than 'thought thinking', *pensiero pensante,* or the act of thinking that thinks, actuates, creates, itself.

3. The abstract/concrete division

Careful readers may notice that Gentile refers to *pensiero pensante* without specifying an object. By referring to thought at this level of generality, has he then inadvertently fallen into the same kind of absurdity of which he accused Kant? If so, it is hard to see how he could have done otherwise. To say anything at any level of specificity there is a need for a class of concepts that are *clear*, in Leibniz's sense of the word (i.e. they are *identifiable* on successive occasions), if not wholly *distinct* from the particular objects to which they refer. Viewed through the act of thinking, which always occurs in a context, even a commonplace object is not precisely the same from one moment to the next.

---

[33] 'Metodo', in *Hegeliana* [223].

Supposing this object is a chair, for example, it is at one time 'the chair at time T_1' and at another time 'the chair, which I thought about previously, at time T_2'. The latter has relational and temporal properties different from those of the former. Without the clear idea of 'the chair', it would be impossible to conceive of the chair as an object existing in time. The object would have no continuity or identity, existing solely on the shifting sands of contingent particularity. Reality so conceived would be incomprehensible, imposing itself on S from moment to moment as unconnected and unfathomable intuitions.

A problem arises: how can Gentile simultaneously insist on the idea of *pensiero pensante* and account for a class of objects or concepts at any level of generality? His solution is to draw a distinction between 'concrete' and 'abstract' thought. Concrete thought is thought as act, *pensiero pensante*. This is 'the only thought that is really thought', and is 'absolutely ours' and 'absolutely actual', in that S is constantly and necessarily subject to it.[34] Being 'actual' — which, let us remember, has in Italian the double meaning of 'of or pertaining to an act' and 'current; of the present time' — concrete thought is timeless, existing always in the present. It comprises both the medium and content of reality, incorporating subject and object in a single act. It is also universal and singular, since there cannot be more than one concrete thought or act of thinking. For S to think about someone else's act of thinking, she must posit it as an object of thought, and as such it would not be an act, but a fact, an abstract creation of S's concrete thought.

This last point leads us to a second conception of thought. S can *think about* another's thoughts, or past, future or possible thoughts, even if she cannot *think them* directly without making them present, concrete and hers. Thought conceived in this way is 'abstract' and unreal; it is *pensiero pensato* (literally 'thought [already] thought), or thought conceived as the object of actual, concrete thinking. Abstract thought consists of descriptions or concepts that cannot be conceived concretely and actually except by contradicting themselves. This does not mean that statements containing abstractions are necessarily nonsensical. Instead they refer to unreal objects, or objects incompletely realised in *pensiero pensante*. Nonetheless they play an important role in concrete thinking. We very often think about objects that existed in the past, will exist in the future, or may exist subject to as-yet-unsettled conditions. By reference to such *pensieri pensati* we can account for objects persisting over time and in space, with continuous identities amid changing contingencies. It is only when viewed through the steady lens of abstract thought that concrete thought is distinguishable

---

[34] 'Pensare', in *Hegeliana* [183–5].

from mere contingent experience. S must draw names, relations and inferences from the realm of abstract thought in order to orient concrete thinking. One critic has claimed that concrete thought is 'imprisoned' within abstract thought, since actual thinking relies on abstract thought to provide concepts and truth conditions necessary to make sense of contingent experience.[35] But we could not know anything about objects of abstract thought without actual, concrete thinking. The two are dialectically linked, united in that act.

The 'unity' of thought enables Gentile to anchor his theory in the method of immanence, rather than a subjective but transcendent method like the one he attributes to Plato. His admission of abstract thought should not be understood as a concession to transcendent realism. To be clear: all forms of realism presuppose the existence of certain true facts prior to S's act of thinking about them, and are thus relegated to the abstract logos; but because Gentile ties abstract thought to concrete thought, he avoids the realists' conclusion that these abstractions subsist independently of S. The concrete/abstract distinction is not the same as Kant's distinction between phenomena and noumena. Certainly the noumenon, or thing-in-itself, is an abstraction, but we cannot hope to know anything about its content, and much less say that it is real and permanent, without thinking about it. That, of course, is a logical impossibility, for once it is thought or spoken or known about, it ceases to exist independently and in itself.[36] Gentilean abstractions have no pretentions of independence, permanence or universality. They are particular and contingent creations of the act of thinking, and differ from concrete 'phenomena' only in their generality and unreality.[37]

It is also important to note the relation between subject and object in actual idealism. Only abstractly is there a subject plus an act plus an object. No object can be concretely known except through its 'synthesis'

---

[35] Fabio Gorani (1995) 'Logo concreto e logo astratto nel pensiero di Giovanni Gentile', *Idee*, 28-9, pp. 139-60 [152]. Gorani is here describing Armando Carlini's view. Note that he actually refers to the abstract and concrete 'logos', not thought, but the two are interchangeable for my purposes here.

[36] *Atto puro* [248-9]; Carr translation [259-60].

[37] Gentile notes some problems with Kant's noumena-phenomena distinction before the advent of actual idealism proper. See Gentile (1904) 'Fenomeni e noumeni nella filosofia di Kant', *La Critica*, 2, pp. 417-22. Although this work appeared before he worked out the details of actual idealism, he notes that 'Kant taught that we cannot say whether the noumenon is [...] different from or identical to the phenomenon', since we can define it only negatively [420-2]. In this early version he follows Kant (or rather, he tries to give an accurate account of what Kant thought). The fuller theory is developed in the sixth chapter of *Atto puro*.

with S. This means that S must think about it; and in so thinking, she changes something about herself. She becomes the act of thinking about that object rather than any other. Thinking about objects is what grants them an ontological status of any kind. It is by thinking that claims about them are true (and therefore not false) or false (and therefore not true) that truth becomes possible. This reinforces the idea that Gentile is a radical constructivist, embracing what earlier I called 'epistemological constructivism'. Since thought is a constructive act, and nothing is knowable except through the act of thinking, nothing is or can be excluded from the scope of construction. Thinking is not an activity in the same way as others. There is not thinking (in the sense of pondering, cogitating, deliberating) and then acting, but instead a permanent and universal act of thinking that underpins and creates all other acts. It is not simply a predicate in other propositions, but the entire medium that makes the proposition possible. So understood, the universality of Gentile's concept of thinking is more comprehensive than anything we see in Kant or elsewhere. As Enrico Berti puts it,

> the Gentilean act can be understood effectively as practical activity — one that is transformative, creative, and revolutionary. In this way it acquires a fullness of content infinitely superior to that of the Kantian's simple 'I think'.[38]

4. Truth in the method of immanence

As we saw earlier, Gentile believes that 'transcendent' methods rely on inadequate theories of knowledge, since they reduce S to the role of a passive 'spectator' on reality, mediating truth claims that are presented directly to her. The phenomenal world's content is imported wholesale into the consciousness of the thinking observer. As a result there is no room for S to exercise her will, to make conscious and intentional changes to the world, or actively to endorse or reject the appearance of reality as it is (seemingly) revealed to her. Hence the 'problem of logic': if truth claims are to mean anything — if there is to be any meaningful sense in which a proposition can be *false* — it seems that there must be some test of 'universality' to demonstrate 'the exclusion of the possibility that other subjects, or the same subject under different circumstances, would think differently'.[39]

This is much-trampled philosophical territory. Gentile's response is ambitious, and rests on two important claims. These are that (i) any 'transcendental method' must be rejected and replaced with a 'method

---

[38] Enrico Berti (1988) 'La dialettica e le sue riforme', in Pierro di Giovanni (ed.) *Il neoidealismo italiano*, Bari: Laterza, pp. 45–69 [57].

[39] *Logica 1* [46].

of immanence'; and (ii) all previous attempts to design a method of immanence have failed because their authors have retained elements of transcendent doctrines. Gentile's preferred method 'has nothing in common with those instrumental and canonical conceptions of the search for truth'.[40] The real difficulty is to locate plausible and universal truth conditions without conceding the existence of a transcendent reality. In what follows I will describe his account of the will, by which truths are 'affirmed', and the conditions in which this can occur; then the underlying coherence theory by which 'thinkable' claims are distinguished from 'unthinkable' others.

4i. The will and truth

Earlier I mentioned that Gentile distinguishes true claims from false or nonsensical claims partly by reference to *la volontà* (the will). This is an unusual position for him to adopt. Traditionally the 'practical activity' of the will is taken to be the basis for physical actions, and is distinguished from the 'theoretical activity' of the intellect, which is the basis for knowledge.[41] Since concrete *pensiero pensante* is a single ongoing act, not several acts occurring simultaneously, we need to explain how the apparently separate activities of thinking and acting can be resolved into it.

Gentile thinks that the commonsensical conception of 'physical activity' is self-contradictory.[42] Anything that is purely physical is not an activity, for an activity must be *performed* rather than merely *occurring*. As such it is inconceivable without S, who consciously acts in order to achieve some end. The will belongs to

> an ideal reality, not in space, but in spirit; and not in time, but eternity. [This is] a reality where the laws of [... nature] no longer hold sway. Instead there are those of liberty and of ends. Events no longer occur because they cannot do anything but occur, given what went before; but everything is made to happen with some end in mind, which is to say, because it has to happen, [but] freely, without taking precedent into account. And human action concurs with the creation of this ideal

---

40 Gentile (2003b) 'Immanenza', in *Hegeliana* [196].
41 *Sommario 1* [79]. Gentile notes that 'empirical psychologists' sometimes add sentiment as a third 'category of psychic facts'. He sets aside the question of whether there are properly two or three categories, insisting that the issue of the division between thought and action or intellect and will is of 'supreme importance'.
42 *Diritto* [62–3].

reality, which, coming from man, is inconceivable except as [the] work of an author of nature, [...] the constructor of a good (or of an evil).[43]

The will is identified not only with the desire or intention to act but also the action by which S's aim is realised. Intention without accompanying action is not will but *velleity*, which is separate, abstract and literally inconsequential, with no bearing on concrete reality. Willing involves S positing a 'self in front of [her]self' and moving from one state to another 'without a point of departure really distinguishable from the point of arrival'. Thus 'the end is not cut off from the subject that pursues it.' When S pursues this abstract version of herself and the world that she occupies, she acts in accordance with the 'dynamic and analytical nature' of concrete thinking.[44] In simpler language, this means that S's will consists in acts that she performs with the intention of bringing about some end that she believes to be valuable. This is an endless process, since it refers to an as-yet-unrealised aim. Once the action is completed and the aim is met, the results become facts, things of the past, *pensieri pensati*. S must then act in this new setting.[45]

The will also plays a role in the creation of knowledge. The truth cannot be assumed to present itself to S directly and fully formed. This would make S a passive spectator on reality, which conflicts with the idea of mediating the world through abstract concepts of the understanding, and belies the possibility of error, since if truths are imported wholesale into S's consciousness, we are unable to account for confusion and clarification, certainty and uncertainty, possibility and impossibility, truth and falsity.[46] It would also make S an empirical

---

[43] *Sommario 1* [80]. Note that Gentile includes indefinite articles alongside 'good' and 'evil' in the original Italian.

[44] *Diritto* [63]. In *Sommario 1* [83], Gentile explains why he writes of S creating herself, rather than the world. At the moment of completing an action, 'the material with which [S's] action must work is no longer remote from nor opposed to [her]; but, [having] already entered into the sphere of [her] dominion [...] is one of the constitutive elements of [her] actual personality. [...] So [her] desire will create a world; but this world will be the desire itself. [...] Whence the infinite value of good and the infinite disvalue of evil: [hence] in the good will there is a good universe, and in the bad [will] a malign universe.'

[45] *Genesi* [25]. The idea that moral value is found in acts, rather than things or facts, supports my contention that Gentile's doctrine is a constructivist one. See Korsgaard (2003): '[A]ccording to constructivism, normative concepts are not (in the first instance [...]) the names of objects or of facts or of the components of facts that we encounter in the world. They are the names of the solutions of problems, problems to which we give names to mark them out as objects for practical thought' [116].

[46] *Logica 2* [12–14].

thing, robbed of the capability to act on and thereby change the world. Thinking and experience — the whole of human life — would be nothing more than a stream of consciousness, its entire contents imposed from the outside. S's experiences of desire, aversion, effort and anticipation would be empty illusions, for really her life would proceed along a course over which she, *qua* subject, has no control.

To reconcile the fluidity of experience with knowledge, Gentile insists that *to know is to act*. Compelled by the insistent desire to think the truth, S must tell herself: *I want to know the truth; I want to make sense of the world*. She finds the truth by thinking, which is something that she must do (and to that extent *will herself* to do), not an event that she passively observes. She can never find a whole or objective truth, but she must cling to the belief that there is value in what she currently holds to be true. She constructs the most coherent and convincing account of the world that she can. This may be revised as she finds reasons to think differently or as circumstances change, but, until that occurs, her beliefs are true for her; they constitute knowledge. She does not (necessarily) assume that what she currently holds to be true must be and will always be so. But neither can she assume that what she currently thinks to be true is *untrue* without contradicting herself in the process. After all, the claim 'None of my beliefs are true beliefs' is itself a truth claim.[47] Thus the dialectic of thinking develops: there is truth in the concrete logos, which exists always in the present tense, just as the unformed and abstract future becomes fixed in the abstract past of *pensiero pensato*.[48]

4ii. The Gentilean will: being and Being There

Gentile claims that it would be absurd to presuppose the existence of a reality outside thought. By thinking that an external world exists, we are surely creating it as an *idea* of reality, which is an internal world of thought. Hence our original problem would go unsolved. Instead of confirming the existence of an external or non-ideal world, we would have instead created an internal and ideal one. We cannot know that this created world reflects a pre-existing reality. Two significant problems arise from this account of epistemological constructivism. Because they are related, I will discuss them together. The first is broad, and can be stated in several different ways; it concerns the persistence and regularity of reality. This I will call the *Being There Problem*. The second

---

[47] I am grateful to Graeme Garrard for suggesting this response to outright scepticism in a conversation we had in February 2012.

[48] '[T]he spirit resolves all of time (past and future) within the actuality of the present, which is its eternity.' See *Logica 2* [93].

problem, which I call the *Torturer Objection*, extends from the first, and concerns the implications of Gentile's description of the will.

Being There begins with the observation that a world is persistently presented in certain ways that we seem unable to alter. Events sometimes occur unexpectedly or (seemingly) inexplicably; we sometimes face conditions with which we feel unable to reconcile ourselves, regardless of how much we would like to or how hard we try. We can forget or ignore features of the world only for them to persist when we next encounter them. But Gentile thinks that the notion of those objects *already existing*, prior to our thinking about them, is absurd. He adds that for something to exist concretely it must be subsumed to S's will, meaning that she must consciously affirm that it exists. But if there are strict limits to what she can think, or certain things that she is bound to think—or, to put it more strongly, if propositions' contents come from somewhere, even if it falls to S to assign them their truth-value—then this constructivist doctrine appears less radical than Gentile claims. Beneath his dramatic language of *creating* the real is the banal observation that to think about and subsequently believe something is to perform an act, and it is in the course of this act that the qualities of 'true' and 'real' are assigned. Certainly they are created *qua* objects of knowledge. But if there are certain objects or relations between objects that S *cannot help but create*, or if the range of options is confined to one, then S's 'absolute creativity' looks doubtful.[49]

This is not strictly an objection. Nonetheless Roger Holmes identifies it as 'perhaps the most serious difficulty which Gentile's actual idealism is called upon to meet'. It entails a concession from which it is difficult for Gentile to recover without committing himself to a conception of reality that he sets out to avoid. It demotes Gentile's 'absolute creativity' to an amplified sort of noticing and suggests that 'his metaphysics is meaningless', leading us round on a long circle to the conclusions we would have accepted as true anyway. If the world somehow conditions the act of thinking, it is unclear what is ruled out by Gentile's bold assertion that the world is created by that act. For all the purported power of thought, the world is presented rigidly and fully formed, leaving it to S to notice it and recognise it as the proper measure of truth. Holmes writes:

> Thought might create for itself a world in which water ran up hill, but for all its creative power it is in some manner compelled to 'create' the

---

[49] George de Santillana asks 'how Gentile is going to lift himself up by his own braces', or rather, how can Gentile make sense of the idea that thinking refers to thought itself and not to a prior outside world? See (1938) 'The Idealism of Giovanni Gentile', *Isis,* 29 (2), pp. 366–76 [369].

world in which we live as a world in which water runs down hill. We may well believe that the order and uniformity of nature are a creation of thought, yet the specific character of that order and that uniformity is quite evidently beyond the power of thought to alter.[50]

My chosen name for this problem comes from H.S. Harris. He draws a distinction between 'real' objects and those that are 'certainly there',[51] accounting respectively for those things whose ontological status we have (positively) confirmed, and those that are just *there*, outside the purview of current thought, yet bound to become real when S notices them. Again it would be strictly absurd to claim that such an object *is*, or *exists*, or anything of the kind. It is no less absurd to say that it *is not*, or that it *does not exist*. To do this would be tantamount to answering a question without knowing that it has been asked. What, then, is the object's ontological status? Suppose, following Harris, we accept that these objects are *there*, but do not (yet) have a definite positive status: they are not *real*. For now we might label them *ontologically indeterminate*. But if we suppose that they hang together in some sense, amounting to a world of possible experience that awaits our discovery of it, our hesitation in accepting them as 'real' amounts to a pedantic (and optional) formality, deferring but in no way altering our conclusions. If this is true, actual idealism's pure constructivist promise gives way to something like common-sense realism, and differs from it only in the criteria by which ontological claims (X exists/does not exist) are ascribed.

The related *Torturer Objection* is so called because of a colourful example that Julius Evola once used to illustrate it.[52] He writes that Gentile would have us recognise every instance of 'inner capitulation [and] conformism' as the product of S's own will. Every proposition or fact about the world that S affirms in the act of thinking is taken to have been willed. It matters not if she disapproves of the facts and wants them to be different, for the present facts are still the concrete manifestation of her will. They are just the 'negative moment' in the will's

---

[50] Holmes (1937b) [114–16].
[51] Harris (1960) [36]: 'What [Gentile] really means is only that the natural world is certainly there: it acts, it resists, it is stubborn. What we call "our" will as opposed to the brute persistence of natural facts is really *thought striving* to objectify itself, *to make itself will*, that is to make itself count in the world.' On a similar note, Harris writes that 'The *fact*ual character of an experience is the *limit* of our actual comprehension. This limit *is always there*, but it is never final: we can never get to the bottom of Nature. It is in this sense that actual idealism affirms transcendence' [18].
[52] Julius Evola (1955) 'Gentile non è il nostro filosofo', *Ordine Nuovo*, 1 (4–5), pp. 25–30.

dialectic. If she is powerless to change the facts, she is condemned to go on suffering them indefinitely, lumbered with the useless consolation that she has (apparently) willed her unhappy circumstances into being. To press this point home, Evola offers 'a drastic example from the most banal domain':

> Subjected to torture, the Gentilean would have to recognise that [her] 'concrete will' is that of [her] tormenter, while the will that rebels and suffers would only be [her] empirical and 'abstract' ego—[the] only [thing] through which reality can be different from the will.

The Torturer Objection extends the Being There Problem by claiming that S's will is limited by the contingencies of a transcendent real world. Evola's example shows that S does not have unlimited power to do whatever she wants or create the world in whatever form she prefers. S does not decide to be tortured, and no doubt as the torture is taking place she feels an overwhelming desire for it to stop. If Gentile insists that, when subjected to torture, S's suffering really *is* the product of her own will, he must explain how the free and unconditioned will he describes is distinguishable from a stream of consciousness over which S has, at most, limited control. Otherwise his bold claims about the will and the constructive capacities of concrete thinking would tell us nothing about how S should decide how to act in the more familiar senses of these words. Desire and expectation would be nothing but 'particular' and 'abstract' moments of a will that is made universal and concrete on the crest of the continuous present, which could be described just as well without reference to it.[53]

These problems are not easily addressed. If they go unsolved, they risk exposing Gentile's concept of the will as normatively indeterminate, referring only to what currently is rather than what could or ought to be. The most plausible solution, I think, is as follows. Gentile's claims about the 'absolute creativity' of thinking are intended to emphasise that thinking is an act and S is an agent. This is uncontroversial. S must be an agent in order to ask herself whether or not she is an agent; strict determinism is to that extent ruled out. S can also imagine counterfactual states of affairs and intentionally work to bring them about. These aims are abstractions inasmuch as they are

---

[53] I take it that it is in response to these concerns that George de Santillana (1938) writes: 'the developments of [Gentile's] doctrine in action have proved so embarrassingly lunar and irrelevant that it is best to draw a chaste veil of silence. It is at this point that the irony of Fate overtakes idealism at last. For the unique Act becomes demonstrably, in the light of common day, actual passivity[, or r]ational, persuasive, albeit half-hearted yielding to the winds as they list' [375].

imaginary, but they are made concrete as S realises them. This is what Gentile means when he says that the true object of concrete willing is S herself: the will and moral value exist always in the present moment in which S acts. She must assign value to her acts by conceiving of them as constitutive of the ends they are intended to achieve. S works in the present toward an imagined future, which, by the time it becomes present, is no longer future. Here again we see the dialectic of thinking borne out. All of this requires S to engage in reflection, deciding what is valuable and what is not, just as she must reflect on her ideas and beliefs in order to determine which are true and which are false.

4iii. The value of truth and its construction

Gentile treats values, norms and truths in an unconventional fashion. Two points should be noted. First is that he emphasises the 'value' of truth claims. He maintains that it is impossible to believe that a claim is true without attaching to it the value of *universal* truth. S cannot think that something is true while doubting it or otherwise suspending judgement on its truth-value, for this would be entirely self-defeating. If she claims, 'I think that X is true and Y is false; but the reasons for holding this belief are inferior to those for thinking the reverse', she does not really think that X is true.[54] Suppose, for instance, that S was once a devout Christian, and although she now claims to have ceased to believe in God, she is at the same time afraid that God will punish her for her loss of faith. On Gentile's account, this person is deluding herself about what she really believes. One belief must give way decisively to the other, or else she must concede that she does not really know what she thinks. In the reality of her thought, God exists, does not exist, or is unknown (in which case He does not positively exist). Hence truth claims demand 'faith in truth', or the belief that what S currently holds to be true is equally true for anyone (it has 'concrete objectivity'). Those truths would appear as such to any person who had proceeded through the same processes of thinking, equipped with the same assumptions, to arrive at a conclusion.[55]

Gentile also refers to the central importance of 'faith in thinking'. He writes: 'There is no philosophical or scientific investigation [... nor] thinking of any sort [...] without the spontaneous and unshakeable

---

[54] There is no contradiction in the simultaneous claims that (I think that) X is true and (I think that) I may be mistaken. I may be unsure whether I'm right; X may be my best guess in light of the available evidence. It only becomes a problem when I add that (I think) I am probably wrong — that is, when the second assertion undermines, rather than reserves final judgement on, the first. See Harris (1960) [28 and 28–29n].

[55] Gentile 'Pensare', in *Hegeliana* [183].

conviction of thinking the truth.'[56] The major difference between 'faith in thinking' and 'faith in truth', as far as I can see, is that the former applies not only to truth claims, but also to the reasoning used to reach them. The structure of thought, or logic, imposes considerable demands on S and the reality she creates. It would be absurd for her to affirm that such-and-such a claim is true while consciously believing that an incompatible and contradictory claim is simultaneously true. Of course, this does not mean that such inconsistencies do not occur. They may go unnoticed.[57] In several places Gentile refers to the fundamental and universal duty to think, for S to assess and test her beliefs against each other in order to find a manageably coherent conception of reality or 'universal truth'.[58] Gentile's point here is that, once noticed, an instance of incoherence forces S to revise or abandon one or both of the affected truth claims. Logic is integral to the nature of thinking, so while it may be impossible to find purely objective truths, it is possible to eliminate incoherence and inconsistency within a set of beliefs already held. In this way we can discard any account of reality that relies upon simultaneous incommensurable claims. This reveals the extent of Gentile's coherence theory of truth: the criteria by which a claim is judged to be true (for a given subject) are *actual affirmation* and *coherence with existing thought*.[59]

---

[56] 'Pensare', in *Hegeliana* [183].

[57] Note Rik Peters' objection: 'In principle Gentile was right that we are all philosophers, but he used to overlook the fact that we are not philosophers all the time. In daily practice we do not do all our activities as self-conscious philosophers. A painter may draw a line and not know why he draws it as he does, scientists and historians ask questions, although they do not know always exactly why they ask the questions as they do. Even philosophers, *pace* Gentile, are sometimes not entirely aware of *all* the implications of their thought.' See Peters (1998a) *The Living Past: Philosophy, History and Action in the Thought of Croce, Gentile, de Ruggiero and Collingwood*, Nijmegen: Katholieke Universiteit Nijmegen [515].

[58] *Genesi* [45–8]; see also *Educazione* [137] on Gentile's equation of goodness and truth. In a rare example of an article explicitly dealing with Gentile's ethics, Valmai Burwood Evans affirms that 'to think is [...] a moral responsibility. Man feels that he *must* or that he *ought* to think as he does think. Every resource of his reason must be employed in his thinking. It is a moral duty.' See (1929) 'The Ethics of Giovanni Gentile', *International Journal of Ethics*, 39 (2), pp. 205–16 [215]. Note that for the most part this article is exegetical rather than analytic; the author summarises Gentile's views on ethics in the same roundabout fashion as Gentile himself.

[59] See, for example, *Sommario 1* [172], where Gentile writes: 'If I think of such-and-such an argument reaching a certain degree of truth, that is, of clarity and evidence, when I later go back to think it, I achieve a higher grade of

5. Coherence and construction

What theory of truth does Gentile support? I think that it is a thoroughgoing kind of coherence theory, but I shall have to argue for this point, since it has been disputed. For example: in his influential book about coherence theory, Nicholas Rescher remarks in a footnote that in the 1920s and '30s, 'there were rather more coherentists [on the Continent than in the UK], Carlo Gentile perhaps the most prominent among them'. 'Carlo' is surely a mistake: Giovanni Gentile is the only plausible contender for this role.[60] Meanwhile, Roger Holmes flatly denies that Gentile 'seek[s] a coherence theory of truth'.[61] Discounting 'Carlo', there is an obvious contradiction between these claims. Which one is correct? Unfortunately, Rescher states his claim without arguing for it, so more work is needed to build up his side of the argument. To offer an intelligible answer to this question, we must ask what coherence theory entails. Coherentism is unorthodox among today's philosophers and was by no means ordinary at the time Gentile was writing. Since it bears directly on the moral and political theory that is elaborated in chapters 3 and 4 of this book, it is worth trying to understand this difficult part of actual idealism, even if the subsequent parts of the book do not assume that the reader affirms the tenets of its metaphysics.

'Truth', writes Gentile, 'is relation; so too is logic. This relation is knowledge, which is possible only if there is an *a priori* relation between object and [a] subject that posits the terms [of the relation between them],[62] and does not presuppose them.' He continues:

> [I]t is clear that: first, a truth transcending the subject is neither truth nor knowable reality; second, nor is truth immanent within the subject while transcendent of the subject's act of knowing; [and] third, nor is truth a truth immanent within the same subject that knows, but transcendent of the actuality of this knowing in a naturalistic conception of thought. The only truth that we can embrace and fix with cast-iron certainty [...] is that which is born out of and develops with the subject, inasmuch as [she] knows [it] in act.[63]

---

truth; and to think on it a third time means an even higher grade, and so forth.'

[60] The mistaken reference appears in Nicholas Rescher (1973) *The Coherence Theory of Truth*, Oxford: Clarendon Press [25n]. Regarding the Carlo/Giovanni mix-up, Rescher confirms that 'there was a slip of the pen/mind there' [email correspondence with author, dated 4/1/2012].

[61] Holmes (1937b) [123]. Note that Harris, in his introduction to *Genesis and the Structure of Society* (1960), also identifies Gentile as a coherentist [21].

[62] Literally 'posits its terms' ('*pone i suoi termini*').

[63] *Logica 1* [65].

It seems, then, that Gentile favours a coherence theory of the *nature of truth*. This means that he believes that truth 'consists in' coherence, rather than in some externally existing world that *happens to be coherent* (as does F.H. Bradley).[64] But he also affirms a coherence theory of knowledge, in that S can be said to *know* a truth if it coheres with her other beliefs. In fact, given his insistence on the continuity of consciousness, the impossibility of consciously holding two contradictory beliefs simultaneously, and his repeated insistence on the concept of truth, Gentile seems to argue for what Ralph Walker calls 'a pure form of [...] coherence theory'.[65] This means that he affirms coherence theories of

i. truth ('the nature of truth' consists in coherence; and 'for a proposition to be true is for it to fit in with some designated set of beliefs');[66]

ii. knowledge (we know X if and only if we believe X and it coheres with our existing beliefs B); and

iii. justification (hypothesis Y coheres with existing beliefs B better than hypothesis Z coheres with B; this justifies the belief that Y is true and Z is not).

Unlike 'impure' coherence theory, which might rely on 'a correspondence account of straightforward "factual" truths about the world around us, but a coherence account of evaluative truths, or of truths about possibilities and necessities',[67] Gentile's theory constitutes an attempt to do away with any kind of unjustified presuppositions, and to invest solely in coherence and the concept of the subject as the act of thinking. He also means to forestall the collapse into mysticism—that is, reliance upon unsupported, vaguely understood or speculative beliefs—which, he believes, characterises the majority of earlier attempts to explain reality. These stand as evidence of other thinkers' failure to apply their convictions with sufficient rigour or consistency.

There are several definitions of 'coherence' and what it means for claims to 'cohere'. In general, coherence theory is distinguished from

---

[64] For some good indications of Bradley's view, see (1909) 'On Truth and Coherence', *Mind*, 18 (71), pp. 329–42 [*passim*], and (1909) 'Coherence and Contradiction', *Mind*, 18 (72), pp. 489–508 [also *passim*].

[65] Ralph C. Walker (1989) *The Coherence Theory of Truth: Realism, Anti-Realism, Idealism*, London: Routledge [15]. Note that Walker is not describing Gentile's theory, but instead a form of coherence theory to which Gentile's theory corresponds.

[66] Walker (1989) [5, 7].

[67] Walker (1989) [6].

correspondence theory by its concern with the relations between propositions in a given set, not between these propositions and a real world to which they 'correspond'. To be coherent and true, claims in a set must imply or at least not contradict each other.[68] On some accounts, propositions are true when they cohere with one another *and* with some other set of propositions, such as the beliefs of an omniscient and infallible God, those constituting nature or a Hegelian Absolute[69] — a comprehensive set of insuperable, permanent, necessary and mutually coherent truth claims. Such halfway-house positions are at least superficially attractive. They allow us to say that mere coherence among the things we have noticed indicates *the possibility* of truth, or a *plausible version* of truth, rather than the genuine version that awaits our discovery. 'The truth', which is authentic, objective and secure, is revealed in piecemeal fashion. While we have incomplete knowledge, then, the best we can do is to rely on the kind of provisional near-truth that coherence (among other things) offers, edging toward this real, genuine, authentic truth, although aware that we will never reach it. This distinction helps to reinforce the idea that there is a single truth to which all truth claims should aspire, even if we can never know it completely or directly. By the same token, it denies that there could ever be simultaneous mutually contradictory truths: where two people hold concurrent conflicting beliefs about the same object, at least one of them must be wrong. This is true regardless of whether there is any third subject to insist that one or both of the parties is mistaken. Correspondence theorists view the truth as though from the position of one who is already in possession of the facts.

Correspondence theorists' suspicion of coherence theory is understandable. Very often, though, this relies on a mistaken understanding of what coherence entails, assuming that 'coherence' is equivalent to 'non-contradiction'. For one instructive example, suppose that each person starts life without any fixed beliefs, as an Aristotle- or Locke-style *tabula rasa*. Any claim can be affirmed with equal ease. How does anyone make the jump from this starting point to anything like know-

---

[68] The problem with coherence as compatibility is that 'there seem to be as many cohering systems of propositions as there are possible worlds', so coherence by itself leaves us unable to 'distinguish the class of true statements from a self-consistent fairytale'. See Francis W. Dauer (1974) 'In Defense of the Coherence Theory of Truth', *Journal of Philosophy*, 71 (21), pp. 791–811 [794]; Mautner (2005) [109–10]; and L. Jonathan Cohen (1978) 'The Coherence Theory of Truth', *Philosophical Studies: An International Journal for Philosophy in the Analytic Tradition*, 34 (4), pp. 351–60 [352–3].

[69] Walker (1989) [4]; and Michael Inwood (1992) *A Hegel Dictionary*, London: Blackwell [298–301].

ledge or certainty? Without any standard against which hypotheses can be tested, what is there to prevent the acceptance of nonsensical claims which subsequently inhibit the acquisition of workably coherent beliefs? Surely this would lead to people holding all kinds of arbitrary but mutually supporting beliefs, and viewing all alternative claims with invulnerable incredulity. How, then, can we explain the near-consensus on so much of reality?[70]

This conception of coherence is mistaken. While coherence theory operates without any concept of a free-standing complete or permanent truth, it would be incorrect to assume that any combination of non-contradictory propositions has equal claim to be true. Several authors have written about the importance of 'comprehensiveness' in assessments of equally coherent sets of propositions.[71] Wolfgang Künne, for example, writes that 'a set of beliefs α is *more comprehensive,* and to that extent more coherent, than a set β if α answers not only all questions answered in β but also at least one further question which remains unanswered in β.' He continues:

> [T]he very word 'coherence' carries the suggestion that coherence is a matter of how well the parts of a manifold 'hang together' [...] Consider the following consistent subset of my beliefs: {[Oxford has many spires], [Caesar was assassinated], [My name is "WK"]}. It is more comprehensive than any of *its* subsets, to be sure, but one is inclined to say that the elements of this helter-skelter collection do not 'hang together'. [... W]e can say that a set of beliefs is coherent only if its members support each other like the poles in a tepee. This support can be only due to justificatory connections within the set.[72]

---

[70] Walker acknowledges these problems. He argues that 'no pure coherence theory is tenable', precisely because '[a] tenable coherence theory will have to leave room for certain truths whose nature does not consist in coherence. These will have to include truths about the beliefs that define the system and determine coherence. Otherwise, the theory cannot get going.' Walker (2001) 'The Coherence Theory', in Michael Patrick Lynch (ed.) *The Nature of Truth: Classic and Contemporary Perspectives,* Cambridge, MA: MIT Press, pp. 123–58 [149].

[71] Aside from Künne (below), see Dauer (1974) [794].

[72] Wolfgang Künne (2005) *Conceptions of Truth,* Oxford: Clarendon Press (originally 2003) [383–4]. Note that the proposition 'Caesar was assassinated' echoes essentially the same example in Bernard Bosanquet's 1922 article, 'A Word About Coherence', *Mind,* 31 (123), pp. 335–6 [336], and may have precedents prior to that. On the idea of propositions that 'hang together', compare Rescher (1973) [173], who claims that '[t]he essential distinctiveness of the coherence theory lies in its utilisation of the following precepts: (1) The truth of a proposition is to be determined in terms of its relationships to other proposition in its logical-epistemic environment. And consequently, (2) The true propositions form one tightly knit unit, a set each

If coherence is to be the measure of truth, these justificatory connections between claims must be more than requirements for consistency. If I have just begun to learn about Roman history, the claim 'Caesar was assassinated' (call this Caesar Hypothesis 1, or CH_1 for short) does not contradict any of my existing beliefs. This cannot be enough to tell me that it is true, for the claims 'Caesar died of pneumonia' (CH_2) and 'Caesar committed suicide' (CH_3) would bring about no contradiction either. I have no doubt that Caesar is dead, for I am told he lived more than two thousand years ago, and people do not live that long. I am similarly confident that he cannot have died from assassination, pneumonia *and* suicide, for each person dies only once. What am I to believe? Should I suspend judgement indefinitely, assuming that this list of hypotheses is not exhaustive, and other possibilities would cohere equally well with my beliefs? (Caesar might have died in an accident, and my assassination-, pneumonia- and suicide-affirming sources might be misinformed or otherwise trying to deceive me.) How can my belief in any one of the hypotheses be justified at the expense of any other? Without an external or transcendent reality in which necessary relations obtain, how can I ever know that a currently held system of beliefs coheres fully, rather than merely *appearing* to do so?

Gentile's answer to these questions is to identify coherence broadly with 'thinkability', leaving S to identify and apply other forms of justification or evaluation to the particular problems she faces. The appropriate kind of justification depends upon the question being asked. She must be convinced that her conclusions are sound and supported by the strongest arguments she can articulate. Returning to my Caesar example, I cannot *know* that CH_1 is true (*viz.* that Caesar was assassinated) with the same sort of certainty I could have about something that is more immediately available to me, such as a claim about something that is occurring now, or that occurred recently, within my memory, such as 'The book I placed on my desk earlier today is still there' (call this *Book Hypothesis*, or BH). The number of justifiable beliefs, which for now I will take to mean, 'beliefs that I am prepared to accept as true', that would lead me to believe that CH_1 is true, while CH_2 and CH_3 are not, is far smaller than the number of beliefs that I can draw upon to support my current belief that BH is true. (I distinctly

---

element of which stands in logical interlinkage with others so that the whole forms a comprehensively connected and unified network.' Also Linda Martín Alcoff (2001) 'The Case for Coherence', in Michael Patrick Lynch (ed.) *The Nature of Truth: Classic and Contemporary Perspectives*, Cambridge, MA: MIT Press, pp. 159–82 [161] for 'minimalist' vs. 'stronger' versions.

remember placing the book on my desk; I locked the door to my study, etc.) I cannot provide a chain of firm and coherent beliefs to connect any particular CH with my present belief in BH.

My belief in CH_1 is less easily verified and for that reason less certain than my belief in BH. CH_1 is at least minimally plausible, since, as I have said, it does not contradict any of my beliefs about the mortality of man. Mere plausibility is inadequate justification for a belief, however. A huge number of incompatible claims are simultaneously plausible, including (it seems to me, in my ignorance of Roman history) CH_1, CH_2 and CH_3. But in favour of CH_1 I can also draw on the support of many sources. Even if I learn rather more about the history of ancient Rome, I cannot provide the claims necessary for comprehensive coherence to support any of these claims (all these historians might have colluded to deceive me). But the historical consensus still gives me evidence that Caesar was *probably* assassinated, rather than dying of pneumonia or by suicide. To think otherwise would commit me to another, far more ambitious hypothesis, namely that all my CH_1-affirming sources are either mistaken or deliberately misleading. Again, this *could* be true. Nothing excludes it entirely. Even if I cannot hope to be absolutely certain about how Caesar died, I believe that it happened, and if I am to hold any specific beliefs about how it occurred, I must appeal to reasons—the best available evidence, say—rather than believing some arbitrary and groundless proposition.

Note that one key difference between coherence and correspondence theories is that the former hinge on some *subject* who affirms a set of *beliefs* and tests propositions against them. To a large extent correspondence theories can do away with such subjects. The claim 'A proposition is true [if and only if] it agrees with reality'[73] does not appeal to any subject's belief, knowledge or assertion that this proposition is true. We might say that it would be true even if there were no one able to entertain the idea. The 'reality' referred to in the claim is doing the work independently of any subject. It is to this that true claims 'correspond' in correspondence theories. At a small stretch, we might call this conception of reality and truth 'transcendent' of our knowledge of it. It exists free-standing and independent of anyone's knowledge of or thought about it. Our role when seeking the truth is to find the propositions that correspond with it. To put it another way: the truth is out there, and our job is to find it. For Gentile, this unknown, transcendent

---

[73] Richard Kirkham (1997) *Theories of Truth: A Critical Introduction*, Cambridge, MA: MIT Press [22]. Kirkham offers this as 'an ideally expressed extensional theory of truth'.

truth can only be a presupposition. We cannot know that it is there until we know what it is, having already constructed it.

6. Actual idealism's positivity and the unknown

Gentile argues that thinking 'realises' truth. The construction of truth is a strictly positive enterprise; falsity is not realised except in the sense that '[I think] *it is true* that X is false.' We may then wonder how he conceives, or can conceive, of doubt and the unknown. To understand his position, we can assess his responses to the three famous sceptical hypotheses in Descartes' *Meditations*. These are the 'madman' and 'dreamer' scenarios, which run as follows. Descartes wants to offer reasons for doubting what seem to him to be obvious truths. He notes that he is aware of people 'whose brains are so damaged by the persistent vapours of melancholia that they firmly maintain that they are kings when they are paupers, or say they are dressed in purple when they are naked'. He adds that his seemingly ordinary impressions of 'sitting by the fire' could equally be mistaken, as he is well aware of having dreamt such things in the past. It is not always obvious to one who is dreaming that one's received impressions are in any way inauthentic. Therefore, Descartes' belief that he is awake is not sufficient to prove that he is awake; or, as he puts it later, 'every sensory experience [he] ha[s] ever thought [he] was having while awake [he] can also think of [him]self as sometimes having while asleep[.]'[74]

Descartes addresses these sceptical hypotheses in the Sixth Meditation. He writes that he can 'almost always make use of more than one sense to investigate the same thing', and that 'dreams are never linked by memory with all the other actions of life as waking experiences are.' When he 'distinctly see[s] where things come from and where and when they come to [him]', he continues, 'and when [he] can connect [his] perceptions of them with the whole of the rest of [his] life without a break', then he can be certain of their truthful existence.[75] What Descartes has presented here is a coherentist argument regarding the *justification* of truth claims. Dream-experiences are recognisable as dreams, as distinct from real experiences, in that they do not cohere with the rest of the reality in which they appear. That is: a dream-subject cannot comprehend and justify the objects of her experience by means of reflection, for the dream does not have a continuous past or present, or indeed any content beyond that which is placed in it by the

---

[74] Descartes, in Cottingham et al. (eds.) (1984) 'First Meditation', in *The Philosophical Writings of Descartes* (Volume 2) [13]; second quotation is from 'Sixth Meditation', same volume [53].

[75] Descartes (1984) 'Sixth Meditation' [61–2].

dreaming mind. But Descartes' appeal to coherence does not make him a coherentist *per se*. Even committed correspondence theorists may appeal to coherence to support or justify their beliefs. The difference is that the correspondence theorist presupposes the existence of an already coherent reality to which maximally coherent truth claims necessarily correspond, whereas the 'pure coherence theorist', such as Gentile, assumes that coherence plus affirmation—which may demand special reasons[76]—*is* truth. Descartes believes in the existence of God and innate ideas, although neither of these can be derived from coherence alone. Their presence in his theory amounts to a correspondence theorist's escape hatch for use when coherence is unable to provide answers.

Gentile cannot presuppose the truth of innate ideas or divine revelation without abandoning his method of immanence, and is left with only coherence and actual will to serve as criteria for truth. This has deeper implications for Descartes' third sceptical scenario, in which 'a malicious demon of the utmost power and cunning' sets out to deceive us. Gentile cannot countenance Descartes' optimistic assumption that faith, innate ideas and coherence tests would expose the demon's illusory world as a fiction. It follows from Gentile's doctrine that if the demon presents S with a coherent illusion of reality, truth claims drawn from within that perceived reality stand up. Once S believes in the demon, and can find compelling reasons to think that the meta-reality in which the demon exists is more authentic than that with which she is presented, she cannot coherently assert that present-world truth claims are, as a matter of objective fact, true. Either assumption can give way to the other: either perceived reality is authentic, and truth claims drawn from it are genuinely true; or perceived reality is inauthentic, and claims drawn from it cannot be true. No intermediate position can be coherently conceived.

This does not explain why Gentile rejects scepticism. Why does he not say: 'I concede that perceived reality could be an elaborate illusion. This illusion may be clearly apparent from a viewpoint beyond the ambit of perceived reality. But there is no reason to assume that within perceived reality there should be any instance of incoherence that would confirm or otherwise alert me to reality's inauthenticity. Hence I

---

[76] Note that I add 'special reasons' to cover cases where S believes (affirms) a particular claim *because there are sufficient reasons in favour of it*, not just because it does not contradict her other beliefs. For example: if I do not know your mother's name, I cannot non-arbitrarily decide that her name was Maria unless I have some reason for doing so—you have told me, for example. The relevant 'special reasons' take different forms for different kinds of belief.

shall not affirm that *any* claim is true'? Gentile's point, I think, is that we must assume that *something* is true, for even 'there is no truth' is a positive (albeit untenable) truth claim.[77] If no incoherence is noticed in perceived reality, then we cannot ascertain any other hypothetical reality's priority over this one; so for the time being, since we *are* subject to an ostensibly coherent and comprehensive reality, we must draw our conception of truth from within that, rather than positing necessarily abstract alternatives about which we cannot make even preliminarily certain judgements. Besides, if we accept wholesale scepticism, there arises another question: how does the demon know that *his* meta-reality is not merely an illusion? Pursuing the line in this direction, we face an infinite regress of hypothetical demons and doubts.[78]

It may be objected that Gentile fails to offer us a theory of truth, or that what he *does* offer is not really a theory of truth, but instead a theory of plausibility, possible truth, or worse, a slippery kind of half-truth without any means to make the leap to final or definitive statement on truth and falsity. To some extent this objection is well-founded. Gentile is unwilling to assume that any hitherto reliable truth claim comes with a cast-iron guarantee. But this does not mean that he is uninterested in or less than serious about truth. He shows a deep commitment to the idea. His argument, in essence, is that we cannot assume that the present offers an accurate indication of what will be or what has always been. He recognises our epistemological limits, and is unwilling to disguise these using concepts that he cannot hope to know or understand. For those who insist on a concept of transcendent truth, he writes,

> [t]he unknown is a great ocean, which all the sciences — mathematical or positive, moral or natural as they may be — are desperately navigating. The short-sighted thinker contents himself with the feeble light that science shines on as much of phenomenal reality as is presented to him, investing his faith in the power of knowledge and reason: but just as he tries to push his sights a little bit farther, a little bit higher, suspicions about the invincible unknown weaken his pride and his certainty,

---

[77] *Diritto* [49].
[78] In one short passage in *Logica 2*, Gentile appears to overstep the margins of pure coherence theory. He is writing about death, but for our purposes, it is worth noting what he says about *dreams*: '[D]eath is frightening because it does not exist, just as nature, the past, and dreams do not exist. There is the man that dreams, but not the things he dreams about. And so death is the negation of thought, but cannot actuate itself [as] the negation that thought makes of itself. As we have seen, in fact, thought cannot be conceived except as immortal, for [it is] infinite' [177].

forcing him to be more modest; disheartened at thought's impotence in penetrating the world, and making him fall suddenly to his knees.[79]

Gentile believes that actual idealism allows him to do away with this gloomy picture of man 'desperately navigating' the 'great ocean' of the unknown. His way around it is to say that reality is no bigger than we think it is. We know reality inasmuch as we know ourselves, the minds that think it. Truth is a construction of thought; it is meaningless without the will. Certain principles of knowledge are necessary to unified thought; non-contradiction and necessity are two of these. We cannot think that two incompatible propositions are simultaneously true (although we might concede that both *could* be true, were it not for the present truth-value of the other). Nor can we suspend judgement altogether and go without any beliefs. As his implicit re-working of the *cogito* shows, to think that nothing is true entails a contradiction that cannot be sustained. S must try instead to piece together (construct) the most coherent account of the world she can.

Gentile presents a theory in which truths may be altered or replaced, but remain constantly true in the present tense for the reflective individual who believes in them. S knows that she may be mistaken about any or all of her currently held beliefs, but she holds them nonetheless. She tests them, where possible, and changes them where she sees that it is appropriate to do so. Her belief is no less authentic for this caveat. She does not slide into blanket scepticism, or worse, nihilism. Hers are not beliefs 'for the time being', held only provisionally until the true facts somehow emerge. The same applies to her moral beliefs: she knows that if she had been someone else, if she had lived in another time or place, her moral beliefs and commitments would, in all likelihood, be different. She also knows that she may change her moral convictions at some point in the future, in light of new ideas and circumstances. They are nevertheless authentic beliefs and commitments. The very idea of a mistaken belief makes sense only in retrospect, and for that reason only as an abstraction. While a proposition is seriously believed—which for Gentile *requires* its coherence with other beliefs—it is concretely true. We have only the ever-changing present in and on which to cast judgement.

I have found it useful to understand Gentile's theory of truth by means of what I call the *Jigsaw Analogy*. Suppose you are presented with a large bag of assorted jigsaw puzzle pieces [propositions], and you decide to fit them together as best you can. However, you do not have anything to which you can match the developing picture [no authentic reality]. It may be that some pieces come from different and

---

[79] *Logica 2* [179].

totally incompatible sets [false or incoherent claims]. You simply try to make the most coherent picture you can with what you have. After you have provisionally matched a few pieces, it becomes easier to make sense of the picture as a whole, and to assess the likely compatibility of a given new piece. It may be possible to fit pieces together in what appears to be a coherent way, but which prevents you from adding other connected groups of pieces. Thus you can build islands of pieces that have no obvious relation to each other. (Your beliefs about what ingredients are used in moussaka are largely independent of your beliefs about how the subjunctive mood is used in Portuguese). It is in your interest to try to build as large and coherent a picture as you can [comprehensiveness]. This is a reason to continue building your jigsaw rather than simply collecting individual pieces: a piece in isolation cannot really show you anything or enable you to make sense of other pieces.[80]

7. Conclusion

In this chapter we have seen how, on Gentile's account, the subject's thinking is, for that subject, the sum of what there is. There are no substantive truths waiting to be found. Rather, truths are created and wholly constituted by the act of thinking. Coherence offers the test of their veracity; but, since propositions are inseparable from the subject's act of positing them, the conditions of truthfulness are *coherence plus belief*. The limits of construction are to be understood as those of the coherently thinkable. Coherence is inherent to the structure of thought, and although *noticing* that thought has a structure might cause us to identify it as a defined and limited object, this impression is mistaken. Anything that occurs beyond the bounds of the thinkable — a necessarily unknown and unknowable realm, which we can describe only abstractly — is unavailable to us as a possible object of thought.

---

[80] Note that this analogy is pure Wakefield and cannot be found in any of Gentile's works.

Chapter 3

The Priority of the Socius

Chapter 2 described the actual idealist conception of the subject and the theories of truth and knowledge that extend from it. Gentile argues that any tenable doctrine must take proper account of *pensiero pensante*'s continuous synthesis of subject and object, which is made intelligible through reference to abstract *pensieri pensati*. Doctrines such as realism and mysticism, which presuppose the existence of transcendent, purely objective domains, are dismissed as speculative and unsound. Extreme scepticism is rejected on the grounds that it is internally contradictory, since the claim that knowledge is impossible is itself a claim about truth and knowledge.

This chapter situates the Gentilean subject in moral theory, promoting a theory of *mind* or *subjectivity* to a fully fledged theory of *the person* by accounting for the role other people play in the constitution of a given subject's identity and values. To achieve this I first discuss and reject the argument that actual idealism's strictly subjective basis makes it impossible for anyone to be bound by moral responsibilities (sub-heading #1). Next I explain how Gentile introduces the idea of a 'transcendental' or 'internal society' to make sense of a plurality of subjects despite the irreducible subjectivity of the act of thinking (#2). I then lay out his account of the 'internal dialogue' by which the thinking subject discerns the demands of the 'universal will' manifest in her conscience (#3), before describing how Gentile politicises his moral theory by having the state act as the ultimate arbiter of moral claims (#4). At the end of the chapter (#5) I indicate which issues Gentile leaves inadequately explained in his account of the internal dialogue. As we shall see in Chapter 4, these inadequacies are exploited and deepened in the extended theory of the total ethical state.

1. Actual idealism and the person

Recall Gentile's conception of subjectivity as *pensiero pensante*.[1] He argues that because the empirical world is known and constructed in the act of thinking, we cannot coherently identify an empirical person as the originator and agent of thought. Instead thought must direct, correct and condition itself, while its subject—the cogito's 'I'—is an abstraction posited in that same act. As the Logical Priority Justification showed, no amount of empirically derived knowledge about how brains work can dislodge Gentile from this position. Some critics have thought that this unusual conception of thought and truth prevents him from making meaningful claims about morality or offering any conception of the person beyond the contingent and ephemeral thoughts in a single stream of consciousness.[2] One version of this objection holds that Gentile is a *solipsist*, or one who believes that only one mind or subject is real, while the objects thought about are not. A related objection holds that, if anything but the subject is real in actual idealism, its existence depends on the subject's beliefs about it, so it cannot yield robust moral responsibilities. Gentile counters the first objection, and can, I think, defend himself against the second. However, the second calls for further clarifications of what actual idealism is intended to model. Both objections, together with replies, are rehearsed below.

1i. The Solipsist Objection

The *Solipsist Objection* holds that by placing S at the centre of a phenomenological universe of her own creation, Gentile reveals himself to be a solipsist, or so much like one as to replicate the problems that such a

---

1   Note that I say 'subjectivity' and not 'subject'. This is because *pensiero pensante* is strictly subject and object in one. Either taken in isolation is an abstraction.

2   A. Robert Caponigri notes that 'it has been charged that the humanism of Gentile [...] is a humanism without the person, which is but a small remove from the paradoxical assertion that it is a humanism without man' [61]. See Caponigri (1963) 'The Status of the Person in the Humanism of Giovanni Gentile', *Journal of the History of Philosophy*, 2 (1), pp. 61–9. The point is reiterated in Caponigri (1977) 'Person, Society and Art in the Actual Idealism of Giovanni Gentile', in Simonetta Betti, Franca Rovigatti and Gianni Eugenio Viola (eds.) *Enciclopedia 76–77: il pensiero di Giovanni Gentile* (Volume 1), Florence: Istituto della Enciclopedia Italiana, pp. 171–83 [175–8]. Note that the non-person and solipsist objections are not mutually exclusive. For example, George de Santillana (1938) explicitly omits to tackle the 'grievous question of solipsism', but concedes that in Gentile's system, 'the empirical person [...] is brushed aside', and '[t]he Concrete Logos inhabits a perplexing world of inconcrete people' [373].

doctrine entails for moral philosophy.[3] Solipsism's central claim is that only S is real.[4] Other objects, including other persons, are considered unreal or else permanently in doubt. Their existence depends upon S, who cannot know any mind other than her own. Propositions about other persons as *subjects* are therefore nonsensical, and these others cannot be the originators of moral claims upon S. Reasons for thought and action count only if S recognises and believes them to do so. If she believes she has as-yet-unrecognised reasons to pursue any particular course of action, she is deluding herself, for those reasons do not obtain in her universe. They and their purported originators are unreal phantoms trespassing on her unique reality.

There is an obvious superficial resemblance between the solipsism just described and the actual idealism described previously. Gentile was aware of this, as well as the serious problems the equation of actual idealism and solipsism would have for the former's potential as a moral theory. Even in the early essay 'L'atto del pensare come atto puro', he distinguishes his own view from any solipsism for which 'the world [is] closed inside the self'.[5] Later, recognising the durability of the Solipsist Objection, he offers a lengthier explanation. Actual idealism is not solipsism because

---

[3] Such views were particularly popular among readers of Gentile before and shortly after the war. Some examples: Roger Holmes explicitly affirms that Gentile is a solipsist [112]. Isacco Sciaky does not endorse this view but claims that one of the most 'common' and 'easy' criticisms of actual idealism was that 'it would make it impossible to understand the multiplicity of [...] individuals' [332]. W.G. de Burgh thinks that Gentile fails to explain 'who, in [the] concrete act of thinking, can truly be said to think'. Gentile's answer leaves 'the living thinker [...] circling restlessly, like a squirrel in a cage, between two abstractions [*viz.* subject and object]' [22]. While this falls short of an explicit accusation of solipsism, it captures something of the strangeness of actual idealism's conception of 'the living thinker'. See Holmes (1937b); Sciaky (1956) 'L'io e i molti io e il significato dello spirito come atto', *Giornale critico della filosofia italiana*, 3, pp. 332-54; De Burgh (1929) 'Gentile's Philosophy of Spirit', *Journal of Philosophical Studies*, 4 (13), pp. 3-22.

[4] There are different kinds of solipsism, and not all of these are described in the broadly idealist terms used here. For the description given here I retain the distinction between thought and experience even though this is not included in actual idealism. Also bear in mind that even Holmes, who most explicitly describes actual idealism as a solipsist doctrine, stops short of claiming that Gentile thinks other people, objects etc. and just 'figments of the imagination'. (See sub-section 2 of the present chapter.)

[5] 'Pensare', in *Hegeliana* [190]. Some of these ideas are further echoed in *Atto puro* [253]; Carr translation [264].

> the solipsist's ego is a particular and negative ego, which as such can feel its own solitude and the impossibility of escaping it. So the solipsist is [an] egoist [who] renounces goodness just as [she] renounces truth. But [her] ego is negative because it is identical to itself; and that makes it a thing, not spirit. Its negativity is the negativity of the atom, which is always [and only] that, incapable of changing. It can absolutely exclude other atoms from itself, and is itself excluded in turn from them, precisely because it lacks the power to negate and change itself.[6]

Gentile believes that the solipsist's subject is the solitary real thing amid a multiplicity of unreal things, without any meaningful relation to them or the power to alter them. He contrasts this with the subject in actual idealism, who constantly changes, creating her world through the position and subsequent affirmation or rejection of claims. (Where she rejects a claim that she formerly affirmed, she 'negates' herself.) Actual idealism's concrete subject, S, is identified with the 'infinite and progressive universalisation of the ego', meaning that she contains the whole of her reality within herself, but, as a progressive act that affects and forms[7] the world, she is not limited to any single state of being. Neither is the world that she constructs. As her knowledge and understanding of it are increased in the endless process of correction and revision, she strives to attain universal knowledge, or that which is justified so any other rational thinker, faced with the same considerations, would reach the same conclusions.[8] She is not 'imprisoned in a world of illusions',[9] but instead constructs and is part of the only genuine reality there is.

This does not quite disarm the accusation of solipsism. Gentile has distinguished his position from that of the extreme solipsist, who may never have existed except as a caricature, as Socrates acknowledges of Protagoras in *Theaetetus*.[10] But actual idealism's account of the relation between thinker (or thinking) and the world thought about is a strange one, and as a descriptive term 'solipsism' may be the best we can hope to attach to it. This is Roger Holmes' view. He distinguishes Gentile's

---

[6] 'Concetti fondamentale dell'attualismo', in *Introduzione* [35–6].

[7] It is tempting to say that S *interprets* the world, but this would expose me to the objection that for something to be interpreted, its existence (and availability for interpretation) must be presupposed.

[8] I am deliberately echoing Gentile's characterisation of universality as 'the exclusion of the possibility that other subjects, or the same subject under different circumstances, would think differently'. This was cited in Chapter 2, sub-section #4.

[9] Harris (1960) [17].

[10] See Plato's *Theaetetus* [171c–e]. Harris (1960), too, asserts that 'no-one is actually a solipsist' [30n].

position from Protagoras's 'crude and early' solipsism,[11] but maintains that other terms volunteered as descriptions of Gentile's position, such as 'mentalism' and 'subjective idealism', are inappropriate because

> Gentile's idealism is actual, not subjective: and, contrary to mentalism, it denies the existence of other minds. There is no single word which describes his position exactly. Although in its very derivation it refers to the self, which Gentile finds unreal, 'solipsism' has been selected for use in this wider meaning because among recent thinkers it has become more than either of the other two symbolic of those very obvious difficulties which actual idealism must face. If solipsism is untenable because it denies existence to everything but the self, actual idealism is even more so [...] because it denies existence even to the self. [...T]o go beyond the self to the act of thinking as the only existent is to carry the solipsistic trend to its extreme. In this sense Gentile is a solipsist.[12]

Holmes' designation is better understandable in this light. Nonetheless, I do not accept it. This is not just a matter of words. To construe Gentile as a solipsist is to situate him among philosophers radically different from him. Actual idealism resembles solipsism in its basic assumption that it makes no sense to say that any specific claim is true unless one knows it, and knowledge is inconceivable without a knower. But solipsism's *other* major tenet—that nothing except S is real—is reflected in Gentile's theory only because the two have markedly different conceptions of what S is and how far her identity extends. Gentile affirms that one cannot say anything about what is true or real without thinking about it, positing the idea of an object (or rather: the object as idea) and attaching to it the label of truth or untruth, reality or unreality. This is very different from the solipsist's view of S as a mind or person without an epistemological handle on the world, and as such suffocated under blanket scepticism.

1ii. The Conditionality Objection

'If a moral reality exists,' writes Gentile, 'it exists inasmuch as man makes it exist. Its moral character consists in precisely its existence as [the] product of the human spirit.'[13] It might be thought that his insistence on the 'absolute subjectivity' of thinking means that nothing can be true unless S thinks it is true, which in turn means that there can be no binding moral claims on S—indeed, no morality at all—unless S currently believes herself to be so bound.[14] If this were true, moral

---

[11] Holmes (1937b) [111].
[12] Holmes (1937b) [113n].
[13] *Diritto* [7].
[14] The phrase 'absolute subjectivity' appears in *Atto puro*: 'Throughout the ages a profound and invincible need has made the human mind hold back

theory could never get started, for morality's contents and structure would depend upon S's unaccountable beliefs, or lack of beliefs, about them. Call this the

> *Conditionality Objection.* Moral claims apply to S if and only if S presently thinks they apply. She cannot act rightly or wrongly unless she expressly thinks she is doing so (she cannot be mistaken in this belief). The claim that S *ought* to perform certain actions cannot be sustained, since any such moral claim's authority is conditional upon an unaccountable belief that S may or may not hold.[15]

On this account, claims about morality would be like claims about deliciousness: true for S only if S thinks they are true, but neither necessarily true for nor falsifiable by other persons (assuming they exist at all) who may think differently. Actual idealist moral theory would be reducible to a description of S's current beliefs, rather than about standards consistently applicable to actions of people in general or to S at other times. This could yield a very thin conception of morality, according to which S acts morally when she believes she is acting morally, but not one in which S could be mistaken about this belief. She would act wrongly only when she behaves in a self-consciously hypocritical way, doing what she thinks she ought not to do. 'Morality' would be an empty category, open to be filled with any content whatsoever.[16]

---

from affirming the unmultipliable and infinite unity of the spirit in its absolute subjectivity. The spirit can neither detach anything from itself nor go outside itself' [33]; Carr translation [30].

15 I take it that it is for these reasons that Richard Bellamy notes '[i]t is hard to see what political consequences are likely to follow from this theory [of spirit as pure act] beyond the anarchism of *bellum omnium contra omnes*' (the war of all against all). See Bellamy (1987) *Modern Italian Social Theory: Ideology and Politics from Pareto to the Present*, Stanford, CA: Stanford University Press [104]. Here it is worth noting that Gentile explicitly rejects the idea of the *bellum omnium* in both *Genesi* and the earlier *Diritto*. He connects the *bellum omnium* to the atomistic Hobbesian conception of the person that he means to deny. See *Diritto* [71-2] and *Genesi* [123--4]; Harris translation [281].

16 I trust that the meaning of this sentence is clear. To elaborate: according to the Conditionality Objection, S's belief that an action of type X is morally good means only that X-type actions are good for S. By the same logic, if S believes that actions of type Y are supercalifragilistic, then (tautologously) Y-type actions are supercalifragilistic for S. The quality of being morally

Actual idealism is less vulnerable to this objection than it may first appear. As we have seen, S exists in the continuous present, but she can reflect on the past and anticipate or otherwise imagine the future. She conceives of herself as a person whose identity persists over time, and for whom the future could take any of several different courses. She has at her disposal an array of abstractions, and although memories and imaginary constructs are not *concretely real* in the truth-determining sense, they enable S to make sense of concrete reality, giving her what earlier I called a 'steady lens' through which to view the ever-changing present. Such abstraction also enables S to conceive of herself as one person among others, and of other persons as thinking subjects, even though her own necessarily subjective standpoint prevents her from thinking (being subject to) their thoughts. She can imagine what other people would think about judgements she is making, and thus construct abstract standards for her own thinking. This idea substantially reduces the force of the Conditionality Objection, for while actual idealism requires S's morality to be her own construction, she has the resources to review her beliefs and the reasons for them while the construction is in progress. This provides critical space between her present, contingent thoughts and the abstractions she uses to evaluate and refine them. She can show herself to be wrong about her beliefs, and engage with moral theory as she works out what the relevant standards should be.

1iii. Persons and personalism

Actual idealism's view of the person is deceptively ordinary. It does us no good to take the day-to-day business of thinking about and interpreting the world, only to re-describe it in such a way that it is disguised or misrepresented, however valid, elegant and ambitious-sounding the resultant theory might be. If Gentile were not describing a kind of thinking that we could recognise as our own, the detailed content of the theory would be arbitrary to the point of uselessness. Yet the basis of the theory is undoubtedly sound: each of us really *does* experience a single life in the continuous present, feeling ourselves to direct our thoughts; and it is only through this act that we can make sense of the world inside or outside our present experiences, interpreting sense data, emotions, truth and falsity using a catalogue of words.[17]

---

good means only that it is believed to be so; the phrase 'morally good' means nothing in itself.

[17] Language is perhaps the best illustration of the fact that persons *need to assume that they share a world with others* if any of their claims are to make sense. Gentile notes in *Sommario 1* that 'if men needed to make themselves

This view is supported by A. Robert Caponigri, writing in the 1960s and 1970s, and Antonio G. Pesce, writing today. They describe actual idealism as a kind of 'personalism', emphasising that its conception of the person includes but is not identical to the (abstract) subject of experience. Rather, as *concrete subject,* it incorporates the immanent dialectic by which thought reflects upon and adjusts itself. S recognises both what she *actually, actively* thinks and what she *could* but *does not* think, as well as the reasons for affirming the former but not the latter.[18] Her self-conception as one person among others is needed for this dialectic to take place.[19] The question of how Gentile can make sense of a concrete, socially embedded subject without overstepping the margins of actual idealism is addressed over the remainder of this chapter.[20]

---

agree to understand "red" by the word "red", they would then need to make themselves agree to see it as red! And it is no more embarrassing — [for] whoever sets himself to thinking of the multitude of [*tante*] human souls as mutually impenetrable worlds, [or] independent unities without windows, as [... Leibniz] said — to take account of the way in which men attain certainty of seeing [...] with different eyes, each taking its own account [of what it sees], positing the same red for the same stuff. When God thunders in the sky, do we not all hear the same noise?' [59–60].

[18] Caponigri (1963) writes that Gentile's 'manifest humanism deserves the [...] designation "personalism" in a sense far more intimate and profound than usually accompanies the attribution' [69; see also 64–6]. Pesce even has '*il personalismo di Giovanni Gentile*' (Giovanni Gentile's personalism) serve as his book's subtitle. He notes that actual idealism relies on a fluid conception of the person that responds to others and so changes itself [15–16]. Here Pesce is referring to the *dialogo interno,* which we will encounter later in this chapter. See Pesce (2012) *L'interiorità intersoggettiva dell'attualismo: il personalismo di Giovanni Gentile,* Rome: Aracne.

[19] More accurately still, S recognises that what she now thinks is just one of several things that she could think.

[20] For a useful comparison, consider David Hume's 'bundle theory' of the self, in which what is commonly called 'the subject' is really just a composite or 'bundle' of thoughts, experiences, memories and so on, constituting a single entity in the same way that many countries collectively constitute a 'commonwealth'. The mistake, thinks Hume, is to imagine that there is *a subject* that must be added to this collection in order to make a person. On the contrary, the subject *is the bundle.* Actual idealism's subject is not far removed from that. The difference is that Gentile supplies a more demanding and fluid account of S as 'the act of thinking that thinks itself', and thus tries to have it incorporate a wider range of experience than Hume, as an empiricist, can address. As has been noted, what are commonly called 'the thinker' and 'thought' are, viewed in isolation, abstractions. This does not mean, as Holmes seems to think it means, that the person is erased altogether. Instead her existence is acknowledged in something like its

2. Socialising the pure act

We have seen how Gentile can make sense of a plurality of points of view despite the 'absolute subjectivity' of thinking.[21] On the evidence we have seen so far, his solution to this problem treats other people as *mere abstractions*, no different from persons S imagines for her own amusement. Since S can imagine a potentially limitless variety of different people, and any claim S imagines being made of her could be countered with an opposing claim, how (if at all) can these abstract persons impose moral claims upon her?[22] To answer this question, we will need to show that S is not only capable of conceiving of other people, but also capable of using their 'otherness' to determine her own substantive moral responsibilities.

Given that Gentile had to work hard to counter the accusation that he was a solipsist, it is remarkable that he readily refers to 'the absolutely social nature of the human spirit' and man's 'primordial sociality'.[23] Even in explicitly metaphysical works like *Atto puro* and the *Logica* he alludes to the multiplicity of things, including other individual spirits:[24]

> The language that we speak, the institutions that govern our civil life, the city in which we live, the artistic monuments that we admire, the books and records of our civilisation, and the religious and moral traditions by which, even without any special historical interest, we feed our culture[; through these] we are connected by a thousand chains to spirits not belonging to our own time, but who present themselves to us,[25] and [are] intelligible only as free and spiritual reality.[26]

This spiritual metaphor reveals a conception of the person far removed from solipsism. Gentile's account is compatible with the idea that,

---

proper complexity. See David Hume w/L.A. Selby-Bigge (ed.) (1978) *A Treatise of Human Nature,* Oxford: Oxford University Press [259–61].

[21] The phrase 'absolute subjectivity' appears in *Atto puro*: 'Throughout the ages a profound and invincible need has made the human mind hold back from affirming the unmultipliable and infinite unity of the spirit in its absolute subjectivity. The spirit can neither detach anything from itself nor go outside itself' [33]; Carr translation [30].

[22] These issues are raised in *Genesi* [20–1]; Harris translation [86–7].

[23] *Diritto* [74] and *Genesi* [123]; Harris translation [181].

[24] As numerous critics of Hegelianism and other idealist doctrines have noted, the term 'spirit' is notoriously hard to define. We might ask whether a plurality of spirits *entails* a plurality of subjects, since (it might be argued) a person without subjective experience could not be described as a 'spirit' unless each and every object were also described as such. Tempting though it is, I will not pursue that issue any farther here.

[25] Literally: 'whose reality is presented to us' ('*la cui realtà è presente a noi*').

[26] *Atto puro* [193]; Carr translation [203].

empirically speaking, persons live individual lives, and have correspondingly individual identities, experiences, thoughts and so forth. But they are embedded in society, shaped by their surroundings, and live within a complex of institutions, values and conventions. At no point is S (or anybody) *purely and simply* an individual, possessing an identity but no social or socially imposed baggage. This is part of her identity from the beginning. For the duration of her life she is a part-constituent of a social group or groups[27] that may have existed before she was born and may persist after she is dead. Society, incorporating all of these groups, is prior to its members, but cannot exist in their absence; so inasmuch as society determines who S is and how she defines herself, it is part-author of her. It 'speaks through [her] mouth, feels with [her] heart, and thinks with [her] brain'.[28]

These remarks explain how Gentile can justify his reference to a plurality of 'spirits' in the passage quoted above. Although S is the only thinker who truly thinks, she still identifies herself as a member of society that also contains others. She cannot be directly subject to the thoughts and experiences of those other people, but she can re-think or re-construct their (presumed) thoughts for herself, even if those others 'do not belong to [her] own time', and are not empirically present. Others' thoughts can be communicated to S in a variety of ways, but most obviously in speech or writing. The potential to direct present thinking along the lines of past thinking distinguishes written language from shapes drawn on a page, speech from noise, and empathy from passive observation. S remains the active centre of the process by which she constructs her own self-consciously social identity. Other people exist only insofar as S thinks they exist, but since S thinks in a social context and as an irreducibly social animal, the issue of their non-existence does not arise. Gentile compares the issue of the 'primitive savage' to whom the idea of other people never occurs with that of a sleeper who is unaware that she exists. Even *to raise the question* of whether she truly existed while she was asleep, she must be conscious (and self-conscious); likewise, now the socialised thinker conceives of

---

[27] I include 'or groups' for two reasons. One is that S may be a member of many groups (in *Diritto*, Gentile suggests friendship groups, families, schools, states and the Church) at once [74]. The other reason is that S may change her allegiance and identity over the course of a single life. For example, she may emigrate to another country and identify herself with that, ceasing to identify with the society where she used to live.

[28] *Genesi* [15]; Harris translation [82]. Note that Gentile here refers to 'the community', but I take it that the same claims can be made of society without altering his meaning.

herself as a person among persons, the possibility of her not being so is only abstractly conceivable.[29]

2i. The internal society and the conscience

Actual idealist moral theory hinges on the distinction between the particular will of the individual and the universal will to which that is subsidiary. As we saw in Chapter 2,[30] Gentile believes that the will cannot be separated from the action to which it corresponds. To will an end is to imagine it, identify it as valuable and set about realising it. As such the will is more complex than desire or inclination, which has no need of any rational basis. S can simultaneously desire two or more mutually incompatible ends, but she cannot *will* them in Gentile's sense, since that would entail their realisation, which is impossible. Nor is willing a case of desiring only mutually compatible ends; S could be making her decision on the basis of misinformation, faulty inferences or caprice. For her (potentially flawed) will to generate moral claims, it must be 'resolved into the universal [will]' manifest in her 'moral conscience'.[31] This is achieved dialectically by reference to the 'society inside the person' (*la società in interiore homine*). Even the fictional castaway Robinson Crusoe, alone on his island, is a member of this internal society. He conceives of himself *as Robinson Crusoe,* an English sailor,

---

[29] *Genesi* [42–4]. The claim that *no one thinks there are no other people* might be thought unconvincing, since it does nothing to explain why someone who *did* hold such a belief, even if no one *actually* does so, would have reason to change it. Harris and Holmes both offer some help. Harris (1960) [24] writes that 'although the philosophy of the pure act may be a system of necessary and universal knowledge, its very necessity and universality will render it valueless unless it helps us to deal with the personal problems of our lives as individuals.' Holmes (1937b) [11–12] similarly insists that 'Gentile does not mean that there are no objects in our rooms or rooms in our houses, nor that there are not men and women in the world, nor that there are no natural laws. He does not mean that these things are figments of the imagination. He argues only that the demands of logic limit the conclusions that may be reached in our thinking about these entities and laws, that they may be studied in and for themselves but that such a study will not lead to an understanding of reality. And the understanding of the real is the problem of philosophy.'

[30] Chapter 2, sub-section 4i.

[31] A note on language: the Italian word for 'conscience' is *coscienza,* which is difficult to translate into English. It is distinct from *conoscenza* (knowledge) but covers the same ground as 'awareness' and 'consciousness', which have no specifically moral connotations. This is worth bearing in mind wherever I point out a reference to 'conscience' in Gentile's writings. Sometimes any of several words can be used as it is unclear which English word best captures his meaning.

interpreting and understanding the world by means of a language and a set of beliefs and values presented to him by society.[32] These are not separable from him; no complete description of him could omit them. As a thinking subject, he does not consist of an essential identity and a number of optional social embellishments, but instead as a composite of elements that, while individually available for revision or jettison, cannot be viewed from a solid, permanent or fully objective standpoint.[33] He reflects on his choices and measures the value of his actions against the standards other people once imposed upon him, and continue to impose even when they are empirically absent.[34]

When he first introduces the idea of the internal society in *Diritto*, Gentile omits to explain how S can use it to unlock the content of the universal will. It might be thought that Gentile is suggesting, by means of a metaphor, that individuals' consciences are socially constructed, and morality is whatever S's conscience tells her it is. S internalises the values held by the people around her, and her conscience comes to berate and chastise S when her actions fail to meet those socially and self-imposed standards. The will would be 'universal' inasmuch as (S

---

[32] Daniel Defoe (1987) *Robinson Crusoe*, Leicester: Galley [80-1] for some of Crusoe's frequent appeals to God and the ideas of Good and Evil (capitalisation sic). Also relevant is Crusoe's attempt to educate the 'poor savage' Man Friday on [243-61], and especially with reference to moral matters and God [251 and 257].

[33] There is an obvious resemblance between this idea and Otto Neurath's famous remarks about 'sailors who have to rebuild their ship on the open sea, without ever being able to dismantle it in dry-dock and reconstruct it from its best components'. See his (1983) 'Protocol Statements', in R.S. Cohen and M. Neurath (eds.) *Philosophical Papers 1913-1946*, Dordrecht: Reidel, pp. 91-9. This essay first published 1932 [92]. Another analogy may be drawn with the debate over Wittgenstein's idea of private languages. Plainly Gentile does not believe that subjects think in 'mentalese' and translate these thoughts into a 'public language' when they want to express them. While interesting, this debate extends beyond the margins of this book, so I do not pursue it here beyond this brief comment.

[34] This example, together with a description of the relation between individual and universal will, appears in *Diritto* [70-5]. The idea of the internal society is echoed in a telling passage in *Educazione*, where Gentile claims that so long as Italian expatriates living in the United States remain 'tied by the natural bond of common origin, [… and] we continue to speak to each other in our old language'—note that Gentile here uses the first-person collective pronoun, *noi*, although he was not an expatriate himself—'always feeling ourselves [to constitute] a special community, with common interests and peculiar moral affinities, Italy has crossed the ocean with us, and we have preserved our nationality, although divided and far distant from our ancient peninsula'. *Educazione* [14]; Bigongiari translation [10].

thinks) it is sanctioned by S's society. This would make Gentile's moral theory a kind of intuitionism undergirded by a social constructivist account of how individuals come to hold substantive intuitive beliefs about morality. The right thing for S to do would be whatever her conscience demands, or whatever she *feels* is right. These demands would always be immediately or intuitively plain to her, and the conscience would have unimpeachable authority.

This would be a crude moral theory. It would assume that S already knows what the conscience and, by extension, morality require of her. Thus it would neglect the most obvious problem motivating moral theory: *we* (or S) *do not always know* what morality requires; the conscience can respond inconsistently or ambiguously (and sometimes not at all) to the actions we perform or propose to perform. This theory would also fail to explain how morality is created or constructed. There would be no dialectical process, for the universal's will's content would come to S fully formed from an external source (the society of other empirical persons) without her thought mediating it in any way. Instead the conscience would be the voice of S's 'internal' society only inasmuch as S notices it. The claims that it has authority over S, or that it provides decisive and morally binding reasons for S to conform to it, would be presuppositions without rational justification. This combination of social constructivism and unmediated intuitionism casts the internal society as a reflection of an external society constituted by many empirical persons, and the universal will as an aggregate of their individual wills. These other persons' wills differ from both the universal will and each other. There is no guarantee, then, that these will inform any unified or coherent set of standards for S, who may even be ignorant of what other people (would) think about the choice she faces. If Gentilean moral theory identifies morality with the universal will of the internal society, it must provide some way for S to untangle the sometimes contradictory expectations that society, broadly conceived, might have of her.

2ii. The internal dialogue

Diritto contains no detailed description of the procedure by which S determines the universal will's content and to what extent her personal, particular will corresponds to that. However, the book does include important stipulations about how S's social nature is developed. The fact of socialisation means that a great many ideas are more-or-less directly imported into S's thinking. These include values, concepts of right and wrong, and some associations[35] with which she comes to identify herself. These contribute to her identity and will. The socialised conscience is formed as S battles two 'enemies': the 'external enemy', namely 'the evil about which we warn others', which is generally countered through education; and the 'internal enemy', which is 'the egoistic and irrational inclination that each vigilant conscience finds from time to time [...] at its lowest ebb'.[36] The egoistic inclination (selfishness) is irrational because it ignores the fact that S is a product of her society, so presenting an *abstraction* in the guise of the *concrete subject*. In inviting S to overcome the 'internal enemy', or ego, Gentile is arguing for neither perfect altruism nor conformity, but instead for her to give due regard to her irreducibly social identity when considering what she wants and wills. By reflecting on how other people would view her actions, S overcomes her ego and begins to act according to a self-consciously moral and universal will. That other people are socialised to hold the same values and ideas about what is *not* desirable (the external enemy) helps her to understand what other people think. S's recognition of others as fellow holders of a shared identity, Gentile claims, constitutes a bond of empathy and even *love*.[37]

A more elaborate explanation is offered in Gentile's last book, *Genesi*, where he describes the 'internal dialogue' taking place in the 'transcendental society'[38] comprising the ego, or the narrowly personal part of S's identity, as she considers her particular interests and circumstances; and the 'socius', or the part voiced by other people as a whole,[39] which presents itself to S as an 'alter-ego [which] joins [her] in a dialogue, speaking and listening as [her] partner in life's drama'. This 'dialogue' between these two abstract parts of S's 'absolutely social' identity enables her to identify the demands of her conscience, or the universal will, and distinguish these from the contrary demands of her

---

[35] Only 'some' because persons can, of course, enter associations voluntarily. This is less true of others, like families or nations.

[36] *Diritto* [68]. Note that in the passage cited, Gentile refers to the ways in which we ensure that *la volontà buona* — the good will — 'prevails' over its internal and external enemies.

[37] *Sommario 2* [42–4]; *Genesi* [45–6]; Harris translation [110–11].

[38] Note that 'transcendental society' is interchangeable with 'internal society'.

[39] In the chapter of *Genesi* immediately after the discussion of *la società trascendentale*, Gentile refers to our need for the 'otherness' (*alterità*) of other people, even if we 'reduce [their] external otherness to the otherness that is within us', in order for the 'interior dialectic of our existence' — that is, of thinking — to take place, 'closed in the circle of the active synthesis of our restless spirituality' [46]; Harris translation [111].

internal and external enemies.[40] In more ordinary language, the dialogue represents the process of *moral reasoning*. The socius is cast as an

> interlocutor and actor in this drama of the transcendental society, wherein man is, absolutely speaking, a political animal [... The] ego reflects on itself and is placed in a synthetic unity of the self and the other, as opposites that are therefore identical[.][41]

This 'synthetic unity' entails the construction of the conscience. If this dialogue is to be any kind of conversation, it must allow meaningful interaction and change on each side. The socius (hereafter A, for 'alter-ego') cannot be directly identified with the agent of the universal will, for that will is the *outcome* of the dialogue, not a contributor to it. If S always knew what the universal will (and morality) required, there would be no need for any dialogue. S must reflect upon, respond to, *converse* with A in order to know the universal will's content, and in the process re-align her own will to match it. The reason S must re-align her will with the result of the dialogue is that this represents the will of the 'universal subject' or 'universal man' to which S continually aspires, all the while conceiving of herself as subject to incomplete knowledge, sometimes erroneous thinking, and wrong choices. She does so because 'the universal man is always right': the conclusion to which S's best thinking leads *is the right conclusion* by virtue of its derivation.[42]

---

[40] Note that Gentile does not explicitly refer to the internal and external enemies in *Genesi*.

[41] *Genesi* [38]. Note the similarity between this reference to man as an 'absolutely [...] political animal' and those to 'the absolutely social nature of man', written in *Diritto* more than two decades before. H.S. Harris translates less literally but perhaps more clearly when he writes, 'The drama in which this interlocutor takes part is the transcendental society, which is what makes man a "political animal" in an absolute sense, from the moment when he is reflectively aware of himself and becomes a real individual, a synthetic unity of self and other as opposites which are therefore identical; or even from the moment when he is an individual *implicitly*, when he has still only a *feeling* of self.' See Gentile w/Harris (trans.) (1960) [103].

[42] The idea of the 'universal *subject*' (my emphasis) is discussed in *Atto puro* [90–3]; Carr translation [92–5]; *Diritto* [73–5]; and *Religione* [89]. The quoted sentence about the 'universal man' appears in *Genesi* [55] where Gentile refers to the need for moral judgements to be 'actual', in that they are, in the language I have been using, actively and consciously constructed by S in the continuous present. Note that I have altered Gentile's punctuation. He actually places 'universal' in parentheses: '*L'uomo (universale) ha sempre ragione.*' Harris translates this as 'The universal spirit of man is always right' [119], but the addition of the word 'spirit' in this case gives the sentence the feel of a sweeping rhetorical declaration that it does not, or need not, possess in Italian. A final important point is that this phrase obviously echoes the Fascist slogan '*il Duce* is always right' (*il Duce ha sempre ragione*). It might be

3. Constructing the universal will

The internal dialogue models S's method of determining which single course of action is the right one for her to perform. The very necessity of the dialogue suggests that S lacks direct access to the answer to this question. The socius, or A, cannot be identified directly with the universal subject, but somehow enables S to discern the universal will's content. It is striking that Gentile places this dialogue between S and her 'moral conscience', for this implies, unusually, that S *cannot directly perceive her own conscience*, or at least what she can directly perceive — call this her 'particular conscience' — does not represent the universal will. This distinction between the particular conscience and the genuine article helps to overcome the problem of the (particular) conscience's unreliability, inconsistency and ambiguity. As S participates in dialogue with A, she *constructs* the universal will, using rational procedures to distinguish it from the contingent demands of her particular conscience.

Earlier I claimed that A represents 'other people as a whole'. Even Gentile's early critics found his conception of the social nature of the individual 'intolerably ambiguous', so to make sense of this concept and its role in the dialogue, we must define it in more detail.[43] It is an idealised 'other' with whom S identifies herself and to whom she refers when she wants to know whether her actions are justified.[44] Gentile characterises this figure in a variety of ways. He suggests[45] that A represents the unified voice of the society or community to which S

---

thought that this implies that Gentile identifies the universal man (or subject) with Mussolini; but, as I shall argue in this chapter and the next, I find it more plausible that *il Duce* is a specially constructed ideal to which political leaders ought to aspire.

[43] W.G. de Burgh complains of the 'intolerably ambiguous' idea of 'the I that is We' that occurs in *Atto puro*. See de Burgh (1929) [11].

[44] Antonio G. Pesce offers an apt description of the socius as '[one's] perpetual companion on the path of life, standing in for [*cambiano*] friends, the people we remember from our early years [...], even the people we have freely loved and with whom we have formed stronger commitments, but nevertheless *company*, [...] which [provides us with] reason so long as it illuminates our spirit'. See Pesce (2012) *L'interiorità intersoggettiva dell'attualismo*, Milan: Aracne [167].

[45] Note that I say 'suggests' because Gentile refers explicitly to the internal or transcendental dialogue only in *Genesi*. Nevertheless, he elsewhere refers to other people and the derivation of universality out from the immanent dialectic of the self and other people, and I take it that the same underlying thought motivates his claims there. The citations offered below point to only a few of the copious relevant passages.

belongs,[46] the people that S loves and to whom she feels an emotional bond,[47] *any person* with whom S interacts and tries to understand,[48] God[49] and the state.[50] Considered as discrete entities or groups, these might conceivably lead S to different conclusions about what she ought to do. The state's expectations of S — defined by the law of the land, say — might be incompatible with the moral code prevalent in her society. It may even be unclear what society as a whole requires of S, for its members do not necessarily share a single, coherent system of values. Even if it were possible to eliminate value pluralism by means of social engineering, the *plurality of persons* would make it difficult to ascribe a single will to society. Individuals have personal interests and relationships to each other, and live correspondingly individual lives. Each one, as an empirical person, must live in some particular place, know particular people, and otherwise have experiences that at least some others will not share. Even where all members of society share a single conception of value, these basic differences may lead them to will different ends.

I suspect that these problems are insurmountable, so it is fortunate that Gentile's moral theory does not require a solution to them. He even *denies the possibility* of a full resolution of the social milieu, broadly conceived to include God, the state and all the rest, into one homogeneous entity. As we have seen, it is precisely the difference between S and A that makes the internal dialogue possible. Without that difference, no such dialogue could occur. The outcome of and motivation for the dialogue is the universal will, or the will of the universal subject. To claim that the will is universal is no different from claiming that a factual claim is universally true. S recognises that she does not know the whole truth, and may be deceived or confused. She also knows that other people hold different beliefs, and that she herself has held different beliefs in the past, but they too may be (and, S must assume, in fact are) mistaken. Likewise each person has contingent desires, plans and values. If these various actual and hypothetical persons are to generate authoritative claims about what S *ought to do*, they must be subsumed to some kind of universal authority. More simply: for S to believe that she ought to perform one action and not another, she must believe that some claim about what she ought to do is *true*. By extension, claims that

---

[46] *Diritto* [70–5]; *Genesi* [15–16]; Harris translation [80–2].
[47] *Sommario* [18–19]; *Religione* [79]; *Logica 2* [171]; *Genesi* [45–6]; Harris translation [110–11].
[48] *Atto puro* [16–17]; Carr translation [13].
[49] *Religione* [78–9]; *Genesi* [18–19]; Harris translation [84–5]. Gentile identifies universality with divinity in *Sommario 1* [20].
[50] *Introduzione* [179–82]; *Genesi* [passim].

she ought to perform other actions are false, even if other people do not believe them to be so. If S's belief is to be anything but the result of an arbitrary choice between possible accounts of what she ought to do, she must find one that is *universally true*, meaning that it is supported by the best thinking she can manage.[51] The universal will has the property of universality *because S imposes it*; it does not represent some fact or feature that happens to be shared by all the entities referred to in its construction, but instead an ideal synthesis of their differences in a single will. We might say that it represents the best discernible answer to S's question, 'What ought I to do?'

3i. Internality and indeterminacy

The suggestion that the universal will is constructed by S gives rise to a variant of the Conditionality Objection discussed earlier in the chapter. Call this the

> *Particularity Objection.* If S constructs the moral will, and in doing so acts as the arbiter of its universality, that will is not universal but particular. Its alleged universality depends upon S's judgement, so the will's specifications—its prescriptions for S—are contingent on who S refers to in the internal dialogue and what method she employs to reduce the plurality of claims to one. Despite her *aspirations* to know universal truths, S is always at least potentially subject to false beliefs, irrationality and ignorance or misinterpretation of the relevant facts. The moral will cannot be universal unless all thinkers are actually subject to it.

The problem is that the dialogue's conclusion hinges on S's contingent beliefs about what other people in her society think and how their various claims contribute to one will. There is no guarantee that any two persons conducting internal dialogues will reach the same conclusion, even if they believe themselves to belong to the same external society. Each can dismiss the other's conception of the universal will as a mistake; and because each is the arbiter of her own conception—each must decide for herself when she has reached the right conclusion—neither can decisively show the other to be wrong. There is no *fact of the matter* regarding what society or the state *really* wills. A claim cannot be universal while it is applicable to only one subject, for if it were, universality would be indistinguishable from particularity. No member of

---

[51] *Sommario 1* [20–2].

society can make claims that are automatically privileged above those made by others, so unless there is genuine unanimity, to call any particular conception of the moral will 'universal' is illegitimate.

The following variant of Gentile's Robinson Crusoe example illustrates his position. Call this

> *Passé Castaway.* In Crusoe's absence, the accepted moral code in his native England has changed so radically that what his conscience tells him no longer correlates with the norms prevalent in that (or any) real society. He identifies with a community that no longer empirically exists. He is now *the only person* who continues to believe in his conception of right and wrong.

Set apart from the other members of society, Crusoe cannot use empirical means to establish what the universal will requires. He can neither ask other people whether they agree with the conception at which he has arrived, nor what reasons they have considered in favour of their different conceptions. Crusoe can refer *only* to the internal society. Since in this example it is supposed that his beliefs about what the relevant people would say are mistaken, and his internal society does not accurately reflect any society of empirical persons, does he act wrongly when he believes he acts rightly? Can he legitimately claim to have identified and acted according to the demands of the universal will?

The actual idealist conception of truth suggests that Crusoe can make legitimate moral claims. If the internal society were an exact reflection of an external entity, and its power to justify S's (or Crusoe's) moral claims depended on its correspondence to that, any claim about the internal society would be reducible to a claim about the external one. The internal society's *internality* would add nothing to the theory. This would have major implications for the claims of persons in ordinarily social contexts. Societies are large, complex and ever-changing institutions, including people who do not necessarily know each other, and who certainly do not have intimate knowledge of each other's thoughts about all topics and at all times. S cannot comprehensively survey the ideas of every member whenever she needs to make a decision, for then the decision would never be made. She must instead work with what is available to her, even though her internal version of society is only an incomplete and imperfect reflection of its external counterpart. Crusoe's predicament is an extreme version of the challenge facing anyone who tries to make a moral judgement according to the universal will, but their problems are two of a kind. Although he is estranged from other people, Crusoe can still have a meaningful dialogue with himself, assessing his current beliefs, or propositions whose truth-value he has not yet determined, against his past beliefs and beliefs he can hypothetically imagine himself holding. This is made possible by the 'internal doubling of the spirit' requisite to self-conscious reflection: S posits herself as simultaneously an abstract object of contemplation, such as a will already willed or a thought already thought; and the concrete, living activity of thinking, which constantly revises, re-evaluates and corrects itself.[52]

3ii. A schematic for the socius

The Particularity Objection so far remains unanswered. We have not yet seen how the internal dialogue enables S to derive the universal will from the internal society. The dialogue is a subjectively bound process, and while it may yield a private, provisional morality, applicable exclusively to S at the moment she consciously evaluates her thoughts and actions, its outcome depends on what its participants (S and the socius, or A) say to one another, which in turn depends upon what A is imagined to represent. If this were left to S's discretion, her dialogue might follow a course different to that of anyone else faced with the same considerations. It may also follow a different course if she faces those considerations a second time. Unless A's identity is reasonably settled, S could refer to versions alternately based on God, society and those nearest and dearest to her, finding different conclusions each time.[53] To anchor the dialogue in such a way that moral judgements are

---

[52] *Sommario 1* [97]. Note that Gentile's word is *geminazione* (gemination), which I have rendered as 'doubling' to avoid confusion with 'germination'. First published in 1913, this marks an early and somewhat crude description of the dynamic that makes the internal society, first described three years later in *Diritto*, possible.

[53] In the course of his career, Gentile made remarks that could be extended to support various different conceptions of what the socius is supposed to represent. In *Religione*, for instance, he presents himself as a Catholic (of sorts), and emphasises actual idealism's Christian heritage. The socius could be identified with God, and the image of the individual subject struggling to overcome her selfishness, conversing with a single alter-ego that is somehow part of her, reflects a Christian image of the repentant sinner trying to reconcile herself with the perfect image of her creator. But this leaves open the question of how the subject knows what God wants, especially with regard to issues on which the Gospels are unclear or internally incoherent. Nor is this convincing as a general moral theory. What about subjects who are atheists or followers of a non-Christian religion? Note that Gentile's own religious beliefs are disputed. Antonio G. Pesce insists that 'there is in fact no doubt that Gentile was a Catholic', but Gentile occasionally identifies himself as an atheist, albeit one who is still *culturally*

more than a matter of opinion, we will need a more detailed picture of the socius.

Consider why we might reject the contingent and subjectively bound version of morality described by the Conditionality and Particularity Objections. On my account of actual idealism, S does not simply do what she wants to do, following her intuitive, brute desires. Nor do her beliefs come to her without her intervention, in a continuous and unreflective stream of consciousness.[54] She has an idea of what someone else might think, or what she herself might think under different circumstances. If S is going to settle on a conclusion or change her mind about something previously affirmed, and this is not just a mistake, she needs a reason for doing so. Since there could be reasons in favour of several mutually incompatible conclusions, S must have in mind some standard by which these reasons can be assessed and the strongest ones identified. This standard applies not only to S but to the reasons other people have (or might have) for thinking whatever they think. The dialogue between S and A represents S's attempt to identify the *best reasons* for thought and action. The support of these reasons grants the dialogue's outcome *universal* status. This suggests that A cannot be an arbitrarily selected alter-ego. There must be some connection between it and those reasons.

From here we can extrapolate four distinguishing features of the socius and the reasons connected to it.[55] These features overlap, and each is open to a degree of interpretation, but among them there is no real order of importance. The first feature is that A should present S with *reasons*. The second is that A must be *distinguishable* from S. It must be possible for A to present S with reasons *other than those that S presently affirms,* for otherwise A would be redundant, and A and S would have nothing to say to one another. In effect, S would be talking to herself in an uninterrupted monologue. The third distinguishing feature, connected with the first, is that A's reasons must purport to be

---

a Catholic. See Pesce (2011) 'La fenomenologia della coscienza in Giovanni Gentile', *Quaderni Leif,*, 5 (6), pp. 39–54 [quoted 52n; also 42–3]; and Gentile (1922b) 'Le ragioni del mio ateismo e la storia del cristianesimo', *Giornale critico della filosofia italiana,* 3, pp. 325–8.

[54] This is debatable. We might say that some beliefs come to S without her intervention, such as those affirming simple claims like 'my feet feel cold' or 'this book is red'. But this is not true of *all* her beliefs. Some require her to draw inferences and make judgements, which are undoubtedly actions on her part.

[55] It is important to stress that these features are not made explicit in Gentile's work. Rather, they are included here because the logic of Gentile's theory appears to demand them.

authoritative for S. Once S has determined what morality[56] requires of her, she must have decisive reasons to do what it demands rather than what she personally wants to do. (This reflects Gentile's claims about the flight from morality's 'enemies', including selfishness.) A fourth and final feature of A is that its reasons should be both *shared* and *stable*. This means that for S to recognise A's reasons as good reasons, they must count as reasons for other rational people (hence *shared*), and for S in circumstances that could but do not presently obtain (hence *stable*). These features are particularly important for establishing the *universality* of the conception of the will derived from the dialogue. Otherwise A's reasons might be those that just happen to occur to S at the moment the internal dialogue is commenced, with the result that the authority of the will constructed from them is illusory.[57]

4. Politicising the internal society

I have laid out some strictly formal specifications that the socius must meet if it is to determine the universal will's demands. If this interpretation is correct, the internal dialogue is an explicitly constructivist device, providing the procedure needed to promote an *epistemological constructivist* theory to a *procedural constructivist* one.[58] The central motif of refining universality from particularity aligns Gentile's theory with some of the best-known constructivist doctrines, and especially those in the Kantian tradition. We should note, however, that Gentile does not pursue his moral theory in this direction. Instead he turns to the political implications of his theory, arguing that the state must act as the embodiment of the universal will. To do this he draws on two elements of the theory that we have seen already, namely, the social construction of the individual and the equation of the universal will with the moral

---

[56] Since actual idealism holds that subjects have a duty to think as well as they can, any factual statement has a moral character. Hence what *morality* demands of S extends to what *reason* demands of her.

[57] Some of these features, and especially the claim that reasons should be shared and stable, reflect John Rawls' conception of 'reflective equilibrium'. As we saw in Chapter 1, Rawls uses this term to refer to the matching of abstractly derived principles of justice to the considered judgements of the persons subject to them, weighing both sides (that is: the principles and the judgements) until the two overlap. The same dynamic can be seen in the derivation of 'universality' from the internal dialogue, except here S *begins with the reasons she presently affirms,* rather than an abstractly derived set of principles, and throws these into contention with the reasons already held by others. These themes will be taken up and elaborated in Part 2 of this book. See Rawls (1971) *A Theory of Justice* (original edition), London: Belknap Press [48–9].

[58] These terms were defined in Chapter 1, sub-section #1.

conscience. I trace the development of Gentile's theory of the total ethical state in Chapter 4, but my final aim for the present chapter is to assess the extent to which the politicisation of the internal dialogue is compatible with the rest of actual idealist moral theory.

4i. Internal and external dialogues

The politicisation of the internal dialogue relies upon a close correspondence between the internal society and some external reference point. At its simplest, the dialogue could be the process by which, whenever she faces a difficult moral dilemma, S checks her judgement against that of some other person whom she considers authoritative — a trusted friend, family member or expert in the relevant topic, for example — and, in the event that their judgements differ, adjusts hers accordingly. Such an internal dialogue would be subsidiary to a conventional, external dialogue or announcement in which the authority figure has made a relevant view known to S. A would be an internal or imaginary substitute for something or someone external. In cases where S does not know what, if anything, the authority thinks about the issue at hand, she may instead refer to more general maxims, codes or reasons that she considers authoritative. She may alternate between the two, following the explicit commands of an authority figure (an appointed leader, say) when such direction is available, and conforming to a code (perhaps the law or some more locally specific set of rules) when it is not.

What kind of external entity (call this *EA*, for *external alter-ego*) could meet the requirements specified in my schematic account of the socius? To meet the second, of being distinguishable from S, is straightforward: EA has an explicit view to which S's more or less accurately conforms. EA's very externality means that it cannot consistently reflect what S happens to think. The *authority* requirement is met if S recognises EA as an authority that gives her *reasons* to do as he says. (Given Gentile's conception of S as the sole arbiter of truth, it is strictly these reasons that have authority, not the institution or person who gives them.) Less clear is what follows from the demand for EA to be shared and stable. Crudely stated, this could be reduced to the requirement that EA's advice is not partial, arbitrary or irrational. S does not follow EA only because he might withhold future good advice if she does not conform; that would be a threat, and would amount to a reason for S to follow EA's advice, whatever this advice demands, provided that this is more desirable than for him to put the threat into action. This would make EA *unstable,* in that the reasons to follow his advice depend upon him actually being present to dispense it.[59] S cannot make moral judgements unless she knows what EA thinks. One solution to this problem would be to ensure that S knows, if only approximately, by what rationale EA makes his decisions. This could involve a process of rational justification[60] or consistent rule-following. For example, it might be that EA's past decisions constitute rules for subsequent ones, as in a common law system. Thus S can, with reasonable confidence, refer to similar past cases to determine what EA would (probably) say about the present one.

This account of EA is extremely demanding. One objection is that no actual figure can possibly anticipate and answer *every possible question* S might face. Even if this is deflated with the observation that S does not *need* an answer for every possible question, since the range of contingencies *likely* to arise is, in fact, manageably small, there remains the problem of how EA's content is determined in the first place — or how, if EA is identified with a person or office, he is to determine what to advise S. The figure identified by other people as EA cannot refer to EA in order to know what to do, and must at some stage justify his choices in another way.

For ease of reference, let us say that there are two related problems here. Call the first the

> *Regress Problem.* If EA is necessarily authoritative and always external to S, the person identified as EA must refer to some further external figure in order to determine what S ought to do. The burden of justification is transferred from S to EA, but EA must transfer it to a further EA, and so on *ad infinitum*. Unless the chain of justification is brought to an arbitrary arrest, it extends to an endless regress.

Call the second the

> *Recognition Problem.* If EA is morally authoritative only if and because S recognises it as such, its authority has no rational foundation. S need not have any *reason* to think that EA is authoritative; its authority, or the

---

[59] More abstractly, if EA is the law of the land, S would need to know exactly what (if anything) the law says about the issue at hand. She would be unable to act unless she had access to and a sound understanding of the relevant legislation.

[60] This would allow A to be wholly internal. It may be external if the rationale is imported from the outside, in the form of a series of maxims, say.

reason-giving power of its claims, is founded not on reasons but on an arbitrary belief that S may or may not hold. One person's version of EA can be wholly at odds with another's, even if those persons believe themselves and each other to be subjects of the same social group and moral code.

4ii. The state and the universal will

A partial solution to these problems can be found in Gentile's characterisation of the relationship between society, the state and the individual. We have already seen that he considers persons to belong to a 'social system' insofar as they are conscious of living together in society.[61] This society does not have a clearly defined and authoritative voice; this is supplied instead by the state. In *Genesi*, for example, the state is identified with the 'common and universal will', and as 'the individual in [her] universality'.[62] Given what we have seen so far, this suggests that the state is the outcome of the internal dialogue, and that the dialogue represents S's means of determining what the state wants. But the state plainly is not, or is not exclusively, an imaginary ideal constructed by a particular subject. Gentile explicitly claims that an individual will is rational (and to that extent universal) insofar as it corresponds to the will of the state. 'The political community', he writes, 'is a form of universality'; the state is the 'universal personality' of its members; and the individual 'truly wants' when she wants 'what the state wants [her] to want'.[63] These remarks suggest that the state has a will that its members do not necessarily share, or at least that they do not yet *appreciate* they share. Otherwise the claim about the state wanting S to want what it wants would be an empty tautology. Gentile pushes this point further when he claims that the state actively shapes

---

[61] *Genesi* [13]; Harris translation [80].
[62] *Genesi*, [57 and 67]; Harris translation [120 and 131]. The relationship between the state and society is never made explicit. I will examine the role of the state in the next chapter, but for now I assume, perhaps controversially, that Gentile's account of the internal society shows how S may come to know what the universal will demands of her.
[63] *Educazione* [33 and 36]. Note that I have run together two versions of the same idea: in the first instance, Gentile writes that 'As a citizen, I want what I want: but, when I look more closely [*quando si va a vedere*], what I want coincides exactly with what the state wants (me to want)', and on the second, 'I truly want when within me is the will of the state to which I belong.' See [29–31] in the Bigongiari translation.

the consciences of its citizens to fit the will of *il Duce*.[64] The relation between the particular and universal wills does not arise organically; it is instead the result of deliberate intervention, even social engineering, by political actors.

The state's will, which is usually expressed through the law, determines what S wills, or, less directly, the background assumptions enabling S to ascertain whether her particular will is morally licensed. The 'universality' of S's will depends upon, or is at least limited by, its compatibility with the law. She identifies herself with the state and the law because her self-conception has grown out of that particular social context, and she cannot ignore her social self-conception (*viz.* her self-conception as a member of a specific social and political community bound by specific laws) when she decides what she ought to do. The moral authority of positive law ultimately comes from the persons subject to it. S must recognise that the law is hers, and that she, as a member of her society or state, ought to conform to it. This account of the law's moral authority allows the content of morality to be imposed artificially by the political state, though *licensed* — assigned its moral authority — by S.[65] If S affirms that, other things being equal, all members of the group (community, state) to which she belongs *ought* to conform to laws imposed by a recognised authority, she has effectively sanctioned those laws as applied to herself.[66]

To what extent can this conception of the state address the Regress and Recognition Problems? Of the two, the Recognition Problem is the

---

[64] *Origini* [268]. I discuss this general theme in Chapter 6 and this specific passage in sub-section #3.

[65] This idea can be extended to the view of the socius as God. If S thinks that some set of precepts accurately reflects God's will, and that God's will is authoritative over hers, she can use those precepts to check that her personal will has appropriately impersonal (divine) sanction.

[66] This could be question-begging. If subject S believes that (Pi) all members of group G ought to comply with law L, and (Pii) S is a member of group G, then S thinks that she, S, ought to comply with L. But this could be re-worded without the normative 'ought': (Qi) all members of group G *are required* to comply with law L, and (Qii) S is a member of group G. This does not require S's self-imposition of any moral duty. It may be a pragmatic decision; suppose we add the claims that (Qiii) all non-complying members of G will be horribly punished, and (Qiv) S does not want to be horribly punished, and nor is it in her interests for this to happen. S is rationally, though not morally, motivated to comply with L. What matters for Gentile is that S must identify with the law and recognise it as authoritative over her; only in this way can it give her reasons for action.

more easily addressed, at least in theory.[67] The state that somehow *brings it about* that its citizens recognise it as a moral authority has effectively made itself morally authoritative for them. This might be achieved by means of extensive propaganda and education (or indoctrination) or by less direct means, such as cultural programmes designed to cultivate pre-existing patriotic sentiment and national identity. The Regress Problem is less easily addressed. The solution to it, I think, must be as follows: while the state may set out to cause citizens to identify with it, it cannot do so by *forcing* them to hold an arbitrarily assembled set of beliefs.[68] The state's laws and policies must have the support of *good reasons*. If they are to draw their moral authority from the individuals subject to them, they must be potentially subject to review and revision by every such individual. This means that the legislator to whom citizens refer when making moral judgements must himself refer not to a further external source, but to the ideal of universality, entailing maximum coherence and rational justification for each person.

This is a crude sketch of the Gentilean model of the state. It is important to remember that it describes an ideal. After all, a state could equally impose laws that no one is prepared to accept or identify as her own. Such laws would not occupy any place in S's conscience. They would be abstractions with no connection to S's will, and, for that reason, no moral authority over her. Nor is positive law guaranteed to provide clear and unambiguous prescriptions for every situation in which S might need to make a choice. Laws could be mutually contradictory or insufficiently detailed and comprehensive in scope to be applied directly to the decision S now faces. S could even be *ignorant* of the relevant parts of the law. In that case, Gentile could conclude that choices about which the law is silent, or about which S does not know what the law requires, are not morally significant, so S could apply any decision procedure (a coin-toss, say) to determine what to do. This solution would contradict the idea of morality's substantive content as a creation of the will, which implies that *every choice S consciously makes*

---

[67] I add 'at least in theory' because there remains an open question of whether any real state could meaningfully effect such comprehensive social changes.

[68] A nuanced version of the same sentiment is given in *Genesi* [134–6], where Gentile denies that the state can impose its will dogmatically 'with [the] right of "forced currency"'. Instead it must retain a firm basis in truth, which in turn must be recognised 'in human thought'. See [191–3] in Harris translation, and [192n] for a note on the term 'forced currency'. The renewed emphasis on the autonomy of thought is especially striking when this is compared with the version cited above: *Origini* [268].

is morally significant.[69] She would need to refer to something other than the law to determine what she ought to do.

As before, the solution to these problems lies in the idealisation of the state. Gentile ultimately describes two distinct entities: first, the transcendental state, or the state as it should be, which is to say a state that corresponds as far as possible with the ideal of universal truth; and second, the empirical state, or the state as it is, a political institution comprising many individuals, each of whom is potentially subject to ignorance, false beliefs, partiality and incomprehension. The second is to be identified with the first only to the extent that it can justify its actions and its claims of moral authority according to those ideals. The extent to which that is possible is determined by the internal dialogue in which each and every citizen engages. We might say that the empirical state must continually try to match its ideal counterpart, although it may never perfectly achieve this aim. In this respect it is like S as she aspires to know universal truths: for individual and institution alike, moral goodness is endlessly realised through the act of self-consciously recognising and striving after the ideal, not in its conclusion.

5. Conclusion

In this chapter I have offered an overview of Gentile's attempts to extend his metaphysics to make moral theory possible. First I rejected the argument that actual idealism is a solipsist doctrine. Next I showed how Gentile accounts for the existence of multiple thinking subjects by reference to the transcendental society and the internal dialogue that takes place within it. This, I claimed, is the keystone of actual idealist moral theory. However, it is inadequately theorised. Notably absent is a full explanation of what the socius represents, and how the subject can know that her chosen conception of the socius is appropriate and authoritative. Because the internal dialogue is portrayed as a conversation between *two* parties, S and A, rather than many parties, I argued that a more robust account of the socius is required to prevent actual idealist moral theory from collapsing into individualist subjectivism. In the third part of the chapter I rehearsed several versions of what features the socius could have if it were to act as the primary reference point in the process of making moral judgements. In the fourth part of the chapter I discussed the idea that the state might be able to impose a substantive code. I argued that, if it is to be compatible with the rest of actual idealist moral theory, such a state must be viewed under two

---

[69] *Diritto* [13]: 'The will', writes Gentile, is 'conceivable as creator of the moral world only if one thinks [of it as] creator of goodness, and, as creator of goodness, creator of itself.'

distinct aspects: one ideal or transcendental, and the other empirical. It is in its transcendental capacity that the state may represent the socius, which need not have any empirical counterpart in order to generate moral claims. Any moral authority the empirical state has must be derived from its transcendental counterpart. In the next chapter I show how Gentile conflates these ideas in his theory of the total ethical state.

Chapter 4

The Total Ethical State

In Chapter 3 I explained how Gentile expands his theory of the pure act to accommodate multiple thinking persons. To do this he offers an account of the person as a socialised individual, capable of thinking and acting according to both particular (personal, partial) and universal (impersonal, impartial) reasons. These are synthesised in the internal dialogue, where both aspects of the subject interact in order to establish the basis for moral judgements. S weighs her personal reasons against her conception of the 'socius', a social alter-ego whom she identifies as a constituent part of her own identity. The claim that moral judgement takes the form of a dialogue between one's social and individual selves is not much of a moral theory, and, until we have a better idea of what its protagonists represent and how this dialogue might play out, it cannot give rise to substantive conclusions. At the end of Chapter 3, the socius was still unclearly defined, although I specified several formal requirements that it must meet to prevent actual idealist moral theory from collapsing into subjectivism.

My aim in this chapter is to examine Gentile's theory of the state. He sometimes describes this in terms closely corresponding with the socius, and this, understandably, has led some commentators to imagine that Gentile's moral theory is nothing more than 'a parade of Hegelian language' and 'a thinly veiled apology for [state] terrorism'.[1] I argue that this interpretation is largely legitimate, but it arises because of Gentile's conflation of two distinct concepts of state: one *political*, and the other *spiritual*. To remain consistent with the rest of Gentile's moral theory, we must separate the two. Nonetheless, the spiritual state and political state can and in the best case should overlap.

The chapter is structured as follows. At sub-heading #1 I exposit Gentile's theories of the state in his *Filosofia del diritto* and *Introduzione alla filosofia*. At #2 I discuss his critique of Hegel's theory of the state, on

---

[1] George H. Sabine (1961) *A History of Political Theory*, London: George G. Harrap [897–9]. Sabine is critical chiefly of Gentile's political theory, not his ethics. However, since Gentile's theory of the state is given such a prominent place in his ethics, Sabine's point remains relevant to my project.

which his is loosely based, showing how he re-formulates Hegel's 'ethical system' as one in which the state is supreme. Next (#3) I discuss the mature version of Gentile's political theory as set out in *Genesi e struttura della società,* showing how this relies on the conflation of what previously were parallel though mutually distinctive conceptions of the state. At #4 I bring out some of the most forceful objections to Gentile's political theory and the confused conception of the state that underpins it. I then argue (#5) that to save actual idealist moral theory, the empirical or political version of the state must be subsumed to the spiritual or 'internal' conception. To conclude (#6) I explain how this corrected view of the state resolves some of the ambiguities of the internal dialogue described in Chapter 3, before pointing out some further problems to be addressed in later chapters.

1. Gentile on the state in *Diritto* and *Introduzione*

Gentile first attempts to describe a political theory in 1916's *Fondamenti della filosofia del diritto* (Foundations of the Philosophy of Right).[2] As discussed in Chapter 3, *Diritto* contains a nascent transcendental society, with Robinson Crusoe referring to the *società in interiore homine* when making judgements on his island. *Diritto* links this idea with actual idealism's concept of will and the law. It was not until the third edition of the book, published in 1937, that Gentile inserted chapters dealing explicitly with the state and politics as separate objects of concern. By that time the Fascist state, which was at least nominally totalitarian,[3] was in full swing. Amid the political uncertainty of 1937, when the PNF set about re-aligning its policies with the racist and warlike programme of the National Socialists in Germany, it was expedient for Gentile to re-align his philosophy of right with the extant regime. With one hand he held tightly to the ongoing Fascist project, but with the other he signalled for caution, insisting that Italian authoritarianism

---

[2] Note that Harris, for example, translates this as *...Philosophy of Law.* Gentile's word is 'diritto', which can be translated as 'law', but which connotes the broad sweep of legal culture, including 'right' (in Hegel's sense) and 'rights' (entitlements). Law in the narrower sense is 'legge'. Gentile certainly uses this term in the book. However, since the book's topic is the *moral status* of law, I deem it appropriate to preserve the '*...of Right*' translation.

[3] Historians of Fascism have often remarked that the Italian state, in which the adjective 'totalitario' and noun 'totalitarismo' first arose, was less successful in putting the idea of totalitarianism into practice than either Hitler's Germany or Stalin's Soviet Union. This is a general claim, but for some revealing statistics, see Stanley G. Payne (1995) *A History of Fascism, 1914–1945,* Abingdon: Routledge [117].

retain a measure of legitimacy and reminding his peers what their spiritual conception of the state meant — and, perhaps, how it differed from that of their increasingly ruthless and vocal ally.[4] We cannot assume that these new chapters are a straightforward elaboration or clarification of the first edition's content. To judge their congruence with the theory that went before, and how, if at all, the state should feature in our model of Gentilean moral constructivism, we must look closely at Gentile's treatments of the state in his systematic works.

It is tempting to think that Gentile's state is included in his later moral theory solely as a means to square actual idealism with the political status quo, thereby ensuring the author's continuing prominence in Italian politics and culture, albeit at the expense of his intellectual integrity and, by extension, his theory's value. This suspicion, echoed time and again in the literature, would be irresistible if the concept of the state was introduced to actual idealism only when Gentile and his employers stood to gain from it. However, Gentile's conception of the state has a pre-Fascist pedigree. In his 'Clarifications', written in 1920 and added to the second edition (1923) of *Diritto*, he claims that the only 'true and real' state is 'the state inside the person' (*lo Stato in interiore homine*).[5] This is an important departure from the earlier version in which society is cast in the same role.[6] There can be no such state, he writes, without a moral character. A merely empirical and abstract state is unreal and therefore without concrete value. This is broadly consistent with what Gentile writes later, but here the concept looks worryingly Procrustean, with the state defined so as to fill a lacuna in Gentile's moral theory (*viz.* the unspecified content of the moral law), rather than the theory adjusted to accommodate the concept of state as it is ordinarily understood.

---

[4] *Diritto* does not refer directly to empirical politics, so this conclusion must be inferred. Still, it is telling that, after adding a brief essay and 're-touching [his] exposition to make it clearer and more precise' in the second edition (1923) [see *Diritto* 'Avvertenza', no page number], he overhauls the book for the third edition (1937), just as the German and Italian states draw closer together. The third adds chapters on the state and politics, as well as a lengthy introduction in the form of an essay on 'Practical Philosophy and the Moral Life', written in 1914 as the conclusion to his editorial commentary on Rosmini's *Il principio della morale*. The moral foundations laid out in the introduction help to counteract the authoritarian implications of the later chapters. See Harris (1960) [338–9].

[5] *Diritto* [137].

[6] See Amato (2011) [95–8] on this issue.

After the second edition of *Diritto*,[7] Gentile's next major philosophical account of the state is the 1929 essay 'Lo stato e la filosofia' (The State and Philosophy).[8] Here he writes that the state

> is the nation conceivable in its historical unity. It is man himself, so far as he realises himself universally, determining this universality in a certain form. [This is a] necessary determination [in the same way] as it is necessary to speak using certain words. [... N]one of the material or moral elements that belong to the life of a people is extraneous to this wholly spiritual form that is sealed in the self-conscious [bond of] of nationhood that is state.[9]

This can be expressed more simply. Gentile is here equating the state with the nation 'in its historical unity', meaning, roughly, *the nation viewed as an entity persisting over time*. The state of Italy exists so far as people recognise themselves and each other as members of the Italian nation and its political institutions — hence 'the self-conscious [bond of] nationhood that is state'. The phrase 'historical unity' means that viewed over the course of a century, say, the specific individual persons constituting 'the people of Italy' will change due to births, death, immigration, emigration and changes over the course of each of those lives. There may also be diversity in or changes to what those people understand by the idea of shared nationality or state membership. Despite these concerns it is possible to talk about an unbroken super-personal identity called Italy. Gentile aligns this with the internal society, writing that 'the man who in his singular personality feels himself to be outside [the state] is an historical abstraction: [...] he might be immoral, and not feel the universal conscience pulsing in his own.' He adds that 'all its external manifestations[, like] territory, the executive force under its control, [and] the men representing [its] various capacities [...] draw their value from the will that recognises and wants them as necessary to and constitutive of the state's historical and actual form.'[10]

The novelty of totalitarianism was its assumption that persons grow to fit their circumstances and that by engineering those circumstances it

---

[7] As mentioned, the 'Clarifications' were added to *Diritto's* second edition as an appendix.

[8] 'Lo stato e la filosofia', in *Introduzione alla filosofia*. This chapter originally appeared in (1929) *La giornale critico della filosofia italiana*, 10, pp. 161–70.

[9] *Introduzione* [181]. Note that I have added 'bond of' and 'nationhood' to clarify Gentile's meaning. He refers to '*l'autocoscienza della nazione che è Stato*' (the self-consciousness of the nation that is state), which, literally translated, leaves ambiguous the question of whether it is the nation or self-consciousness of it that Gentile identifies with the state.

[10] *Introduzione* [181].

is possible to cause persons to fit a prescribed form. Thus Gentile's political state acts as a coordinating device, and, insofar as it succeeds, it invests itself with spiritual value through S's recognition of it as an extension of herself. The internal state is identified with the universal conscience, and the universal conscience is identified with the socius, which is the key to true moral judgements. Therefore that property also belongs to the state, which assumes responsibility for constructing S's personal identity by means of education and establishes laws to give the socius a voice. S knows what her social alter-ego thinks precisely because its thoughts are already set out in law. In this way Gentile's legislator not only manipulates but also *creates* the individual conscience in whichever of its possible forms he deems best. Really all that qualifies the political state as the closest earthly manifestation of the internal state is that it is (or was, in the world as Gentile saw it) uniquely able to create, impose and enforce laws, as well as controlling the educational and cultural institutions that would determine how those laws were received.[11]

The substitution of the transcendental state for transcendental society prompts a question. What is the relationship between these, and how can Gentile justify exchanging the two? At least a partial answer is given in the chapters added to *Diritto*'s third edition (1937). Here Gentile examines Hegel's theory of the state, which is one part of the 'ethical triad' alongside civil society and the family.

2. Gentile on the Hegel's ethical state

For Gentile, the originality of Hegel's state theory is its *positivity*. Before Hegel the state 'was always conceived as something negative'. It limited the individual subject's capacity to realise herself.[12] This negative conception resulted from the presupposition of the individual as 'an absolute *prius*' to which the state would be added later. Doctrines of natural right and law [*giusnaturalismo*] proceed from this position, loading the individual with inalienable entitlements and duties before situating her in an ethical/political context. The state is confined by these unproven predicates, which 'it must recognise, because they pre-exist it as conditions of its existence'.[13] These conditions require any legitimate

---

[11] The explicit link between state *qua* extended moral personality and *qua* institution distinguishes the conception of the conscience from the nascent version in the first edition of *Diritto*. In this late version, the state's 'external manifestations' are identified directly with the spiritual universal to which individuals consider their beliefs subsidiary.

[12] *Diritto* [103].

[13] *Diritto* [104].

state to secure natural rights and submit to natural laws, or else manifest itself as a despotic power, outside the ambit of moral life.

Hegel also rejects 'contractualism' (social contract theory) which, like natural rights theory, begins with the concept of asocial individuals, and uses the state as 'the *means* of liberty's realisation'.[14] The method of determining rights' and laws' proper contents takes the form of hypothetical or actual agreement among individuals.[15] On some contractualist accounts, there exists a set of laws and rights to which contracting parties *must* agree, or are constrained to agree if they are to live together in reasonably stable schemes of social co-operation. In the technical language of contemporary philosophy, we might call these rights and laws *necessary corollaries of the contract's meta-ethical set-up*. Even if this is so, contractualism differs from natural rights theory in that it does not assume that laws are readymade objects awaiting discovery. Instead they are constructed. So the contract does not, or does not entirely, presuppose what Christine Korsgaard calls 'substantive moral realism',[16] but instead acts as a means of constructing moral precepts that, in order to make sense, may be able to take only one form.[17]

As conceived in both these doctrines, Gentile complains, the state imposes a limit on S, 'a simple reality of fact', without any independent value or agency.[18] Social contract theory leaves the state wholly subject to the terms of the agreement by which it was created, and that agreement reflects the contingent will of the 'pure individual' — the asocial, transcendental subject. This agreement constitutes the beginning and the end of the state's 'constructive process' and its whole *raison d'être*.[19]

---

[14] *Diritto* [104]; emphasis in original.
[15] For more on Hegel's rejection of individualism and subjectivism, see Judith N. Shklar (1976) *Freedom and Independence,* Cambridge: Cambridge University Press [102–10]. An earlier, shorter version of the same material is to be found in Shklar (1973) 'Hegel's *Phenomenology* and the Moral Failures of Asocial Man', *Political Theory,* 1 (3), pp. 259–86 [esp. 261–2]. Bruce Haddock offers a nuanced interpretation of Hegel's view of contractualism in (1994) 'Hegel's Critique of the Theory of Social Contract', in David Boucher and Paul Kelly (eds.) *The Social Contract from Hobbes to Rawls,* London: Routledge, pp. 147–63.
[16] This phrase appears in Korsgaard (1996a) 'The Normative Question', in O'Neill (ed.) *The Sources of Normativity,* Cambridge: Cambridge University Press, pp. 7–48 [35].
[17] I will elaborate on this theme in the second half of the book, and especially Chapter 7.
[18] See *Diritto* [105]. The phrase 'reality of fact' ('*realtà di fatto*') rings strangely in Italian and English alike.
[19] *Diritto* [105].

On the natural law account, it is similarly confined by the dictates of some transcendent reality. For both, the moral law directly connects the source, which is the contract or natural law, to each individual. It is unclear how the state, or indeed any other conception of community or collective identity, can fit into this picture. Gentile insists that the logical consequence of this 'liberal individualism' is 'anarchism', with individuals thrown together as a jumble of materially distinct objects, and bound together by capricious and contingent agreements. Society is no more than 'an aggregate of individual humans, each closed in on itself, without any necessary relation to each other'.[20]

All of the foregoing is common to both Gentile's view and that which he ascribes to Hegel. The way to avoid the anarchistic conclusion, Gentile explains, is 'to deepen the concept of the individual'.[21] Hegel does this in his *Phenomenology*, systematically showing the development of consciousness into self-consciousness, and all the moral, social and political relations that come with it. This is echoed in Gentile's conception of S as a self-consciously fallible agent working to construct true judgements: she is one thinking subject among others, and as such a part of the universal thinking subject.[22] It is as a contributor to and subsidiary of the universal subject that she comes to recognise laws, duties, permissions and so forth. For these to count as moral principles for her, rather than presenting themselves in opposition to her or otherwise limiting her freedom, they must be internalised so she wills herself to conform to them.[23]

Only in the *Philosophy of Right* does Hegel explicitly identify the state as the chief manifestation of the universal subject's 'ethical life' (*Sittlichkeit*). The justification for this move is notoriously unclear. It contains a non-sequitur: why should identifying oneself as a particular subject necessitate the existence of a corresponding universal subject? Why should S identify the universal subject with the (political) state, rather than some other, smaller entity or group of which S sees herself to be a part, like 'dentists' or 'diabetics'; or some larger inclusive concept, like 'rational beings' or even 'the universe'? Could she not recognise herself as an example of a particular type (that is: as a person), rather than extending this to any kind of universal (the universal person)? Or rather: could she not recognise that as one who thinks, she belongs to the universal class of *thinkers*, without needing to

---

[20] *Diritto* [106].
[21] *Diritto* [105].
[22] *Diritto* [107].
[23] *Diritto* [111]; also G.W.F. Hegel w/A.V. Miller (trans.) (1977) *Hegel's Phenomenology of Spirit,* Oxford: Oxford University Press [esp. 104–38].

say that the universal thinker is, concretely, a thinker who thinks? The move has transcendent overtones, echoing Plato's theory of the forms. As such it seems especially alien to Gentile, who so fiercely opposes the idea of transcendent realism.

These concerns do not strike Gentile as problematic. He claims that the link between the parts and wholes was established in Spinoza's works.[24] There is little doubt that Hegel also had Spinoza in mind when choosing the term *Sittlichkeit* (ethical life, of which Hegel considers the state a constituent part). After all, he wrote that 'thought must begin by placing itself at the standpoint of Spinozism',[25] and both this neologism and the concept to which it is attached are reminiscent of Spinoza's holism. But this does not settle the question of why *the state* is uniquely suited to this all-encompassing role. Spinoza, of course, assigns that same role to God.[26] A conventionally omnipresent and omniscient God is hard to situate in Gentile's metaphysics, since it requires the presupposition of something transcendent of human knowledge and understanding.[27] Yet Spinoza's equation of the ethical category and God is in some respects more comprehensible than Hegel and Gentile's placement of the state in the same role. An infinite and permanent God can be described as a *ne plus ultra* without embarrassment. The political state, meanwhile, seems anything but infinite, as the existence of other states suggests.

Gentile's first step in resolving this problem is to re-assert the difference between the ethical and empirical manifestations of the state. In doing so he quotes Louis XIV's claim that *'l'état, c'est moi'* (the state is me; I am the state). Gentile's aim is not to endorse political autocracy, though. Rather, he means that if it is to have ethical status and the

---

[24] There is a good discussion of Gentile's thoughts about Spinoza in Hervé A. Cavallera (1995) 'Gentile e Spinoza', *Idee*, 28–9, pp. 185–212 [esp. 188–92].

[25] G.W.F. Hegel w/E.S. Haldane and Frances H. Simson (1955) *Lectures on the History of Philosophy*, New York: The Humanities Press [257]; Merold Westphal (2003) 'Hegel between Spinoza and Derrida', in David A. Duquette (ed.) *Hegel's History of Philosophy: New Interpretations*, Albany, NY: New York University Press, pp. 143–63 [144–5].

[26] For Spinoza, God is the *only* substance. See Benedict de Spinoza w/Edwin Curley (trans.) (1996) *Ethics*, Oxford: Oxford University Press [3–13; Part 1, Propositions 1–15].

[27] This is not to say that he did not identify himself as a Catholic, nor that Catholic readers have not tried to reconcile Gentile's *spirito* with the Holy Ghost and the *atto puro* with Aquinas's *actum purum* (which 'belongs to God alone'). See (1927) *Summa Theologica*, I–II, 50, 6: 'Whether there are habits in the angels' [24–7]. But this resemblance is specious: the substantial bulk of Catholic theology is wrung out in its passage through the actual idealist mangle.

power to issue morally binding commands, the state must be recognised by S as an authority *of her own creation*. She must identify the state with herself and its will with her own. The state is Louis, for sure, but it is also each and every one of its other constituents. This is what Gentile means when he says it must be internalised. An external state, removed from the individual will and self-conception, is no different from a foreign or historical state: it is abstract and morally insignificant. Only once it is internalised so the will of one matches that of the other can S and the state simultaneously possess 'true and real liberty'.[28]

Gentile believes that Hegel grasps this idea but fails to follow it to its proper conclusion. If the state is to be identified with *Sittlichkeit* and the 'true and real liberty' mentioned above, it cannot be limited by other entities. Hegel's state, writes Gentile, is limited in three ways, all stemming from Hegel's mistaken concessions to empirical methods, which try 'to view spiritual reality from the outside'. These limitations are: first, the state's conception as *a state* among others; second, its identification with 'objective spirit', an intermediary moment between 'subjective' and 'absolute' spirit; and, third, its relation to the family and civil society, which also occupy the domain of objective spirit, and provide the state's 'necessary foundation'.[29]

The first limitation runs contrary to how we ordinarily talk about states. The problem is that to think about states in this way is to ignore what makes the state (our state) distinctively *ours*. This is to make the ordinary mistake of treating the world as if we were viewing it in itself from an external, impartial and impersonal standpoint. He compares the status of the term 'the state' with the term 'mother': 'everyone has one, but no one has more than one; and no one can speak of the world in general without speaking of her own unique world in which there is only one mother.'[30]

Is the state's special status just a matter of words? Of course, when I say 'mother' I might mean *my* mother, a specific person who is related to me in a specific way. No one else can be my mother; her status is an office that can admit only one person. How does this formal necessity arise? Is it a question of biology? On Gentile's view, it cannot be so. To clarify this point, consider the situation of someone who has been adopted. This adoptee might call an adoptive parent 'mother', since she is performing the day-to-day role most often filled by a biological parent. The adoptee may be aware that she is adopted, and that there is

---

[28] *Diritto* [113–4]. Note that Gentile refers to Louis XIV's dictum in *Genesi*, but there he emphasises its authoritarian implications [62].
[29] *Diritto* [114–5].
[30] *Diritto* [116].

or was once someone else who, by some definition, is also her mother. A non-adoptee might reject the idea of having a mother: perhaps she feels terribly wronged by or otherwise alienated from her biological mother, and denies that the term—or what Gentile might call its *spiritual significance*, vis-à-vis its relation to her self-conscious identity— can be applied to her or else to their relationship.

To clarify. What Gentile means to emphasise is that, while I can refer to your mother, French mothers, or what have you, and can probably assume that you identify with yours in a way different to that in which I identify with mine, these other mothers are only abstractions unless they have some concrete meaning for me.[31] That is: I know the person in question, and the term 'your mother' connotes a specific person, with some relation to me. Likewise I can talk intelligibly about other states. For example, I might say, 'in 1870–1, France was at war with Prussia', without ever having been French, Prussian or alive in the nineteenth century. But for these to have concrete significance, and to have any impact on *my will,* I must conceive of them in relation to the state that I identify especially as mine, as an extension of my personality. Hence we must distinguish between, first, states 'that we know to exist', but whose existence neither helps nor hinders the continued existence of ours, and, second, those with which our state stands in direct or indirect relation. Firmly attaching S to the state with which she self-consciously identifies, the idea of other states as limits on her state ceases to be a problem. S's own state, as a super-personal extension of her personality, still defines her will, aspirations and relations. The state presents itself to her as *her* alter-ego, rather than as some hypothetical, possible alter-ego, which could be saddled with any sort of convictions or will, but which, lacking the power to cause S to identify with it, cannot affect her will or self-consciousness in any way whatever. (Gentile does not here refer to the transcendental society or internal dialogue, but the link is plain.)

The second limit on Hegel's state results from its placement at the intermediary stage between subjective and absolute spirit. This is likewise removed through careful application of actual idealism's metaphysical principles. According to Gentile, the triad of subjective, objective and absolute spirit is 'fictitious and arbitrary'. As we saw in Chapter 2, on Gentile's account there can be no *pensiero pensante*

---

[31] What if you are my sibling? When we each say 'mother', we refer to the same empirically distinct person. But the connotation is still different; that I recognise the person my sibling calls 'mother' as my mother is a coincidence. A different relationship is implicit in each sibling's utterance: that between me and my mother and that between my sibling and her mother (who happens also to be mine).

without an object. That would be an act of thinking without a thought or any object thought about. Nor is it possible to conceive of an object without a subject, since the very act of conception demands a subject to perform it. Thus the distinction between subjective and objective spirit dissolves. 'Absolute spirit', which comprises absolute categories of art, religion and philosophy, has no place in actual idealism. The absolute cannot exist transcendent of the thinker, for this would make it a presupposition. If it is *not* transcendent of the thinker, it must be thought; its special elevated status is unwarranted. S cannot step entirely out of her social world in order to become pure and absolute spirit. The only alternative is to ground her conception of the social world in a theory of immanence, set within the limits of what is thinkable.[32]

Gentile's approach to removing the third limit is crucial to understanding his conception of the state. It clears the way for totalitarianism. To Hegel's triad of objective spirit, with family, civil society and state all supporting each other, Gentile has two objections. One is that Hegel places the family, the first and simplest stage of objective spirit, in *opposition* to the state, which is the last. The family cannot be 'interior ethical reality' recognised by all its members, a 'true form of self-consciousness' and 'the spirit in its effectual existence', if these same characteristics also belong to the state in which it is contained. For the two to co-exist, S would need two identities, one as citizen and another as family member, as well as two wills, two self-conceptions, and so on. This would make moral responsibilities impossible, ruling out any meaningful appeal to a 'universal will'. A person with more than one will effectively has none. So for Gentile, the family must be absorbed into the state, and its distinct claims on the individual annihilated.[33] Is this justified? I do not see how it can be, assuming that the state is understood in conventional terms as a politically if not morally authoritative institution. To assign this special role to the state seems arbitrary, and Gentile is no more entitled to demand the family's absorption into the state than he is to demand the state's absorption into God, humanity or members of supranational organisations, or else the family into (international) ethnic groups, classes and so on.

Gentile's view is better understandable if we take 'the state' to mean not the empirical institution, but the ultimate constructed arbiter to which S refers. There is no doubt that Gentile accepts that persons

---

[32] *Diritto* [118-9]; a nice summary of Gentile's position appears in Giacomo Rinaldi (1994) 'Italian Idealism and After: Gentile, Croce and Others', in Richard Kearney (ed.) *Continental Philosophy in the 20th Century*, London: Routledge, pp. 350-89 [357].

[33] See *Sommario 1* [142-3 and 149-50] and, for more on Gentile's view of the family, *Genesi* [64-5 and 113]; Harris translation [128-9 and 172-3].

assign their families special importance, and no question of dismissing this institution as a mistaken abstraction. His reference to the use of the word 'mother' attests to this. What could it mean for the family to be absorbed into the state, and its separate status thus 'annihilated'? Gentile cannot mean that persons should identify family and state as the same thing. If this were the case, the whole idea of one's mother's special status would be indefensible. More plausible is the idea that the family should make demands that are compatible with those of the state. Just as family members' individual wills contribute to that of the family, so do families' wills contribute to that of state. They are, in Hegelian language, all part of the same organism.[34] The state is distinguished by its members' *recognition* of its authority and its *scope*. The state is better able to impose its will on the family than any family can impose its will on the state. But it is not simply the state's ability to do this that gives it priority over the family where the two impose different demands. After all, it may be that some foreign state is better able to impose its will on a subject's family than her own state can. Once again, what matters is that the political state is identified with the morally authoritative spiritual state—the socius—with which she identifies herself.

Gentile has much the same second objection and response to civil society. He maintains that it cannot limit the state's authority for the simple reason that it is based on a false concept of the person. Hegel's reference to 'individuals [... as] private and material persons whose end is their own interest'[35] confines them to the abstract logos. We cannot think concretely of persons as social atoms any more than we can talk about an incomplete whole or a square circle. Only what is concrete and real can play a meaningful, active role in society. Abstractions are products of such activity. This argument is difficult to counter within the confines of Gentile's metaphysics. In this way, then, Gentile concludes that 'in spiritual actuality, the family is state, and the state is family', and that 'there is no civil society that is not also state'.[36]

---

[34] There is an interesting question of whether Hegel thinks the state incorporates the family or exists in parallel with it as one of the three components of what Andrew Vincent calls 'the institutional structure of the social world'. See Vincent (1991) *Theories of the State*, Oxford: Blackwell (originally 1987) [123-7; quotation 123 only]. Gentile is certainly more uncompromising in his assertion that the state is the ultimate all-encompassing entity in the hierarchy of institutions.

[35] G.W.F. Hegel w/T.M. Knox (trans.) (1945) *Philosophy of Right*, Oxford: Oxford University Press (originally 1942) [124: §187].

[36] Hegel (1945) [120: §180]. This reference also applies to the preceding paragraph.

3. Gentile's mature state

The theory of the state in *Diritto* is often overshadowed by Hegel's. Gentile criticises his forebear and suggests what his own theory might look like if it were laid out in purely Hegelian language. But, as we have seen in the preceding discussion, he sometimes dismisses an idea as untenable (as with the family as an independent moral claimant and civil society in general) without making clear what he would do with it instead. Does he think, for example, that the family has no concrete spiritual significance? Fortunately, he returns to the state in his last book, *Genesi e struttura della società* (Genesis and Structure of Society). To keep my exegesis within moderate limits, in what follows I shall identify some general points of difference before focusing on the questions left unsettled in *Diritto*.

Prepared in just five weeks, Gentile's last work of systematic philosophy[37] has been compared to 'a drowned man's last testament', in which the author works frantically to justify past words and deeds before a jury from whom he had, under the regime's protection, been shielded.[38] As such its tone is strange, its discussion scattershot and its arguments often faulty. Old material is recast to fit new and uncertain circumstances. The totalitarian state, which had provided the backdrop for most of his earlier discussion of the state as concept, was gone. In its place was a foreign power in the process of losing a war. If we assume that Gentile's earlier accounts of the state were intended to provide philosophical licence for his employers, with all concepts devised to accommodate *de facto* political arrangements, *Genesi* seems less self-assured. Its principal message is no longer that individuals have good

---

[37] Historically oriented works such as *Storia della filosofia (dalle origini a Platone)* (The History of Philosophy: from [its] origins to Plato) were published later, having been left in manuscript form at the time of Gentile's assassination.

[38] G.R.G. Mure (1950) '*Genesi e struttura della società*, by Giovanni Gentile' (review), *Philosophical Quarterly*, 1 (1), pp. 83-4 [83]. The full paragraph runs: '[It reads] tragically [...] like a drowned man's last testament drifting shoreward from a wreck. The faithful toil with which he spins every dogma of Fascism out of man's original self-consciousness, and his somewhat pathetic attempt to show that, despite the inevitability of war, the end of it all is peace and good will through the self-recognition and self-love of man in all men; the occasional parentheses of professional self-defence; the stretches of rather febrile exhortation, and the relatively long discussion of death and immortality in the last chapter—all these are clear traits in the sombre self-portrait of a thinker who through the twenty years of his service to the Fascist *regime* always resent the shadow of his greater master [Hitler] whom Mussolini dared not touch, yet never quite stilled his own philosophic conscience, and now quails perceptibly before the approach of national and personal catastrophe.' (Mure's italics.)

reason to submit to an all-encompassing authority, but a simpler one of solidarity. In the foreword, Gentile indicates that he wanted to show Italians that they were still a people, and still had reason to hold together, in difficult and fractious times (and, we might add, without an authoritarian state to remove the choice to do otherwise). This echoes his concerns about the brief rise and sudden collapse of national solidarity during and after the First World War.[39]

There are some changes in weight and focus. Hegel is moved to the margins; Gentile's language remains unambiguously Hegelian, but there is no real exegesis of or explicit comparison with the *Philosophy of Right*. The discussion of the state is expanded to six (often short) chapters, rather than *Diritto*'s one. These cover 'The State', defining it as a concept and distinguishing it from 'the nation'; 'The State and Economics'; 'The State and Religion'; 'The State and Science'; 'The State and [other] States'; and 'History', in which, once again, Gentile gives special prominence to the state's role.

Diritto's extensive discussion of the role of right, or law (that is, *diritto*), is less prominent in this later version, and compressed to just two pages.[40] (This does not indicate any major change of attitude on Gentile's part. *Genesi* concerns the spiritual conception of the whole gamut of social relations, not the law's moral status as such. There is considerable overlap between the two books, but again, the contents of *Genesi* should be considered elaborations on and not replacements for those of *Diritto*.) His attention is now on the state's will and its relation to S, as well as the various possible conceptions of society and state that might be opposed to her own.[41] The state's role as law-maker is again described as a *moral* office insofar as S willingly subscribes to it. Once she has overcome the law's 'positivity' — that is, her perception of it as a limit on action, rather than a guide and protector of liberty — it 'is resolved into morality' for her. This means that the last word on what is right is whatever the law says is right.[42] Later Gentile reaffirms the

---

[39] See Gentile (2004) 'Origini and dottrina del fascismo', in Renzo de Felice (ed.) *Autobiografia del fascismo,* Turin: Einaudi, pp. 247–71 (originally 1927).

[40] *Genesi* [58–9]; Harris translation [122–3].

[41] One common interpretation of *Genesi,* already indicated in several citations, has it that Gentile wrote it as a desperate *post facto* justification for the regime that had, as he produced it in just five weeks in the Salò Republic, all but collapsed. With the writing on the wall, a politically engaged man like Gentile could see that he would soon need to defend his role in the Fascist experiment.

[42] *Genesi* [59–60]; Harris translation [123–4].

state's role as 'the individual in its universality' and 'the concrete actuality of [the individual's] will'.[43]

Subsequent chapters are spent showing how the concrete elements of moral and social life can be fitted into the state, and that the abstract elements have no real value. This is achieved at a fast pace. The discussion of the state and economics deals mainly with utilitarian[44] conceptions of politics and morality. These are given over to the abstract logos, along with the body (except one's own body, which every subject identifies with her own consciousness), and natural and mathematical theories of economics. The state's character is inseparable from that of religion, since, again, one identifies one's own religion as part of one's personality, bringing it into the fold of concrete spirituality, along with the state.

The relation between family and state is laid out more clearly. However, Gentile does not entirely resolve the issues identified previously. He writes:

> Man is [the] family. He works for himself, but he also works for his children [...] The state has interests in cultivating and encouraging the instinct, which in man becomes a vocation, toward the generation and recognition of offspring. As such it has interests in the formation of the familial unit [literally 'nucleus'] out of which the individual is led by nature to break the crust [*spezzare la crosta*] of his narrow-minded egoism and to widen the sphere of his natural individuality. [...] Woe betide the man who condemns himself to sterile solitude, and woe betide the state that renounces humanity's perennial moral nursery, which is the personality integrated within the family, cemented by love and perpetuated by inheritance.[45]

The lack of spiritual language is especially noticeable here. Gentile has abandoned Hegel's strict terms of reference. This is partly understandable, given his earlier objection to the triad of subjective, universal and absolute spirit; but nowhere here, in contrast to the earlier version, is the family's absorption and annihilation even suggested. Gentile appears to have retreated from his former radical and rather strange position in order to adopt a more conventional account of the family, in which the state 'has interests' in maintaining and protecting its members' 'perennial moral nursery', that domain in which love is especially important, without swallowing or overriding it.

---

[43] *Genesi* [67]; Harris translation [131].
[44] Note that when Gentile criticises 'utilitarianism', he is concerned not with Bentham and Mill, but rather the idea of means-ends practical reasoning.
[45] *Genesi* [113]. Note that the passage has a different structure in Harris's translation [172].

So: has Gentile simply given in to Hegel's view of the family? To an extent he has. The heightened emphasis on love reflects Hegel's description, in which the family is 'specifically characterised' by it.[46] Sentiment, of which love is one variety, serves to orient the individual will toward other people, establishing an impulse toward empathy, understanding and reasonableness.[47] Unlike Hegel, Gentile denies that the family can be just one object among others, as is required in Hegel's move from family to civil society.[48] Gentile leaves civil society out of the picture; the family remains as the anvil on which man's moral ore is beaten out. But this still occurs *within the state*. In Gentile's system it cannot be claimed that family and state sit alongside one another in the sphere of objective spirit, with each preserving some distinct faculty or right that shields it from the other. Instead, the state is the universal spirit, and the family is part of the state. To maintain S's united will, the family cannot impose moral demands contrary to those of the state. This does not mean that one must give way entirely to the other and thus make the losing claimant redundant. Instead the state and family must make compatible demands. These may still differ in their substantive contents, just as when someone's mother is in need of help, say, the daughter has (and feels) a stronger responsibility to intervene than would a stranger. Provided that this does not require her to break any other moral commitments, it is perfectly compatible with the conception of state and family that Gentile proposes. For any individual family member, state and family both appear to exist concretely and uniquely: she does not feel the tug of two families, two states, or family against state. They are all one with her concrete will.

Perhaps the most substantive change from *Diritto* is found in *Genesi*'s chapter on 'the state and other states'. This includes a passage on international law, understood as 'the unification of states by means of treaties'.[49] Gentile warns us that the logical extension of this tendency, namely 'a confederation, a centralised empire, a society of nations, or what have you [...] would not be the absolute realisation of the state but its end'. Without other states to act as our state's alter-ego or antagonist, ours would become nothing more than a *thing*. Deprived of conflict, it would cease to pulse with 'the eternal rhythm of human

---

[46] Hegel (1945) [110; §158].
[47] In *Genesis,* Harris notes that Gentile began to emphasise the importance of love in his *Filosofia dell'arte,* and further in the chapter 'Il sentimento', in *Introduzione alla filosofia.* It should be noted that love is featured in the early works, too. *Sommario* is full of it, but there Gentile does not make its full importance explicit.
[48] Hegel (1945) [122; §181].
[49] *Genesi* [103]; Harris translation [164].

social life', and its spiritual character would vanish. To avoid this outcome, there must be a plurality of states in 'inevitable opposition' to one another, constantly and unendingly trying to transcend that opposition through means including, if not restricted to, war.[50]

Harris correctly observes that this argument is fallacious, and that Gentile 'ought logically to argue that the state does not depend on other states any more than the individual depends on other individuals for society'.[51] Even a solitary state would be able to develop; its whole existence relies on a constantly changing cast of persons, with transient interests, relationships and circumstances. It is even easier to conceive of 'the moment of otherness' in the state than in the case of Robinson Crusoe on his island. As he weighs up his choices, Crusoe is subject to the rhythms of the spirit even though he is empirically alone. The state can do this without even projecting imaginary persons. It contains a plurality of competing individuals, each with her own preferences, opinions and so on. If the state is free and infinite for every individual subject residing within and identifying herself with it, the existence of other states is immaterial. At most, S's acknowledgement of other states' existence, even as abstract entities, is what links the state *qua* spiritual extension of S with the state *qua* political institution. But I cannot see how this link is *necessary*. If those other states did not exist, what S calls 'state' would cease to be *an example of a state,* just as if all mothers but mine ceased to exist, it would no longer be the case that mine was *an example of a mother*. She would still be 'mother' to me. The relation would still mean the same as I saw it. Only her relation to the abstract concept of 'mother' would be affected.

4. 'The real shipwreck of actualism': some standard objections

The changes to Gentile's conception of the state as it approaches its totalitarian endpoint reflect his increasing tendency to conflate two essentially different concepts: the spiritual or internal state, which is at the heart of his doctrine; and the empirical state, which is manifest in a contingent arrangement of institutions. The first does not require the second in order to act as a reference point in moral decision-making. Unless persons associate the second with the first, *recognising* the various manifestations of the empirical institution as bearers of moral authority, the second is an abstraction without moral significance, just as some imaginary otherworldly society is for someone living today. An empirical state may still *act* as though it were a spiritual state, and

---

[50] *Genesi* [103–5]; Harris translation [164–5].
[51] Harris *Genesis* [164n].

try to compel its citizens to recognise it as such, but, as Gentile says of police states, for coercion to be *needed* implies that the spiritual version is not yet properly established. If it were, citizens would already want what the state wants and act accordingly.[52]

Gentile's treatment of the state is the crux of the standard objections to his political and moral theory. Within his lifetime he was accused of 'statolatry' (*statolatria*) providing dubious arguments to justify elevating political contingency to the point that the decisions of certain empirical individuals are treated with uncritical reverence *because of where they originate* rather than because their content has any special qualities.[53] Gentile's attempts to meet this objection only exacerbate the issue.[54] In *Genesi*, he begins a paragraph on statolatry with the claim that '[t]he state, inasmuch as it is the unique reality, is undoubtedly divine.'[55] This is worryingly reminiscent of some of the cruder translations of Hegel, giving the impression that the (political) state is (pretending to be) a substitute for God, with all the infallible truth-affirming qualities that this suggests. Thus Gentile plays into the hands of his critics.[56] However, there is a way out, and the phrase 'inasmuch as it is the unique reality' hints that this interpretation is flawed. As I understand him, Gentile can only be arguing that the *transcendental* state, understood as the widest or 'universal' extension of S's personality, is the entirety of what she can aspire to know. Or rather: the state contains all 'the elements belonging to the life of a people'; anything that an individual knows is, *ipso facto*, also contained within (known by) the state; Gentile's 'pure immanence' requires that we cannot make concrete truth claims about anything that we do not know; therefore, the state is the highest (and, at a small stretch, the 'divine') form of human consciousness.

---

[52] For Gentile's view of police states, see *Genesi* [124–5]; Harris translation [182].

[53] This objection is levelled on a regular basis against Gentile and, often for better reasons, other Fascists and fascism(s).

[54] Note that he also discusses the charge of 'statolatria' in *Diritto*, but there defends Hegel against it. His point, I think, is that the state can be equated with 'the march of God through the world' only while its citizens identify it as the manifestation of their liberty. Once it becomes something material, it is *ipso facto* non-spiritual and therefore non-moral. See *Diritto* [112–3].

[55] *Genesi* [107]. Note that the phrase translated as 'inasmuch as it is the unique reality' comes from the Italian, '*in quanto l'Unico*' (literally, 'inasmuch as [it is] the Unique'). I borrow the less awkward phrase 'unique reality' from Harris's translation [167].

[56] Harris also points out the link with Hegel's 'march of God through the world' etc. in his translation of *Genesis* [267n].

For theorists without Gentile's unusually privileged real-world political connections, the conflation of empirical state and transcendental state might be dismissed as an embarrassing philosophical mistake, an example of an author carried away on his own hyperbole. But since he consciously wrote these works to provide theoretical justification for the Fascist state, the consequences ran unusually deep, and are not so easily isolated and set aside. Gennaro Sasso argues that Gentile's identification of the universal will with the (political) state is wholly unjustified and ultimately damaging to actual idealism's credibility as a moral and social philosophy. S does not recognise the authority of the universal spirit's will and align hers with it through the internal dialogue. Instead the universal spirit's will (which is really the will of a dictator or equivalent political executive) *replaces* S's will. There is no negotiation or justification or recognition; S's will does not come into the equation. Under these circumstances it is senseless to talk about an ethical state, individual freedom or even the state's 'interiority'. Where the state is deaf to the individual will, yet possesses a will of its own, to which S is forced to submit *irrespective of what she personally wills,* the only meaningful will is external, possessed by a person whose arbitrary identity is only obscured by Gentile's spiritual posturing.[57]

Views similar to Sasso's are common in the secondary literature. Some commentators are straightforwardly disparaging, maintaining that Gentile's philosophy was always vague, and could be rendered compatible with any prejudices that its author happened to hold.[58] Few have claimed that the political theory flows directly from the *Teoria*

---

[57] Sasso (1998) [268-9, 507-9 and 528-31]. Gennaro Maria Barbuto has more recently written that Gentile makes the state 'an Absolute: in one way, a universalisation of the state, pure act, free, infinite, unlimited; in the other, its particularisation in a single entity, the state to which one belongs'. He continues: 'Gentile's political thought exhibits an ambivalence. In his works, and above all in [*Genesi*], one can read a great deal about the *alterità* [otherness] of the alter[-ego] that is in us and is our *socius,* [and] about the transcendental dialectic between the ego and the self, which is the origin of society. But, on the other hand, a monolithic absolutisation of the state prevails, constituting the horizon of individual sense.' See Barbuto (2007) *Nichilismo e Stato totalitario. Libertà e autorità nel pensiero politico di Giovanni Gentile e Giuseppe Rensi,* Naples: Guida [24-5].

[58] Harry Redner is a good example of such. Critics like Sabine and Marcuse could be included in this group, but their assessments of Gentile are so uniformly savage that it is hard to say what they think his theory would have been worth if he had not become a Fascist.

generale.⁵⁹ A more common view is that actual idealism has something to offer, but, in one way or another, its political manifestation does its metaphysics a disservice; once the state is granted special discretion over all questions of truth and value, actual idealism can no longer offer a critical standpoint on social and political contingencies. Instead, it seems to guarantee any kind of authoritarian regime the appearance of legitimacy. 'The state' is left so empty a term that it can be filled with whatever the reader likes. In his book *The Living Past*, Rik Peters, by no means a flippant or hasty critic, states this objection in bold terms:

> [T]he real shipwreck of actualism came when Gentile began to confound the ideal of the self-constitutive act of thought with the reality of fascist politics, with the result that he saw fascism as the necessary, universal and self-justifying outcome of history. At this point the *norma sui* principle, which otherwise would have formed the basis of a most tolerant philosophy, turned into its own opposite, and formed the basis of one of the most intolerant philosophies in history.⁶⁰

Bruce Haddock makes a similar point. Since there is no truth outside the mind by which political arrangements can be judged, 'it follows that political orders establish their own terms of reference'. If the state 'creat[es] unity, rather than passively reflecting it[, it is] not enough to value the traditions and practices that had [formerly] shaped a way of life'. Instead, in Gentile's state, citizens '*have to* identify with the organised projection of those values by the state, treating the state as the public embodiment of their personalities'.⁶¹ Gentile's basic criterion of political legitimacy is that the state's will and the individual wills of its constituent persons should align. He does not assume that these conditions already obtain. They must be brought about through active intervention. But he neglects to specify any limits on how much the state may do to bring about such an alignment. His theory, preoccupied with S's 'unity' with the state, removes all traditional limits on the

---

⁵⁹ One example is A. James Gregor, who claims that Gentile's theory was 'betrayed' and misrepresented by its nominal adherents. See his introduction to Gentile (2007) *Origins and Doctrine of Fascism*, New Brunswick, NJ: Transaction [xii]. An account of other Fascists' attempts to deny that actual idealism represented the substance of Fascist doctrine can be found in Gregor (2001) *Giovanni Gentile: Philosopher of Fascism*, New Brunswick, NJ: Transaction [67–80].

⁶⁰ Peters (1998a) [515]. The quotation continues: 'Only at the end of his life, seeing the results of fascism, Gentile did [word order sic] try to reinforce the tolerant aspect of actualism with his theory of the transcendental dialogue according to which society is based on the possibility that we can talk to ourselves.'

⁶¹ Bruce Haddock (2005) *A History of Political Thought: 1789 to the Present*, Oxford: Polity [124]; emphasis added.

state's authority. Even its conceptual structure is designed to eliminate conflicts of interest, as shown by the assimilation and near-obliteration of Hegel's concepts of family and civil society. Indeed, with Gentile's insistence that orders of value must be imposed, he seems to have granted the political state an unlimited amount of power to impose its will upon individuals. The idea of the concrete will, or of the world constantly changing according to subjects' acts of self-realisation, allows him to excuse current problems, such as widespread intolerance or state terrorism or opposition to the state by its own citizens, as unfortunate but inevitable wrinkles in the universal spirit's development. Viewed through the concrete will of the state, what appears to be opposition is just history *in fieri*: the state's will is bound to be vindicated in the future.[62]

There are two problems here. One is that the will is attached to an empirically identifiable entity without adequate justification. Thus we see Gentile endorsing *Benito Mussolini* as the agent of history, rather than the role or office that Mussolini may or may not fill. The second problem is that, having too readily granted the spiritual value of one person or administration, Gentile becomes unable to criticise it. What is the status of a disobedient citizen in a totalitarian regime? From the regime's perspective, the citizen's will represents a moment in the development of its proper form, which will ultimately (and inevitably) conform to the 'universal will' of the state. From the citizen's perspective, the regime is tyrannical, and its will opposed to her own.

Whether Gentile would have supported the Fascist regime in the event that Mussolini had been replaced is a matter of speculative history. The philosopher's death preceded the dictator's by almost a year, so his loyalty was never tested in this way. I do not think that his excessive acceptance of the regime's activities can be explained in terms of his theory. Some authors have claimed, with varying degrees of scorn, that Gentile became caught up in Mussolini's cult of personality and swallowed the Party line on how 'il Duce is always right' (*il Duce ha sempre ragione*).[63] Others portray Gentile not as deluded but as a tragic figure who often disapproved of party policy, but was aware that he was so deeply embroiled in the Fascist project that he could not leave without bearing the responsibility for its wrongs. On this account he felt that he could better employ his moderating influence from inside the regime than outside. A third account has it that he know-

---

[62] The idea of the disparity between the state that is and the state that it is *in fieri* is at the heart of Sasso's general critique.

[63] Harris (1960), for example, characterises Gentile's adherence to Mussolini as a symptom of 'opportunism' [190–1 and 219–20].

ingly betrayed his own principles, producing philosophy to order in exchange for influence—and that he certainly gained, as the owner of a publishing house, the editor of the *Enciclopedia Italiana* and (somewhat artificially) Italy's most prominent public intellectual. Again, though, these are historical and biographical curios. The present study does not claim any insight into Gentile's psychology, but rather his theory.

Fortunately, Gentile's early efforts elaborating his actual idealist system give us enough material to distinguish effective objections from misdirected ones, or those which misrepresent the theory they mean to criticise. A recent example of the latter comes from M.E. Moss. She writes that when the concrete truth-affirming qualities of state are invested in specific individuals, Gentile finds himself supporting a 'romantic concept of the elite person, the *uomo fascista*'. From there it follows 'that any proposition[,] no matter how contrary to empirical evidence or combination of propositions, even if inconsistent with one another, expressed by *Il Duce* must be true'. On the purely metaphysical analysis, an act of thinking is *necessarily* conditioned by that of the state, since that is spirit itself: it represents what S already affirms. Transplanted to the political state, this dynamic implies that any person who wants anything other than what her state (i.e. the dictator) wants must be *mistaken*. The dictator is imagined to be infallible and insuperable. 'This', writes Moss, 'is the path to folly, not to truth.'[64]

I suspect that Moss overstates her case. What she describes is a step removed from even the most far-reaching political authority that actual idealism can accommodate. This is not to say that Moss's claims do not reflect how Gentile and some of his Fascist colleagues sometimes *treated* the relation between the state (or its leader) and its citizens. But as we saw in Chapter 2, Gentile insists on a theory of truth based on coherence and belief. While it is true that he denies the value of empirical evidence *in itself*, he cannot claim that the state's truth claims trump individual beliefs where individuals have compelling reasons (including empirical evidence) to hold the beliefs they do. Nor can the state make claims that are 'inconsistent with one another'. According to Gentile's definition of truth, such inconsistency requires that one or more of the incompatible claims be adjusted or jettisoned. Thinking is primitive; the state's will is not, and is rather *constructed* by individual (albeit socialised) thinking subjects. The state can cause an indefinite

---

[64] M.E. Moss (2004) *Mussolini's Fascist Philosopher: Giovanni Gentile Reconsidered*, London: Peter Lang [54–5]. For more on the idea of what the state 'wants [the citizen] to want', see *Educazione* [33]: 'As a citizen, I want what I want; but, on closer inspection, I see that what I want coincides precisely with what the state wants (me to want). And my will is the will of the state.' (Note that the parentheses are present in the original.)

number of propositions to be true, and can alter citizens' beliefs through propaganda and education, but only within the bounds of thinkability. As such, the state's actual truth claims are available for reasoned scrutiny and subsequent criticism.

5. The ethical state of mind

It is plain that Gentile's identification of the political state with the state or socius in his moral theory is an aberration. In order to present them as the same object, he needs to make untenable assumptions about S's beliefs, namely, that they square with those of the political state, however those are understood. This demands one of several highly improbable arrangements. It could be that the state is able to alter S's will directly, perhaps through a maximally efficient and comprehensive system of propaganda and education. If S were already committed to the idea that what the state wills is what she personally wills, this could be achieved. But this would make her nothing more than a credulous and uncritical follower of an external authority. These thoughts are not subjected to examination, compared with alternatives, checked for coherence and integrity, and subsequently affirmed, but imported from the outside. Under these conditions S cannot be free in the way Gentile thinks requisite to morality. The relation between S and the state would be not a dialogue but a lecture. The privileged few with political power cannot have moral authority over S—who, let us remember, represents every thinker—unless she self-consciously recognises them as such.

The only solution to this problem, as I see it, is to insist on the sharp division between the two concepts of state. There is the empirical, political state and the spiritual, ethical state. These two may coincide, but only in special circumstances. It is crucial that these are not confused with one another. A maximally efficient political administration may be able to marshal the beliefs of its constituent citizens in such a way that they hold reasonably compatible commitments, recognise each other as fellow contributors to a common endeavour, and are otherwise able and motivated to behave in ways that further their collective ends. However, Gentile treats the political state as though its citizens *already* share a collective consciousness and recognise its supreme authority in matters of law, culture and morality. Plainly this was not and was never the case. A moral theory that relies upon a merely *possible* arrangement of empirical circumstances is no more than an abstract exercise concerning responsibilities held and discharged by imaginary people. If the theory does not reflect the facts that actually obtain, it can present S with no morally significant reasons for action.

There is a worrying dissonance between what Gentile insisted the state represented and what was believed by the very individuals he claimed to describe. Persons already identify strongly with groups other than the state, to which they can even be apathetic or hostile. Sometimes these other groups make moral claims on their members that contradict or otherwise cannot be assimilated into those of the state. The state cannot then impose its contradictory order of value and have persons uncritically accept it. Indeed, the state's conception of value would present itself as a moral affront to persons already so committed. This clearly indicates that the political state cannot be assumed to fulfil the role of the socius. Persons with other beliefs may ignore or consciously reject the demands the state makes of them. There is no point at which previously committed persons do not already exist; even under conditions of extreme social conditioning, the existence of persons and commitments *prior* to those conditions remains problematic.[65]

The spiritual conception of the state is more promising. It does not presuppose S's identification with any particular political entity or community of empirical persons. It is instead a model of the best reasons and truest beliefs that she can conceive. Although S is the arbiter of reasons, the demands of the universal will — of morality, in a word — are not just whatever S happens to want them to be. Through careful consideration of Gentile's wider system, and particularly the set-up of the internal dialogue, we can flesh out the socius and fit it into a workable moral theory that can discipline her thinking and identify universal reasons.

6. Conclusion

In this chapter I explained the development of Gentile's concept of the state and showed what role it is assigned in his moral theory. I contend that he fails to justify this insertion. The problem is that he runs together two distinct concepts — the political state and the spiritual state — and tries to cover the difference between the two using unconvincingly adapted terms from elsewhere in his theory. When the political state is identified with the socius, and the state's will is identified as the 'true' counterpart to S's will, the 'internal dialogue' — the process of moral reasoning — ceases to be a conversation. Instead it becomes a monologue, consisting of the state's claims about what its constituent persons 'really' believe, undergirded by the dubious assumption that these claims somehow supersede the beliefs those persons might (mistakenly) think themselves to hold. They are deprived of any critical

---

[65] The experiences of Roman Catholics and Mafiosi in Fascist Italy are relevant (if in most respects very different) examples of how and why these problems might arise.

standpoint, and their personal judgements count for nothing in the determination of what to think or do. This is wholly incompatible with the basic tenets of actual idealism, in which S *must* have the capacity to judge and endorse (or reject) what moral claims are made of her. At the end of the chapter I argued that the solution to Gentile's problem is to distinguish cleanly between the political state and its spiritual counterpart. The two may overlap, and in morally upstanding states any disparity between them will be minimal. But Gentile's attempt to fasten his theory to a nascent authoritarian regime is unconvincing, and requires him to compromise the theory's structure in order to supply a facade of constant legitimacy.

In Chapter 1's brief overview of constructivism I distinguished 'epistemological' constructivism from its 'procedural' counterpart. This first half of the book has shown actual idealism to be an unambiguous example of epistemological constructivism, since it conceives of all thinking, including the subject and object of thought, in an endless process of self-creation. It also contains hints of a constructivist procedure in the form of the internal dialogue. In Gentile's moral theory, however, the constructivist principles are undermined when he equates the political state with the socius and S's will with that of the state. The theory collapses into the assertion that what S ought to do is whatever her political state wants her to do. The content of those commands is left immune from rational scrutiny. Thus moral claims become facts, purely objective features of a realist cosmos. This is anathema to actual idealism's constructivist principles.[66] My task in the coming chapters is to elaborate a more sophisticated version of the socius and the internal dialogue, revealing how, without the (political) state's disruptive influence, Gentile's theory can be rehabilitated as a plausible moral constructivist doctrine.

---

[66] Recall Street's definition of 'constructivist views in ethics [as those which] understand the correctness or incorrectness of some (specified) set of normative judgements as a question of whether those judgements withstand some (specified) procedure of scrutiny from the standpoint of some (specified) set of further normative judgements', in Street (2008) 'Constructivism about Reasons', already quoted in a footnote to Chapter 1, subsection #1.

Part II
Gentilean Constructivism in Moral Theory

Chapter 5

Gentile contra Kant on Practical Reason

To set the scene for this chapter and those that follow, let me briefly summarise Part I. Chapter 2 described actual idealism's conception of the subject as *pensiero pensante,* together with the idea of truth as a process of construction within the bounds of the coherently thinkable. Chapter 3 explained how Gentile distinguishes his theory from solipsism and situates the subject (S) in a world alongside other people. The link between S and other persons, and, by extension, S and morality, is contained in the 'transcendental society' in which the 'internal dialogue' occurs. This dialogue involves S justifying her beliefs through reference to the 'socius', an arbiter that she constructs. Chapter 4 described Gentile's attempts to have the political state fill this role. I argued that this strategy proves self-defeating, since the person or persons representing the political state must refer to a third agent in order to know what they (and the state) will. The third must refer to fourth, that to a fifth, and so on in an endless regress.

Over the second half of the book, and starting with this chapter, I mean to employ Gentile's conception of the socius as part of a recognisably constructivist *internal dialogue procedure,* or *IDP.* Since Gentile's moral theory has not previously been presented as a fully fledged procedural constructivism, I refer to other theories to see what features such a doctrine should have. This will also allow me to show how the IDP is distinguishable from them. Especially important is Kantian constructivism, since Gentile frequently compares Kant's doctrine with his own, praising it for its demonstration of *the possibility* of a doctrine without unjustified presuppositions, despite the residual dualisms that persist in Kant's actual writings. More recent Anglo-American theorists have tried to render Kant's doctrine in fully constructivist terms. I refer to their writings where the contrasts with Gentile's positions are more striking than those between Gentile and Kant himself.

The present chapter is structured as follows. I begin (sub-heading #1) with a summary of Gentile's account of reason as put forth in his *Logica*. From that I extract the IDP's basic outline. I then indicate a number of questions that remain unresolved in this account of the IDP. To see how these might be answered, at sub-heading #2 I describe Kant's various formulations of the categorical imperative (hereafter *CI*), which has been widely interpreted as the centrepiece of the recent constructivist literature. Under the next three sub-headings I assess the extent to which these formulations can be applied to the IDP: the Universal Law Formula (#3); the Kingdom of Ends Formula (#4); and the Autonomy Formula (#5). I find that the Autonomy Formula bears the closest resemblance to the Gentilean theory I describe, but, while a strong conception of autonomy enables us to answer some of the questions raised earlier, actual idealism's unusual structure leaves the full meaning of autonomy ambiguous. (That problem is taken up in Chapter 6.) At sub-heading #6 I comment upon the CI's features that Gentile *does* consider worth retaining, before concluding with an overview of the questions still to be answered (#7).

1. Reason in actual idealism

Part I showed actual idealism to be a thoroughgoing variety of anti-realism. The method of immanence denies the possibility of any independent domain against which claims can be tested.[1] This leaves *pensiero pensante* open to the charge of crude intuitionism, according to which truths are immediately available to the thinker without any need for mutual coherence or consistency. This would deny the possibility of error, for any claim or combination of claims could be simultaneously true at the moment S thinks of them as such. She would be at the mercy of the whims of intuition, her thought determined by what is given to it, without any power to distinguish and thus construct the truth.

Similar charges can be made of anti-realist doctrines in general. We might say that if nothing is independently real, anything can be true, and if anything can be true, the prospects for achieving certainty in judgements look doubtful. Gentile replies to this accusation by appeal to the unity of thought and value. To hold something to be valuable, an argument to be valid, or a truth claim to be justified requires S to affirm a belief about it. This act of affirmation is the basis for actual idealism's distinction between right and wrong beliefs, or thinking well and thinking badly. S must try to find beliefs that are justified, in that they

---

[1] 'If a moral reality exists,' writes Gentile, 'it exists inasmuch as man makes it exist. Its moral character consists in precisely its existence as [the] product of the human spirit.' See *Diritto* [7].

have enough mutual coherence for her to affirm them simultaneously without needing to think two or more mutually contradictory claims at once.

The usual constructivist solution to this problem is to invoke the idea of reason or reasons for belief and action, with different accounts of what S ought to do (including, perhaps, what she ought to *think*) undergoing scrutiny in accordance with some specially designed procedure. We have already seen evidence of such a procedure in Gentile's internal dialogue. In the version presented so far, it is unclear how subject and socius are related. Until we know this, we cannot know how authoritative moral judgements can be reached. A successful account of actual idealist moral theory must operate without presupposing the moral authority of some external agent such as the political state. That would infringe thought's unconditioned liberty. Conversely, if it is possible for the state to act in a morally authoritative way, its actions must meet criteria freely imposed upon it by thought. To see how Gentile achieves this, I turn to the account of reason in his *Sistema di logica*. In what follows I lay it out, drawing occasionally on relevant supporting passages in other parts of the *Logica*. This will give us the basic materials with which to design a practicable constructivist procedure.

Gentile notes that throughout the history of philosophy,[2] it was believed that thought could be divided into discrete events or individual *thoughts* occurring successively over time, enacted by empirically separate subjects, each thinking 'this or that thought' in her own mind.[3] These commonsensical assumptions about the existence of other minds cannot be rigorously defended, as actual idealism's conception of the subject goes to show. However, both actual idealism and the conventional view recognise the need for a unified conception of thought. That is: in order for people to live together, and even for them to think at all, these separate though (sometimes) simultaneous thoughts must 'come together' in the dialectic, wherein thinkers can, first, 'compose and resolve the multiplicity of natural things [...] in a [shared] cosmos and a single being'; and, second, 'gather together and reduce the multi-

---

[2] This is a somewhat liberal interpretation of the Italian. Gentile in fact refers to the spirit's 'historical representation', which I take to mean 'the history of philosophy, construed as one ongoing project'.

[3] Note that Gentile uses the verb 'appropriarsi', meaning *to appropriate* (for oneself). Hence subjects *appropriate* this or that thought. Here we should note the implication that, according to Gentile's view of the 'historical representation of the spirit', the range of possible thoughts is viewed as though it existed prior to anyone thinking them, with the result that thinkers *appropriate* rather than create them.

tude of men under the empire of a single thought, of a unique intellect, of an impersonal reason'. These two postulates,[4] he writes, were 'energetically affirmed' by successive philosophers, showing how much 'faith in thought had been strengthened'.[5]

The first postulate refers to the idea that thoughts contribute to a whole. If S asks herself the question, 'Are these my shoes?' and thinks (affirms) that P (e.g. 'yes; these are my shoes') *and* not-P ('no; these are not my shoes'), she is confused, assuming that she also believes both of these claims to refer to the same object under the same circumstances. Not every combination of thoughts thought (call these 'claims') can be affirmed simultaneously; a claim's truth or falsity is not a property independent of other claims. It is quite ordinary to say that what a person thinks is wrong or that she has failed to reason correctly. The basis for this, and S's motivation for finding coherent beliefs, is the assumption (a *necessary* assumption, unless persons are to retreat to a solipsist standpoint) that, despite the subjectivity of thinking, there are multiple subjects or at least points of view that could be adopted in S's world.

The second postulate extends this idea to inter-subjective reason. Although earlier philosophers assumed the existence of multiple, individual and separate thoughts and thinkers, they persistently referred to thinking as an activity in which all thinkers are engaged and of which every thought is a product. Although people sometimes think differently when faced with the same set of considerations, or come to hold different beliefs, it would be strange to say that they each occupy a separate universe about which they can make accordingly separate, incommensurable claims. Since they assume themselves to belong to a single, shared universe, persons can review, reject and/or follow each other's reasons for thinking and acting in much the same way that they each review, reject and correct their own. The 'empire of [...] impersonal reason' refers to the single, shared conception of reason against which several (and perhaps all) subjects test their own and each other's ideas. Without a conception of a 'united' cosmos, persons face the unedifying prospect of a world 'crumble[d] into the multiplicity of things, parts or phenomena, [before which] the individual feels [her]self [to be] enclosed by an impassable barrier [and] cut off from other

---

[4] A postulate is a claim assumed to be true for the purposes of subsequent discussion or reasoning. In these cases, then, the relevant postulates are strictly (i) *that it is possible* to 'compose and resolve the multiplicity of natural things [...] in a [shared] cosmos and a single being'; and (ii) *that it is possible* to 'gather together and reduce the multitude of men under the empire of a single thought, of a unique intellect, of an impersonal reason'.

[5] *Logica 2* [96].

individuals'. Even when overcome by doubt and uncertainty, thinkers persist in 'peer[ing] through the gloom, searching anxiously for ways to unite [their own thoughts] with the thoughts of others'. This search for unity, Gentile thinks, is driven by 'the very nature of thought itself'.[6]

1i. The internal dialogue re-visited

In Chapter 2, I noted that Gentile's conception of concrete thought is strictly a *positive* one. 'Not thinking P' is not an act one can perform. Instead, one must (positively, actually) think something else. Nevertheless one requires a conception of what one *does not think*, as well as a set of reasons that one does not think it, in order to be able to articulate clearly what one *does* think. An appreciation of this opposition or resistance is the very basis of reason. S needs not only the consensus of other thinkers, but also 'their dissent, their opposition and their resistance to [her] thought'. Gentile asks:

> What does it matter whether [a person] encounters other people empirically, as they are thrown together in political life, in crowds and assemblies; or lives for [her]self according to the cowardly warnings of epicurean wisdom?[7]

His answer is that the second person, who 'lives for [her]self' at the exclusion of other people, 'will never be content with that changeless death'—surely a spiritual death—'that [Epicurus's] wisdom promises', because in losing any resistance to her thought, she also loses the basis for her positive self-conception. That is: without an idea of what she does *not* believe, and why she rejects these propositions as false, S has no way to distinguish her actual, positive beliefs from unjustified assumptions. The abstraction of other persons' ideas is 'overcome' when S re-thinks and rejects or affirms them for herself. Thus they cease to be a 'limit' on her thought. It is in overcoming the limit imposed by other thinkers and other (perhaps hypothetical) points of view that her life as self-creative, self-correcting *pensiero pensante* consists.

This should not be read as a claim that persons empirically isolated from others are unable to think or apply reason. To drive this point home, Gentile unambiguously invokes the internal dialogue:

> In solitude, man speaks to himself. He makes his *alter [ego]* inside himself, and he labours away in the secret conversation with the interlocutor

---

[6] *Logica* 2 [97].
[7] *Logica* 2 [97]. Note that Epicurus thought that pleasure was the sole criterion for a good life. I think that what Gentile suggests here, then, is that a person might live 'for [her]self' in a self-interested, pleasure-seeking fashion, at the exclusion of what other people think.

that he, in the abstract solitude of his particular life, has created, in a drama identical to that which each of us brings to life in the concrete marriage of our being with the whole of our world. And one has no less need to make oneself agree with this secret interlocutor, [by] overcoming or yielding or submitting; finding in him sometimes a satanic tempter, another time a stern or benign mentor, another time a criminal or a judge, and in general a partner.[8]

The most notable difference between this and *Diritto*'s brief description of Robinson Crusoe is the acknowledgement of the variable character of the alter-ego (or socius). This plainly distinguishes it from a hypothetical onlooker at an Archimedean point, like Kant's 'impartial and rational spectator',[9] Hare's 'archangel',[10] or any of countless other ideal observers. It would be strange to invoke and follow the advice of an acknowledged 'satanic tempter' when considering what to think or do.[11] The socius's authority in reasoning cannot be derived directly from its identity, for that would have the IDP hinge on a kind of intuition, with the present state of the socius corresponding to a changeable set of facts already available to S.[12] Figure 1 shows how this implausible dynamic would operate. S is the *subject*, who refers (solid line) to A, the *socius* or *alter-ego*. A is taken to have moral authority (dashed line) over S. The imperative presented by A reflects S's immediate awareness (intuition) of what she ought to do, and is unmediated by reasons. As such it is liable to change, and can be taken to be authoritative only as S recognises it as such.

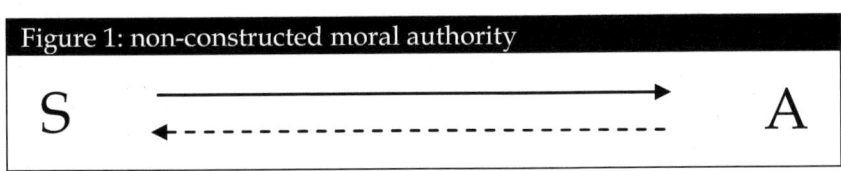

Figure 1: non-constructed moral authority

---

[8] *Logica 2* [97]. Thanks to Matteo Fabbretti for his help in correcting this translation in September 2012.

[9] Immanuel Kant w/H.J. Paton (ed., trans.) (1948) *The Moral Law*, London: Hutchinson [61; 393 in std. pag.].

[10] R.M. Hare (1978) 'Moral Conflicts', in *Tanner Lectures in Human Value*, pp. 171–93, [Online], www.utilitarian.net/singer/by/tanner.pdf [182].

[11] Harris acknowledges this point: 'Even the roles and attitudes here suggested—"tempter", "mentor", "criminal", "judge", "subjection" [for which I have offered "submitting"], "conquest" [for which I have given "overcoming"]—are slightly suspicious' (1960) [110].

[12] To clarify: S cannot refer directly to the socius in order to decide what to do. This is because (i) it would assume that S had the answers already, but was projecting them onto this mysterious 'other'; and (ii) it does not explain the reconciliation of S and the socius in 'a single thought'.

S's awareness that A could appear under a different guise suggests that A can at most feature in the reasoning process as one element among others. Hence S's 'drama' is 'identical' to those of other people only inasmuch as persons recognise each other as fellow thinkers. But for a given thinking subject, the socius remains secret: it is internal, and is not strictly shared with other people. Its characteristics are not wholly arbitrary, of course. S does not create it in a social vacuum. It may reflect other people, specific or otherwise, as S imagines what they would say about the judgement she is making. It cannot be assumed that any two people will reason identically, since each must create her secret partner for herself, and respond to whatever form it might take.

1ii. Universality and objectivity

Recall that, in his later works, Gentile calls the dialogue 'transcendental'. Given his resistance to the idea of transcendent domains beyond the immanent plane of the thinkable, this may seem a poor choice of words. Here, though, the term 'transcendental' should be understood in another sense. Rather than 'removed from the phenomenal plane of existence', it means 'inherent in the way thinking occurs'.[13] Crusoe distinguishes reasoned from unreasonable judgement in consultation with others in the 'transcendental society'. He imagines what other people would say about whatever problem he faces; he reflects on their suggestions and adjusts his judgement where he considers it appropriate to do so. He asks himself, 'If I were someone else, how would I assess this problem?' He overcomes his particularity, recognising the possibility of other points of view and the subservience of his reasons (and those of other people) to those of a 'universal subject' whose reasons are not only unbiased but sound. These are *good reasons* rather than his (or S's) particular reasons.[14] More generically, once S has judged the matter in what she considers the best way she can, viewing

---

[13] This is a generous interpretation. It is notable that Gentile does not refer to the *transcendent* society (which really would be unknowable, and claims about it therefore nonsensical) but the *transcendental* society, which, following Kant's distinction between the two, would make it the society that 'pertains to the necessary conditions of knowledge'. See Mautner (2005) [622].

[14] On a rather charitable interpretation, Gentile might be thought to make this point in *Sommario 2* [34–5] and *Genesi* [20–1]; Harris translation [86–7]. The phrase 'soggetto universale' occurs rarely, in works like *Religione* [89], although variants appear elsewhere and appear to have the same meaning. In *Logica 1* [40], for example, Gentile refers to 'mente universale' (universal mind). Most often, though, he uses the word 'universal' as a noun rather than an adjective.

it from the (imagined) perspectives of people other than herself and deciding how she ought to respond to them, her judgement ceases to be merely subjective and gains objective status.

Figure 2 models a minimal dialogical constructivist procedure. The subject (S) refers to the socius (A), and may or may not accept A's reasons as authoritative. S may also find that her original reasons are superior to A's,[15] and are as such vindicated through the dialogical process. It could otherwise be that some new intermediate position provides the strongest reasons. In this way S can *construct* a universal subject (US), which S recognises to have *the best reasons* available from S and A.

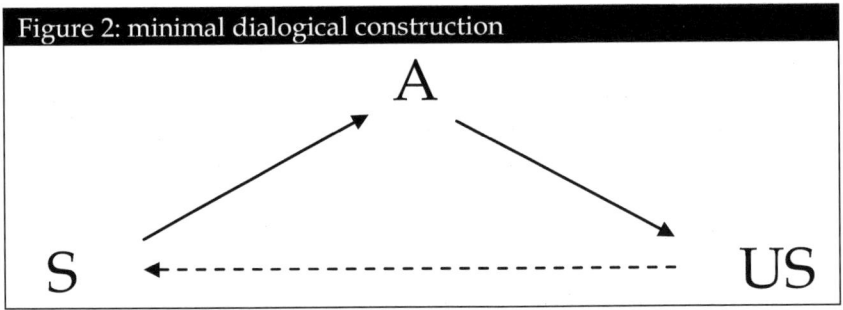

Figure 2: minimal dialogical construction

Recalling the Particularity Objection raised in Chapter 3, it might be objected here that A — the other participant in the internal dialogue — is an invention of S, whose thought is already 'particular', since it includes her contingent characteristics, perhaps including stupidity, ignorance, prejudice and self-deception. Hence the purported universality of its result cannot be anything more than a mirage, and aspirations to it necessarily misguided. Someone who fundamentally misapprehends or is ignorant of the facts of the matter will posit internal interlocutors with the same impediments. If I am very stupid, and cannot think through a problem, I am unlikely to see the correct answer in the clear light of reason because an imaginary alter-ego has put the case to me. Either I have reasoned out the problem for myself, or else those in the internal dialogue will have nothing to say. A judgement made in isolation is necessarily a subjective one, and its aspirations to objectivity via inter-subjectivity are illusory.

Gentile responds to this objection in the *Logica*'s first volume. He equates S's 'process' with the truth's 'dialectic'. So conceived, the process (*viz.* thought) is 'subject and object in one', incorporating both 'the

---

[15] For now, controversially, I take the idea of a good reason's *superiority* to a bad reason to be basic. I will come back to the question of what qualities better or worse reasons have in Chapter 7.

subject's liberty and the object's necessity'. In simpler language, he means that *thought constantly corrects itself*. He continues:

> Against those who would object that our [*viz.* actual idealism's conception of] subjectivity cannot pretend to contain the genuine objectivity which is proper to truth, [we] must reply that that subjectivity in which one finds what one legitimately wants to save in the objectivist conception of truth is not our dialectic[al] subjectivity, but [instead] that abstract concept of transcendent truth statically opposed to the reality of truth.[16]

These objectors are making a mistake by imagining a form of objective truth existing without S. As we saw in Chapter 2, Gentile insists that purely objective truths are unattainable, and cannot, therefore, yield intelligible standards for knowledge. S cannot know a pure object even so far as to be able to compare her own subjective claims with it. Thus 'objective knowledge' is a contradiction in terms, confusing 'the shadow thought projects in front of itself' for an object that conditions and determines that thought.[17] If reason is imagined to be an 'unattainable' object, isolated from S in 'the strong fortress of the abstract logos', out of time and space and isolated from any actual thinker, the problem of describing or meaningfully applying reason would seem insoluble.[18] Gentile's reference to 'dialectical subjectivity' hints at how S might attain a more robust kind of knowledge than unmodified subjectivity allows by responding to alternatives to her reasons for thinking and acting as she does. That will be one of the tasks for the IDP developed over this second half of the book.

The unifying feature of Gentile's account of reason is his claim that thought, actual concrete *pensiero pensante*, is prior to reason. Reason is thought's product, and insofar as thinkers appeal to principles of reason to guide their thinking along a single path that other thinkers would recognise as the right one, they are invoking the authority of abstractions *that are authoritative precisely because actual, concrete thought has made them so*. Two thinkers might think very differently about some contentious problem and come to different conclusions about what solution is best. If they think separately, justifying their respective conclusions by appeals to reasons that they each believe to be sound, they can both be said to exercise reason. It is only when they come together and see that they have each presupposed a different conception of reason that they are prompted to re-assess their judgements. The aim is to attain

---

[16] *Logica 1* [126].
[17] *Logica 2* [240].
[18] *Logica 2* [99].

true and absolute objectivity: absolute because [it is] self-governing, and has no need for external norms to which it must correspond. But without any such external norm, all of thought, in its actuality [as] *pensiero pensante,* is homogeneous.[19]

1iii. The heart of reason

It is often assumed that reason is separate from sentiment.[20] On the conventional intellectualistic account, to apply reason is to think in a structured, logical way. Sentiment, being notoriously capricious, serves mainly to disturb its finely tuned counterpart, which requires care and deliberation to be effective. Emotions that different people may or may not feel are too unreliable to count as universal reasons, however much those subject to such emotions might feel compelled to take them into account. This view prompts the familiar metaphor of the impartial spectator, who reasons out arguments unaffected by troublesome personal preferences or feelings. Gentile insists that this view is mistaken:

> The heart's thought is in the same line of thought as reason: thought belonging to that [species of] reason [...] that is called heart by those who orient themselves toward a conception of truth [using] norms of the abstract logos. Thought, which is the ego being non-ego, does not admit anything [...] outside itself. What is not heart is not reason, and what is not reason is not heart. [What] is not intellect is not sense; nor vice versa.[21]

The significance of 'the heart' in this passage is not immediately obvious, and might, on an uncharitable reading, be dismissed as a poetic flourish. But this would be to concede the whole passage to 'those who orient themselves toward [...] the abstract logos', which is plainly something Gentile means to resist. 'The heart' is something that those favouring a purely objective conception of reason, based in the abstract logos, would eliminate from their method of inquiry. What Gentile has in mind, I think, is S's *considered conviction* or *feeling* that what reason tells her is true. She must countenance the abstract outcome of her reasoning, conceding that it follows logically, say, from the other relevant considerations; but also its concrete outcome, recognising that *she ought to believe the testimony of her own thought.* In more ordinary language, we sometimes speak of a person having *the courage of her convictions,* meaning that she resists the temptation to compro-

---

[19] *Logica* 2 [100]. I have written 'self-governing' although Gentile in fact uses the more technical and suggestive word 'autarcà' (autarchy). I return to this important term under sub-heading #5 in the present chapter.

[20] Gentile points this out in *Sommario 1* [79].

[21] *Logica* 2 [100]. Note that I do not follow Harris in distinguishing lowercase 'ego' (the pure individual, or social atom) from 'Ego' (concrete thinker).

mise on her aims and beliefs. This is distinguishable from stubbornness, which might involve adherence to beliefs that S just happens (but has no good reason) to hold. The Gentilean subject endeavours to justify her convictions and desires, altering them where appropriate, in order to find a coherent, unified self-conception.

Gentile's account of 'reason and the heart' concludes as follows:

> [A] heart will be conquered by a reason, not because the heart was ever destined to succumb in the struggle, but because reason always conquers itself. Or rather: it is an eternal victory over itself. And whoever employs syllogisms to win over the mother's heart, ignorant of exactly this centre [*viz.* the heart] on which the reason of syllogisms must hinge itself, has never suspected this living link between the abstract logos and the concrete, outside which there will be the philosopher's truth, but a truth that will taste of straw for the man to whom the philosopher tries to offer it.[22]

This passage again refers to a conflict between reason and the heart. However, since the heart also 'has its reasons', the two are not incommensurable.[23] Unlike Plato and Aristotle, who divide thought into abstractly distinct functions or faculties,[24] Gentile means to unite them in the dialectic of ego and non-ego, intellect and sense. Logic will not compel S to alter her beliefs until she *feels* that the truths logic has revealed are authentic.[25] They must not be only the kinds of speculative fancy indulged by philosophers, but instead true claims about concrete reality. The idea that the heart can be 'conquered' by a reason[26] suggests that unity can be achieved: the heart, or sentiment, or feelings, must give way to reasoning, which is, after all, a special kind of thinking. We see here again that Gentile's reason is a product and analogue of thought, something endlessly created and re-created in the act of thinking.

To summarise. Reasoning involves the reconciliation of contradictory viewpoints in a single subject's thought. This means that propositions are systematically affirmed or rejected in order to construct a unified and coherent set of ideas that S can recognise as *justified*,

---

[22] *Logica* 2 [100].
[23] Antonio G. Pesce points out that when he says that 'the heart has its reasons', Gentile invokes Blaise Pascal, whom he elsewhere quotes in the epigraph to *Atto puro*. See Pesce (2012) *L'interiorità intersoggettiva dell'attualismo: il personalismo di Giovanni Gentile,* Rome: Aracne [128].
[24] *Logica* 2 [99].
[25] This point is further reinforced in *Atto puro* [99–100]; Carr translation [102].
[26] Note that I say 'a reason' and not 'reason'. This is not a typo. In the Italian, Gentile writes: 'Un cuore bensì sarà vinto da *una ragione*; ma non perchè il cuore sia mai destinato a soccombere nella lotta, sì perchè la ragione vince sempre se stessa' (emphasis added).

supported both positively (in that she believes she has sound reasons for choosing her preferred position) and negatively (in that she believes the reasons for choosing other positions are less convincing). Hence reasoning relies upon the simultaneous recognition of positive and negative reasons for selecting one's position. The process cannot come to a decisive close without S's beliefs becoming presuppositions. Alternative views can be presented directly to her, as in a conversation with other empirical persons, or else in the internal dialogue, in which she imagines versions of the socius challenging her views and implicitly inviting her to alter or re-affirm them in light of theirs. In this way it is possible to achieve *objectivity* in judgements, understood not as pure knowledge of a permanent object (which would rely on implausible dualism) but as subjective knowledge elevated to objective status through systematic justification from a variety of different standpoints. Although the outcome of a given stretch of reasoning can never be fixed with absolute certainty, and may at any time be altered to accommodate superior reasons, S may (and must) still trust the conclusions she has reached. To accept thought's authority only abstractly is to resign oneself to endless doubt. The endpoint of reason is the heart, or rather, S's concrete conviction and *feeling* of being right.

1iv. The IDP in outline

This account of reason is both unconventional and ambitious. It explains how Gentile conceives of reason, not how he proposes to exercise it. From it we can infer what the basic structure of the IDP should look like. Figure 3 models this structure:

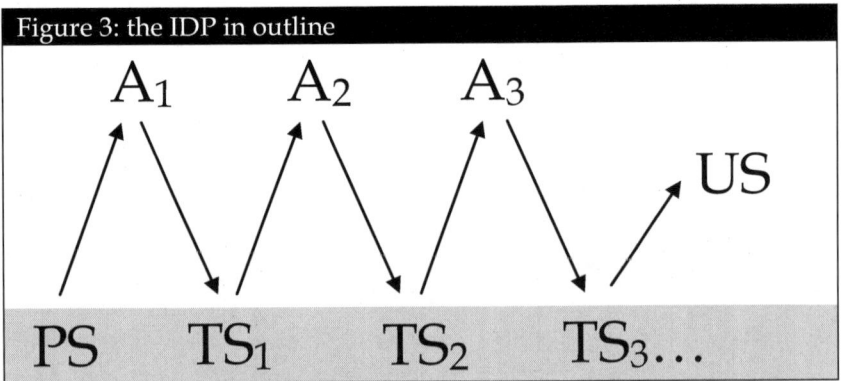

The subject (S) appears here under three different guises: initially as the 'personal subject' (PS), who presents pre-reflective reasons to some appropriately designed hypothetical alter-ego (A); later as the 'thinking subject' (TS), who occupies a series of transient hypothetical standpoints as she refines her reasons; and ultimately as the 'universal subject' (US), who represents the procedure's provisional endpoint.

The outcome of the first exchange between PS and A_1 is manifest in TS_1, who differs from PS at least insofar as her reasons have been tested against A_1. The process continues as S posits a new version of A to challenge her new, provisional reasons. Once again these may or may not persuade TS to adapt her reasons. For S to recognise that any of A's reasons are better than TS's is itself a reason for S to abandon the affected reasons and adopt the relevant superior reasons instead. But TS and A always retain their separate identities. They are separate abstractions posited by S, and although it is possible for S to adopt an A's reasons wholesale, only S has a continuous though changing identity (suggested in this diagram by the grey shading) in successive TSs. Alternatively, if TS's reasons consistently trump A's reasons, TS will continue to present the same reasons to successive As. Every A is a new creation, offering a different point of view from which S can check and challenge the reasons of the current TS.

After an indefinite number of steps, TS is promoted to the status of *universal subject*, or US. The full criteria for this promotion will be developed in the coming chapters, but for now we can define them loosely. TS becomes US when it has been shown that TS's reasons are better, stronger reasons than the others considered, and S knows of no decisive reasons for further changes to TS. This is not guaranteed indefinitely. At any point it could be that new reasons arise, and a previously accepted US must be demoted to TS and thrown back into contention against some new A. But US represents the best and most convincing reasons that S can presently conceive. As such it is the best approximation of 'impersonal reason' that S, whose thought is necessarily subjective, can derive.

2. Kant's categorical imperative

The given account of the IDP leaves some important questions unanswered. Some of these I keep for later chapters.[27] The ones I mean to answer over the remainder of this chapter are: why should S recog-

---

[27] The specific questions I have in mind are: by what criteria can S determine that one set of reasons is *better* than another? Which A-views must be considered before TS is promoted to US status? If this is left wholly to S's discretion, it could be that S considers only those objections she considers most amenable to her original views at PS, and, after an arbitrary number of exchanges, tells herself that her beliefs are vindicated by the IDP. So conceived, the IDP would be a procedure for reinforcing existing beliefs, or else forcing arguments to reach pre-determined conclusions, and thought's freedom to correct itself would be impaired.

nise the authority of US? On what grounds can we justifiably call any US 'universal'? Can S not assume that US is, like TS, potentially vulnerable to as-yet-unconsidered A-objections, and for that reason bracket it as only another hypothetical view that she (S) could hold? My reply refers to Kant's CI, which, in his philosophy, and the theories of several influential constructivists, is used as a test of universality and objectivity. Although not all the CI's formulations are compatible with actual idealism, they can all contribute to a clearer picture of the IDP, how it is distinguishable from similar devices used by other constructivists, and what limitations it carries with it. An ideal solution to these problems would yield some test of IDP-derived judgements' objectivity.

The CI is among the most distinctive features of Kant's philosophy. In its several formulations, this provides the basis for his conception of objectivity in ethics. I will compress Kant's four or five formulations[28] into three:

1. *The Universal Law Formula*: 'Act as if the maxim of your action were to become through your will a universal law of nature.'[29]

2. *The Autonomy Formula*: '[T]he supreme condition of the will's conformity with universal practical reason — namely, the Idea *of the will of every rational being as a will which makes universal law.*'[30]

3. *The Kingdom of Ends Formula*: '[R]ational beings all stand under the *law* that each of them should treat himself and all others, *never merely as a means,* but always *at the same time as an end in himself.* But by so doing there arises a systematic union of rational beings under common objective laws — that is, a kingdom. Since these laws are directed precisely to the relation of such

---

[28] As well as the three presented here, Kant also refers to the End-in-Itself Formula and two slightly different versions of the Universal Law Formula. (See next footnote for details.) I take it that these overlap the three described here to such a great extent that they can be run together without harming the theory.

[29] Kant w/Paton (1948) [88–9; 420–1 in std. pag.]. The wording here is labelled 'the Formula of the Law of Nature'. I take the slightly earlier 'Formula of Universal Law', namely 'Act only on that maxim through which you can at the same time will that it should become a universal law' to express the same idea.

[30] Kant w/Paton (1948) [98–9; 430–1 in std. pag.].

beings to one another as ends and means, this kingdom can be called a kingdom of ends[.]'[31]

Christine Korsgaard points out that 'each formulation [of the CI] is intended to represent some characteristic feature of rational principles.'[32] These formulations are not three separate imperatives, but instead three expressions of the single imperative in accordance with which subjects can test their subjective claims or maxims, which are 'regarded by the subject as valid only for his own will', and elevate them to the status of 'objective, or practical laws [... that are] valid for the will of every rational being'.[33] This unity is implicit in the conspicuous overlap between the various formulations. (1) and (2) refer to the CI's *universality*, although (1)'s reference to 'a universal law *of nature*' emphasises the statement's imperative form, suggesting that persons ought to accord with the CI with the same consistency as if 'a law of nature' caused them to do so — that is, as if they were incapable of doing otherwise. Likewise (2) and (3) can be taken together to capture Kant's conception of humans as rational beings, and all rational beings as ends in themselves.[34] (3) takes up the previous formulations' idea of the will's conformity with reason and extends it to 'common objective laws'. Since all persons, as rational beings, are subjects of the same 'kingdom of ends', any law that they will and thereby impose upon themselves should apply equally to all other subjects if their reasons are to have *objective, universal status*.

---

[31] Kant w/Paton (1948) [100-2; 433-4 in std. pag.]; see also the End-in-Itself formula at [95-6; 427-9 in std. pag.]. It is worth stressing that in the next paragraph Kant adds that 'a rational being belongs to the kingdom of ends as a *member*, when, although he makes its universal laws, he is also himself subject to these laws. He belongs to it as its *head*, when as the maker of laws he is himself subject to the will of no other' [101; 433-4 in std. pag.]. When S thinks of herself as both legislator and subject to these laws, she is forced to engage in hypothetical reflection with imagined others, which is the central motif of the IDP.

[32] Korsgaard (1996b) *Creating the Kingdom of Ends,* Cambridge: Cambridge University Press [106-7].

[33] This is how Kant puts it in his *Critique of Practical Reason* (1898) [105; 126 in std. pag.]. It may be objected that Kant believes his formulations are mutually equivalent. To that I must reply — in much the same way that Gentile rejects the idea of the thing-in-itself — that while Kant says this, we have only his word for it, and when worked out in detail it is by no means guaranteed that the formulations will lead to the same conclusions. Since Gentile shares Kant's aim of subjecting claims or maxims to a test of 'universality', it is appropriate to treat the formulations separately.

[34] This is Korsgaard's method in 'Kant's Formula of Humanity', in (1996b) pp. 106-32.

Kant's followers have interpreted the CI in a variety of ways, prioritising different formulations over others on the grounds that they are, in certain cases or interpretations, mutually contradictory. I will now examine each formulation in turn, starting with the Universal Law Formula, then the Kingdom of Ends Formula (which Gentile can challenge on similar grounds to the Universal Law Formula), and finally the Autonomy Formula. In each case I assess the formula's compatibility with the IDP.

3. The Universal Law Formula

The CI's first formulation is probably the best known, and of the three it is the most programmatic. According to John Rawls, the CI demands that S ask herself, 'Can I rationally will that my proposed course of action (that is: my maxim) should become a universal law, such that persons are compelled to comply with it as though by a law of nature?' If the answer is yes, the mooted action is legitimate; if not, it is illegitimate. By applying this test, S can assess her contingent desire as moral or immoral. She can say, for example, 'I know that it would be rational for *me* to perform this action. At present it seems to me that the results would be desirable. But a world in which everyone did what I now propose to do when faced with an equivalent decision does not seem desirable (or is impossible). My proposed action fails the CI test, and is therefore not morally justified.' Motivated by the desire to do her duty as an end in itself, rather than any further end she means to realise through her action, she can impose a law on herself: do not act on the maxim.[35]

There are several objections to this account of the categorical imperative. One, which we can call the *Practical Application Objection*, holds that the requirement for everyone to be able to act on a legitimate maxim makes practically every possible action illegitimate. Persons do not act in a transcendent realm of universals. There is scope for serious practical difficulties once the decision's outcome is re-applied in contingent circumstances. If treating the maxim as a universal law demands that *everyone* (an indefinitely large number of persons) *must be able to act on the maxim*, a vast array of possible actions must be counted as immoral on banal pragmatic grounds. If I eat some particular biscuit, say, others will be unable to do so. I cannot universalise such a particular, narrow maxim; I cannot will that 'always eat this biscuit' become a universal law for all persons and all possible circumstances.

---

[35] This is basically what John Rawls calls the 'categorical imperative procedure'. See Rawls w/Barbara Herman (ed.) (2000) *Lectures on the History of Moral Philosophy*, Cambridge, MA: Harvard University Press [162–80].

This absurd conclusion is probably a misinterpretation of Kant's meaning, since it refers to particular, phenomenal contingencies (the number of people in the world and the number of instances of this biscuit). For a maxim to be universalisable, it must be expressed as a general statement applicable to a wide range of possible experiences. Hence my maxim could be something like 'always eat biscuits', or — since surely Kant does not expect us to commit to one activity unconditionally and forever — 'it is always permissible to eat biscuits if I so desire and this does not prevent me from fulfilling other moral responsibilities.'[36] Thus S is moved from her contingent, 'phenomenal' standpoint to a universal, 'noumenal' standpoint from which she can freely and rationally assess her proposed maxim without influence from her changeable preferences, interests and circumstances. She cannot create a truly noumenal self, because that, as a product that she has created, would not exist 'in itself' in the way that noumena require. Instead she does the next best thing and posits an abstract version of herself that is identical, or as close as possible, to what she thinks any other rational person would create. This is achieved by ignoring or altering certain characteristics that could otherwise differentiate between them. Being the same, these 'universal subjects' reason identically, despite the diversity of the contingently embedded persons they represent. This grants the shared outcome of their judgements universal, objective status.[37]

---

[36] Derek Parfit points out that such a reading of the CI would logically exclude seemingly admirable maxims like 'Win an Olympic gold medal', 'Become a doctor' and 'Discover the causes of cancer'. To achieve each of these goals excludes others from doing so (there are only so many Olympic gold medals; we cannot *all* be doctors; and the causes of cancer cannot be discovered and rediscovered *ad infinitum*). What Parfit describes are, in Andrew Sneddon's terms, 'puzzle maxims', *viz.* 'principles of volition which seem clearly morally innocuous, yet which fail the CI universalisability test'. See Parfit (2002) 'What We Could Rationally Will', in *Tanner Lectures on Human Value* (Volume 24), pp. 287–369, [Online], http://tannerlectures.utah.edu/lectures/documents/volume24/parfit_2002.pdf/ accessed 06/10/2012] [315–18; quotation 318 only]; and Sneddon (2011) 'A New Kantian Response to Maxim-Fiddling', *Kantian Review*, 16 (1), 67–88 [84–6; quotation 84 only]. While Kantians may object that the impossibility of everyone achieving a goal does nothing to prevent everyone from trying to achieve it, this is not much good for a moral theory concerned with what S actively and actually *does*, rather than remaining content with what could be done.

[37] In an important chapter on 'The Unity of Values' in *Logica 1*, Gentile writes that Kant's strict distinction between phenomena and noumena leaves no tenable position for the subject of knowledge. He notes that Kant claims that the subject acts freely when it exercises its autonomy as a moral agent,

This leads to a second, more explicitly Gentilean problem. There is no fully impartial and privileged interpretation of any given action.[38] For example: imagine S proposes to assassinate a tyrant who she knows to be persecuting his subjects. She perceives her action as *the liberation of a people*, or *the removal of suffering*. She tells herself that this is something she could rationally will to become a universal law. But someone else might interpret her proposed action as *murder*, which would not satisfy the CI. There is potentially a huge range of interpretations of her act, viewing it at greater or lesser levels of generality. I call this the *Linguistic Objection* because, as Gentile makes clear, truth claims are linguistic constructs.[39] A maxim's compatibility with the CI depends on the terms in which it is expressed. This is to deny that there is an objective (noumenal) archetype to which the action corresponds. For that reason there can be no definitively *true account* of what one is *really* doing when one acts. The CI's (implicit) universal subject has no special authority to *define* the maxim under scrutiny; that is something that the actual thinking subject must do before presenting it to the CI for rational tests. Since she has such considerable room for manoeuvre, there are limited prospects for an objective account of the action's legitimacy.[40]

The *Idealisation Objection* refers to the counterfactual abstraction or idealisation on which the CI hinges. The procedure alters or ignores troublesome factors in order to generate consistent results. The question of what should be retained, ignored or altered is deeply controversial, since it can bias the CI in favour of certain outcomes; but if too

---

but 'insomuch as it knows, it sees no need for any liberty'. Kant's first *Critique* portrays the subject as a phenomenon, or an object of knowledge, but for Gentile this is unsatisfactory because phenomena are constructed through the act of thinking, so such a subject presupposes the existence of its creator. Being 'subject to the category of causality', it cannot be *free*. The idea of a noumenal subject is also problematic, since the noumenon's role is to 'make sense of the stuff of the phenomenon', and can only be glimpsed darkly through phenomenal objects. It cannot, therefore, be comprehended by the subject. Only knowledge of the *moral law* enables the subject to see through 'the veil of the unknowable [noumenon]'. This would not make sense without some concept of freedom. It is necessary for Kant 'to make a claim for liberty in the noumenal subject'. See *Logica 1* [108]; and Gentile (1904) 'Noumeni e fenomeni nella filosofia di Kant', *La Critica*, 2, pp. 417-24, [*passim*].

[38] Remember that Gentile denies that an action can be repeated. See *Genesi* [1].
[39] *Sommario 1* [56-65, but especially 60-1].
[40] The Linguistic Objection is the basis for the problem of 'maxim-fiddling', which Andrew Sneddon has discussed and attempted to solve in a recent article (2011) [*passim*].

many factors are left out of consideration, the procedure will prove indeterminate. Even to assume for the sake of convenience that people are equally rational would be, as Peri Roberts puts it, 'utopian reasoning', an 'idealisation' based upon 'illegitimate assumptions about the basic premises of reasons'. Such idealisation differs from abstraction, whereby some details about actual persons are left outside the ambit of inquiry, and rather assumes the presence of features ('illegitimate assumptions') that do not, or do not necessarily, obtain. Hence idealisations necessarily give rise to partial reasons, in that they are biased toward one or more of the features that persons might but do not necessarily possess. The purportedly objective or universal status of any judgement based on such partial reasons would be uncertain. Reasons based on abstractions, by contrast, are 'at worst [...] incomplete', and may even be necessary if it is possible to describe a reasoning process relevantly applicable to problems at any level of generality.[41]

Taken together, the foregoing objections leave the Universal Law Formula open to serious doubt. The Practical Application Objection denies that actions can be universalised except when conceived abstractly as noumena. The Linguistic Objection denies that the noumenal (abstract) realm can provide definitive solutions to phenomenal (concrete) problems. The Idealisation Objection once again suggests that the CI's prescriptions could never be followed by a non-abstract subject. The Kantian universal subject is irreconcilably alienated from the actual, concrete subject it is intended to represent; the two do not share a meaningful identity, and, on the evidence we have seen, the universal, noumenal subject's reasons have no purchase on the particular, contingency-bound subject's reasons for thought or action.

3i. O'Neill on universality

Of all Kant's recent interpreters, Onora O'Neill has done the most to present his theoretical and moral works as one unified constructivist project. She stresses that 'if reason's principles are precepts for seeking the greatest possible unity, these precepts must apply both to thinking and to doing.'[42] Since Kant identifies the CI as practical reason's

---

[41] Peri Roberts (2007) *Political Constructivism*, London: Routledge [85–6 and 88]. Note that Roberts is talking about O'Neill's (Kantian) constructivism at this point.

[42] Onora O'Neill (1992) 'Vindicating Reason', in Paul Guyer (ed.) *The Cambridge Companion to Kant*, Cambridge: Cambridge University Press, pp. 280–308 [288–9].

'supreme principle', it must also be the supreme principle of theoretical reason. O'Neill acknowledges that this interpretation of the CI is 'highly controversial', but for our purposes it is notable for some of the close similarities between it and Gentile's account of reason as described earlier in this chapter. The comparison is relevant because O'Neill claims to describe and interpret Kant's views, rather than adapting Kant or drawing inspiration from him when developing her own theory. As such she and Gentile are concerned with the same texts. Their differing responses to these texts, as well as their differing accounts of what a fully constructivist doctrine entails, are especially revealing in this context.

In *Constructions of Reason*, O'Neill explicitly rejects the idea that Kant conceives of reason as a pure object, something with a 'transcendent basis' that is 'inscribed in us'. She acknowledges that 'we often need to think of reason in abstraction from acts of reasoning', but without assuming any such otherworldly transcendent paraphernalia, we cannot 'think that specific rules and algorithms are what is fundamental to reason'.[43] It is notable that she does not think this is true of the understanding, which Kant spends much of his first Critique describing.[44] But this is no obstacle to O'Neill, who means merely to show that Kant offers a constructivist account of *reason*; and without that, Kant would have no way to develop the complex and seemingly necessary account he offers of the understanding. (This idea of reason as an action or process, rather than an object or scheme, is already amenable to Gentile's idea of the logical priority of thought.)

O'Neill notes Kant's use of judicial and political metaphors in his description of reason. He refers to 'tribunals' and 'trials' by which reasons can be tested for suitability as bases for subsequent judgements.[45] This idea of reason's vindication in the eyes of other people, or by some impartial standard, is reinforced later when O'Neill cites

---

[43] O'Neill (1989) *Constructions of Reason: Explorations of Kant's Practical Philosophy*, Cambridge: Cambridge University Press [24].

[44] O'Neill writes that '[t]he use of reason is not assigned any counterpart to *the reduced, empirical realism that Kant allows the understanding*' [282]; emphasis added.

[45] O'Neill (1989) [9–10]; she refers to Kant's *Critique of Pure Reason* [Axi–xii and Bxvi]. She explains her interpretation of Kant's use of political imagery in (1989) [16–20]. There is another pertinent judicial metaphor in Kant's *Metaphysics of Morals*, where the conscience is described as an 'internal court in man'. This is very similar to Gentile's IDP, although to identify the IDP with the conscience would be to underestimate the range of its applications. See Kant w/Gregor (ed., trans.) (1998) *The Metaphysics of Morals*, Cambridge: Cambridge University Press [188–9; 6: 437–40 in std. pag.].

Kant's claims that '[r]eason must in all its undertakings subject itself to criticism [... whose] verdict is always simply the agreement of free citizens, of whom each one must be permitted to express, without let or hindrance, his objection or even his veto.'[46] In another article O'Neill explains that

> it is because reason's authority is *not* given that it must be instituted or constituted — constructed — by human agents [... who] need, if they are to organise their thinking and doing together, to find — to construct — some common authority. If they cannot, they will not be in the business of giving and receiving, exchanging and evaluating each other's claims about knowledge and action.

Thus it is possible to rule out 'ways of thinking and acting that cannot be followed by differing others', as well as the idea that 'the fundamental principles of thought and action need only reflect some local authority, as the acolytes of [...] communitarianism [maintain.]'[47] This confers the resultant conception of reason *objective status*,[48] and, in its opposition to particularism, plainly reflects O'Neill's view of the CI as the guiding light for *all* reason.

In other works O'Neill elaborates her conception of 'followability' as the key test of universality. This requires that for something to count as *practical* reason, it should 'at least aim to be followable by others for whom it is to count as reasoning'. She adds that '[t]hose who organise action and thinking about action in ways which they take not to be followable by some of those who are to follow, even be convinced by, their claims offer those others no reasons.'[49] Her explicit reference to practical reason should not deter us from extending these criteria to theoretical problems as well; what O'Neill describes here is a normative principle that applies to 'all stretches of thought [that purport to count as] reason or reasoning'.[50] While at this stage she refers to only 'some' of the relevant people, she soon makes clear that her claims have a broad (though at this stage still imprecisely defined) scope:

---

[46] Kant's *Critique of Pure Reason* [A738/B766 in std. pag.], quoted in O'Neill (1989) [15]. Note that even O'Neill refers to the 'materials' used to construct reason: 'manifolds and forms of intuition, categories and empirical concepts' (1989) [21].

[47] O'Neill (1992) [298].

[48] O'Neill (2003a) 'Constructivism in Rawls and Kant' [358]; much the same point is made in O'Neill (1992) [297–8].

[49] O'Neill (1996) *Towards Justice and Virtue: A Constructive Account of Practical Reasoning*, Cambridge: Cambridge University Press [51].

[50] Thomas M. Besch (2008) 'Constructing Practical Reason: O'Neill on the Grounds of Kantian Constructivism', *Journal of Value Inquiry*, 42, pp. 55–76 [55].

> [Some] thinking about and justifications of action must be presentable, hence followable and exchangeable, not merely among an immediate group of participants, or of those present, or of the like-minded, or even among fellow-citizens, but among more diverse and often more dispersed others, whose exact boundaries cannot be readily identified. [...] This formally universal specification of the scope of anything that is to count as reasoned is not in itself informative; its import depends wholly on the specification of the inclusive or restricted domains within which that stretch of thinking is to be followable.[51]

Even here O'Neill stops short of the crude universalism under which an argument or judgement ('stretch of thinking') must be followable by *every person*, or perhaps even *every possible person*, or still more ambitiously *every possible rational being*. Since no one can know for sure how as-yet-unknown others would reason out a problem, it would be senseless to assume that we owe an account of our reasons to those we can conceive of only abstractly. Thinkers on some distant planet, if such thinkers exist, do not yet owe me reasons for what they do. The same would have been true of persons on mutually undiscovered continents in earlier periods of human history. But when these persons encountered each other, or if I encounter these extraterrestrials, and they/we recognise each other as rational beings, capable of expressing and justifying our actions in terms of reasons, then followable reasons are owed by each to all.

3ii. A Gentilean reply to Kant and O'Neill

O'Neill's overtly anti-realist interpretation of Kant has several parallels with Gentile's conception of reason, premised on the IDP. Kant's judicial metaphor is especially apt because it models an IDP-like scenario and ascribes to its participants two features that Gentile does not overtly demand: freedom and equality. In Kant's version the former demand is made explicit where he refers to 'the agreement of free citizens'. The latter is implicit, but still present, since every citizen is permitted to voice objections or even to veto a claim 'without hindrance' from others. In that respect citizens are equal, as there is no meaningful hierarchy among them *qua* reviewers of the reasons under discussion.

Gentile can endorse both of these orienting assumptions, though not for quite the same reasons that Kant offers. For both it is true that reasons cannot be imposed by coercion. S must recognise their authority for herself, in her own thought. No one can be denied the opportunity to challenge reasons presented by others. Thus, to put it in

---

[51] O'Neill (1996) [53–4].

more Gentilean language, *thinkers are free and equal insofar as they think*. Reason's authority cannot be adduced except by thought; its warrant comes from its recognition as authoritative by a jury of thinkers, or rather, by one subject engaged in the IDP and thinking on behalf of each of its abstract participants. Since S articulates and constructs the participants' reasons for herself, she cannot strictly misinterpret them.[52] She and the interlocutors, or their reasons and hers, are equal in that respect. No reason can be affirmed or denied at all without being articulated and evaluated by S. This reflects Gentile's idea of thought as 'homogeneous', relying on no 'external norms'.

Kant's judicial metaphor makes explicit reference to 'free citizens' participating in the tribunal of reason. Elsewhere Kant claims that freedom (as well as God and immortality) is a *postulate of morality*: any tenable moral theory must presuppose it, although it cannot be tested in experience or otherwise demonstrated.[53] All three postulates are working assumptions. Gentile, of course, thinks that thought's freedom as *pensiero pensante* can be demonstrated, albeit negatively, in that nothing can be known to condition or limit thought without thought, so in its logical priority to any possible conditioning object, thought is free.[54] But this is only a thin and formal conception of freedom. As the Torturer Objection showed in Chapter 2, there is very little that the freedom implicit in thought's logical priority can rule out. It is again in the idea of thought's *homogeneity* that we find the full meaning of Gentile's conception of moral freedom.

As we have seen, Gentile's idea of spirit as *pensiero pensante* is a strictly subjective conception of the person. Other people's thoughts are abstractions. This consideration explains Gentile's use of the IDP metaphor in preference to a more flexible third-person formulation, like Kant's tribunal or O'Neill's followability criterion, in which the first-person subject has no clearly defined role. In Gentile's version, S is always present, and the claims of other people, or of hypothetical others, are presented individually and successively before her. S also retains a set of beliefs and ideas, which, as elements of the act of thinking, cannot be detached from her. Like Descartes, who ring-fences

---

[52] This does not rule out the possibility that S misunderstands what another empirical person has said to her, of course.

[53] Kant w/Mary Gregor (trans.) (1997) *Critique of Practical Reason*, Cambridge: Cambridge University Press [100–10; 5: 119–5: 132 in std. pag.]. Garrath Williams (2009) 'Kant's Account of Reason', in Edward N. Zalta (ed.) *The Stanford Encyclopaedia of Philosophy*, [Online], http://plato.stanford.edu/entries/kant-reason/ [accessed 28/03/2012] (originally 2008).

[54] This was discussed in Chapter 2, herein (see sub-section #2 and especially #2i and #2ii).

some beliefs *par provision* while he tests and re-constructs the edifice of knowledge,⁵⁵ S remains actively involved in the reasoning process by which objectivity is established. For her to know that a 'stretch of thinking' is 'followable' she must think it—follow it—for herself. To know whether she can affirm a truth claim she must test it against other claims within its set in order to establish their mutual coherence, then against claims she already believes or recognises herself to have good reasons to believe to be true. To do this she must review her reasons from the 'abstract' positions of other possible subjects, or at least those that are appropriately *rational* according to S's present beliefs about reasons.

The irreducible subjectivity of the IDP places further obstacles before the distinctively Kantian project of establishing 'objective validity'. The Kantian subject need only show what reasons can best sustain scrutiny from the standpoints of other people, culminating in the establishment of objectivity in the judgement of a universalised 'other'. Gentile's S must do this (*viz.* draw an abstract judgement) and then attend to her own concrete beliefs and ideas. That these might be out of sync, with S finding that reason leads her to one conclusion and her personal beliefs another, explains why Gentile invokes the heart in his account of reason. There is no assumption that thinkers applying reason are fully rational; they are instead embedded in personal and social contexts, forming and correcting ideas with reference to incomplete and sometimes misleading information. The endpoint of the reasoning process, if we allow that thinking can be conceived abstractly as a series of discrete processes, is the unity of heart and intellect. Once again: beliefs may be replaced and assessments of a reason's value may change, but thought is always true at the moment of its *attuale* affirmation.

4. The Kingdom of Ends Formula

The idea of treating persons as ends-in-themselves, or else as citizens of one 'kingdom of ends', has offered Kantian theorists an attractive alternative to the cold formalism of the Universal Law. As Korsgaard explains, while universality 'gives us the form of the moral law', humanity is 'the appropriate material for a principle of practical reason'.⁵⁶ This newly humanised CI also allows Kant to deny that a legitimate moral maxim can be followed in order to further some other

---

55 This occurs in the third part of the 'Discourse on Method'. See Descartes w/ Cottingham et al. (1984) *The Philosophical Writings of Descartes* (Volume 1), Cambridge: Cambridge University Press [122–6].
56 Korsgaard (1996b) [106–7].

end. Pragmatic reasons, which can only ever be 'relative' to the contingent circumstances at hand, are not moral reasons.[57] A moral reason must be justified according to universal principles drawn from reason itself.[58] Humanity is special insofar as it is, or at least possesses the potential to be, rational. By thinking and acting rationally, S respects rational (human) beings.

Gentile claims that the Kingdom of Ends Formula takes insufficient account of S's contingent circumstances. She is in the world, encumbered with desires, mores and interests; but is at the same time required to act as a 'citizen of the kingdom of ends, [...] breath[ing] the pure air of the moral life', in which contingency has no place. Gentile claims, predictably, that such dualism is 'impossible', and amounts to 'putting one foot in two stirrups'.[59] Kant cannot have it both ways: S (Gentile thinks) wills and is committed to one course of action or another, and cannot be judged to will one end in the phenomenal world and another wholly separate end in the unreal and abstract kingdom of ends. 'The idea of a horse', Gentile reminds us, 'is not a horse one can ride.' Likewise a merely abstract maxim is not a maxim on which one can act.[60]

This objection echoes those levelled at the Universal Law Formula. With some small embellishments we can bring out the distinctiveness of Gentile's position. His conception of the will suggests that an end or outcome is not an act one can perform. It is necessarily an abstraction, for once it is achieved, it ceases to be an end. It is instead part of the reality in which the subject operates. Despite their abstract status, the values ascribed to ends contribute to the assessment of the worthiness of possible actions. A subject's conception of what she is doing at any given moment contains at once the act, the reasons for it and the ends at which it is directed. In a passage of uncharacteristically plain Kantian inspiration, Gentile writes that

> if you want to find out whether your action is moral, look to the maxim that [the action] obeys. [...] Look not to an abstract maxim that you can propose as the object of mere speculative contemplation, [nor] to the standards by which you come to judge the action; but to the maxim that you in fact follow in what you are doing [*operare*]; that is, to the maxim that is immanent in the action, [and] of whose intrinsic validity you have, by acting upon the maxim, already shown yourself to be con-

---

[57] Korsgaard (1996b) [107–9].
[58] See Kant w/Paton [93–5; 426–7 in std. pag.].
[59] *Religione* [95].
[60] *Atto puro* [83]; Carr translation [84].

vinced. In the end, the maxim is not your abstract ideal, but the inner law of your effectual will.[61]

Some of Gentile's critics, including Herbert Marcuse, have thought that his equation of thinking and acting, manifest here in the resolution of 'action' with 'maxim', means that 'all thought is rejected if it is not [...] immediately consummated in action', leading to a conception of 'aims and norms that may not be judged by any objective ends and principles'.[62] If Marcuse is right, the whole of Gentile's moral theory looks deeply suspect. It is exposed as a theory about something other than morality, and his elaborate accounts of reason, heart and the will must be considered disingenuous. A more plausible reading is that Gentile denies the possibility of purely formal ethics. Once again: S cannot transcend her contingent circumstances and the particular problems she faces. A maxim abstracted for 'speculative contemplation' serves no purpose unless it applies to an actual practical problem. Purely hypothetical situations do not in themselves make moral demands of non-hypothetical subjects. The concrete subject of any moral decision must be recognised and accounted for throughout the reasoning process.[63]

This last point deserves elaboration. Gentile does not strictly deny that human reason is an end in itself. What he *does* deny is the Kantian assumption that it is possible to make intelligible claims of a pure faculty abstracted from the act in which it is exercised and realised. To speak of 'human reason' without recognising S, the singular human subject who employs it, is to misapprehend the nature of thought. S acts in accordance with reason when she recognises the authority of her own thought. Her thought's unity, which amounts to its coherence both now and in an as-yet-uncertain future, is achieved as she identifies reasons that she recognises and (she expects) will continue to recognise as *good reasons* in the future.

5. The Autonomy Formula

So far my attempts to find a role for the CI in the IDP have fallen foul of Gentile's objections to dualism, and especially his claim that *merely*

---

[61] *Religione* [88].
[62] Herbert Marcuse (1955) *Reason and Revolution: Hegel and the Rise of Social Theory*, London: Routledge & Kegan Paul. Second edition; originally published 1941 [408–9].
[63] It may be objected that Kant does not present his categorical imperative as a 'pure formal' test either. Gentile agrees with this. He thinks that Kant's *followers* made his doctrine implausibly formalist. We might think of actual idealism as an attempt to clarify the position uncovered by Kant, removing elements that could prompt a formalist reading and reinforcing its plausibly phenomenological basis.

abstract reasons do not and cannot obtain for real, concrete, contingently embedded subjects. If the same objection could be used to dismiss the CI at a stroke, it would do us no good to rehearse this argument any further. We could shelve the CI as an abstract procedure that necessarily leads to alienating conclusions premised on false assumptions about the nature of thought. (This would have disappointing implications for my attempt to present Gentile as a distinctive moral theorist, since his arguments would add nothing to Hegel's description of Kant's 'empty formalism' a century earlier.)[64] Fortunately, though, Kant's Autonomy Formula is designed to address concerns of precisely this kind, showing how it is possible for a subject to act according to a moral law without thereby infringing her own liberty.[65]

5i. Kant on autonomy

Kant and Gentile agree that freedom is indispensible to any account of moral agency.[66] A subject whose actions are entirely caused by external forces acting independently of her desires and intentions is neither free nor accountable for her actions and the consequences leading from them, just as an inert object (a libellous letter, say) is not morally responsible for the ends to which it directly or indirectly contributes.[67]

---

[64] This famous argument occurs in Hegel (1945) [90; §135n]; and, for the similar idea that 'the laurels of mere willing are dry leaves that never were green' [252; §124n]. Gentile sails particularly close to Hegel when he writes that because it is abstracted from the circumstances in which action occurs, 'a wholly [*radicalemente*] good will is unable to act and so realise [*attuare*] the good. This is the great defect of Kantian formalism.' See *Diritto* [23]. A similar point is made in *Logica 2* [80].

[65] Robert Stern has recently claimed that '[t]here is widespread consensus amongst constructivists that Kant should be credited as holding a constructivist position in ethics at least partly on the strength of his commitment to autonomy[.]' See Stern (2012) 'Constructivism and the Argument from Autonomy', in James Lenman and Yonatan Shemmer (eds.) *Constructivism in Practical Philosophy*, Oxford: Oxford University Press, pp. 119–37 [121].

[66] Note that I interchange freely between 'agents' and 'subjects'. Korsgaard distinguishes them: '[a] person is both active and passive, both an agent and a subject of experiences.' See (1989) 'Personal Identity and the Unity of Agency: a Kantian Response to Parfit', *Philosophy and Public Affairs*, 18 (2), pp. 101–32 [101–2]; also in (1996b) *The Sources of Normativity*, pp. 363–98.

[67] Gentile equates the CI with the Golden Rule insofar as both 'hint at moral activity's sole distinctive character: not desire's conformity to the law, but the will's self-position as law'. Loving one's neighbour and positing one's will as law both involve the subject's recognition of her place 'as pure spirit, as spirit free of those natural limitations that are proper to all objects of our

Kant does not deny that persons are in some respects causally determined natural objects. Their bodies are objects among others. But we do not ascribe responsibility for actions to a person's *body*, even if the body is, empirically speaking, the instrument with which the relevant actions are performed. Instead we refer to the subject so *embodied*, understanding it along the lines of the 'I think' discussed in Chapter 2.

Kant's conceptions of the subject's body and the subject *per se* as possessors of different attributes should not be mistaken for Cartesian mind/body dualism. These separate conceptions are made possible by the use of two 'standpoints': the 'naturalistic standpoint', from which objects appear as particular phenomena, determined by natural laws that obtain independently of the subject who observes them; and the 'practical standpoint', which offers a view of the 'intelligible world', or the world of noumena, governed by laws 'that have their grounds in reason alone'. Kant believes any tenable moral theory must have S 'look upon [herself] as belonging to the sensible world and yet to the intelligible world at the same time'.[68] This is because neither a disembodied subject nor a body without subjective experience is conceivable as a moral agent. Rather than ontologically separate worlds, these standpoints reveal different features of a single world. Neither is intelligible without the other.[69]

Some familiar questions arise. If S freely creates ('wills') the moral law and imposes it on herself, is that law not an exclusively subjective creation without purchase on other persons' lives or ideas? If not, and she is in any way limited by coherence requirements, say, does she really create and impose the laws freely? Not every consideration relevant to an actual moral decision can be known *a priori*. At the very least, S considers the decision in some *particular* context, and very often with reference to *particular* people. So if part of the decision can be influenced by particular, contingent and phenomenal factors, which are already acknowledged to be independent of S's reason, is this freedom not at best partial and at worst illusory?

Kant answers this with his concept of *autonomy*, according to which moral directives are known without reference to any free-standing external authority, and imposed by each subject upon herself as

---

experience'. See *Religione* [87–8]. (I return to this theme in Chapter 7, subsection #4ii, herein.)

[68] Kant w/Paton (1948) [121; 453 in std. pag.].

[69] O'Neill, among others, insists that Kant refers to separate 'worlds' only figuratively. The whole motivation for the theory of two *standpoints* would be redundant if there were already discrete worlds. Note the strong parallel between these claims what, as we saw earlier, Gentile characterised as trying to put 'one foot in two stirrups'.

binding obligations that are discharged for their own sake.[70] Autonomy of the will 'is the sole principle of all moral laws, and of all duties in keeping with them'.[71] This differs from *heteronomy* of the will, whereby its cause is something outside it; the desired outcome is a means to some other end.[72] When S acts autonomously, 'the laws of morality are the laws of [her] own will and its claims are ones she is prepared to make on herself'.[73] It is for this reason that Kant thinks a moral subject may not use other people as means, only as ends in themselves. I have already explained why Gentile cannot follow that step in the argument in quite the way Kant describes it. Ultimately S must not recognise *other people* as ends in themselves, but instead *rationality*, the authority of her own thought, which can only be recognised through the exercise of the same.

5ii. Korsgaard's account of Kantian autonomy

Christine Korsgaard offers a distinctive theory of Kantian constructivism in which the autonomous will is the sole ground of normativity.[74] It is because a maxim is autonomously willed that S ought, or has reason, to act upon it. Korsgaard also appeals to the Universal Law Formula, holding that the will is recognisable as will, as opposed to another kind of volition, *when S is able to will that her maxim become universal law*. This requires that S be able to see the reasons supporting and guiding her will, which would be impossible if she were to take her will solely on credit, as it were, from an external source whose reasons she does not comprehend. Hence on Korsgaard's account of Kant,

> [t]o be governed by reason, and to govern yourself, are one and the same thing. The principles of practical reason are *constitutive* of autonomous action: they do not represent external *restrictions* on our actions, whose power to motivate us is therefore inexplicable, but instead *describe* the procedures involved in autonomous willing. But they also

---

[70] J.B. Schneewind (1992) 'Autonomy, Obligation and Virtue: an Overview of Kant's Moral Philosophy', in Paul Guyer (ed.) *The Cambridge Companion to Kant*, Cambridge: Cambridge University Press, pp. 309–41 [309].
[71] Kant w/Gregor (1997) [30; 5: 33 in std. pag.].
[72] Kant w/Paton [108–9; 441 in std. pag.].
[73] Christine M. Korsgaard (1996a) [19]. Note that most of this passage is also quoted in Christopher W. Gowans (2002) 'Practical Identities and Autonomy: Korsgaard's Reformation of Kant's Moral Philosophy', *Philosophy and Phenomenological Research*, 64 (3), pp. 546–70 [547].
[74] Gowans (2002): Korsgaard's interpretation of Kant is distinctive because she advocates 'a theory of autonomy that grounds normativity solely in the will' [551].

function as normative or guiding principles, because in following these procedures we are guiding ourselves.[75]

It is not yet clear how the Autonomy Formula, which includes an explicit reference to the idea of universal law, differs from the Universal Law Formula already discussed. For Korsgaard, at least, the difference is that while the Universal Law Formula gives us the formal criterion by which legitimate maxims are distinguished from illegitimate ones, the Autonomy Formula allows us to locate maxims' *contents* in contingent facts about the subject. This claim signals Korsgaard's rejection of any moral realist interpretation of Kant, according to which the Universal Law Formula can be used to deduce a complete and freestanding set of fine-grained moral laws.

Korsgaard recognises the contingency of many (indeed, she writes 'most') of the identities or self-conceptions that give persons reasons for action.[76] No one is purely and simply a citizen of the kingdom of ends, a moral agent without a wider, messier identity. Much of what we recognise as true about ourselves is taken for granted. Given names offer a simple illustration of this idea. I strongly identify myself as James while recognising that my identification as James, and not, say, Crispin, is a result of some wholly contingent facts about my upbringing. Doubtlessly if I had been given another name, I would now identify myself just as strongly with that. That my being James is in a sense arbitrary does not make it insignificant. If someone were to take my name away from me, as it were, I would feel deprived of or alienation from an important part of my identity. This need not be a bad thing. I may intentionally and consciously rid myself of my present identity in order to cultivate a new one, and in the course of doing so encourage others to call me by a different name, so as to reinforce my familiarity with the new identity I have made for myself. But in the ordinary course of things, it is important to me that others call me by a name with which I identify, even though my identification with some particular name (James) rather than any other (Crispin) is not rationally defensible independently of contingent facts of my personal history. To call a generically conceived person Crispin is not to abuse him. It is only once he is given some particular characteristics, such that he identifies and ascribes significance to the idea of himself as *not-Crispin*, that such abuse can occur.

---

[75] Korsgaard (1997) 'The Normativity of Instrumental Reason', in Garrett Cullity and Berys Gaut (eds.) *Ethics and Practical Reason*, Oxford: Oxford University Press, pp. 215–54 [219].

[76] Korsgaard (1996a) 'The Authority of Reflection', in *Sources of Normativity*, pp. 90–130 [120]; mentioned in Gowans (2002) [552].

Korsgaard makes clear that any given person typically holds multiple 'practical identities', understood as roles providing reasons (even if these are very weak reasons) for acting. Hence S might be a mother, a daughter, a friend and a member of both the local badminton club and the East London mafia. These roles can come into conflict when simultaneous incompatible claims are made of her. Korsgaard suggests that, in this case, the subject must rank her various identities in order of importance, and perhaps even discard some altogether, ceasing to identify herself with some role (as a Mafioso, say) that she deems either unworthy of her adherence or excessively demanding of the time and effort she would rather dedicate to other commitments. This is very obviously a constructivist procedure. S *decides* how she is to constitute herself, even though she may not have consciously chosen those identities in the first instance.[77] Nonetheless, it is clear that this process of ranking and discarding identities to construct a unified will involves a further value claim, such as 'It is more important that I fulfil my commitments as a friend than as a Mafioso', which cannot be rationally defended all the way down. It hinges on 'particular values [...] that we *just happen to hold*',[78] as basic or non-derivative features of our thinking. Still, on Korsgaard's Kantian account, there remain various tests that we can apply when deciding which of those values are worth retaining. But recognising that one does not have full justification for valuing something is not necessarily enough to make one cease to value it. A value may be strongly endorsed but irrational or rational but entirely unfelt.[79]

5iii. Gentile on autonomy (and autarchy)

Actual idealism's account of reason, which was parsed at the beginning of this chapter, has several parallels with Kant's account of autonomy. According to Gentile, thought that is 'self-governing, and has no need for external norms' is appropriately 'homogeneous'. Underlining the above claim about thought as an end in itself, this means that *the reason for S to submit to reasons she recognises as good* must be justified in terms of thought itself. An unrecognised good reason is not, or is not yet, a reason for S to alter her convictions. This observation explains why the IDP's subject should recognise the authority of the universal subject (US) constructed in the course of the procedure: US's authority over S stems from S's recognition that each step in the dialogical process has

---

[77] Gowans (2002) [553].
[78] Korsgaard (1996d) 'Reply', in *Sources of Normativity,* pp. 219-59 [242]; also Gowans (2002) [553].
[79] I return to this theme in Chapter 6, herein.

been justified using better reasons than the one before it. US is, in effect, the same entity as the subject that constructs it. US has authority over PS (*viz.* the subject's pre-reflective reasons) because its reasons are, and have necessarily been recognised to be, superior. US's authority is legitimate because S remains 'homogeneous' — autonomous, perhaps — throughout the procedure. In this respect the IDP plainly differs from Kant-style universalisation procedures in which S is (potentially) estranged from the constructed subject that legislates on her behalf. The Kantian US is effectively *someone else*, an abstraction applying S's thoughts to unreal and alien circumstances.[80] To borrow Gentile's memorable phrase: for the subject who reasons only abstractly, the procedure's results will 'taste of straw'.[81] The Gentilean US may (but does not necessarily) prescribe the same actions as the Kantian US. However, it arrives at that destination via a long, low road, eschewing more direct routes (e.g. a single-step test) in favour of a larger number of intermediate steps between which the justificatory link between S and US is kept intact.

So: what can Gentile make of Kantian autonomy? He cannot accept the Universal Law Formula implicit within it. If he instead endorses autonomy *without* universality — if, indeed, this is possible — we will need more details to help us determine whether, and how, he can navigate between abstract universality on one side and ungeneralisable particularity on the other. With this in mind it is telling that when Gentile writes of objective thought, he refers not to its autonomy (*autonomia*) but its autarchy (*autarcà*). In some recent literature on moral philosophy, these terms are contrasted in the following way. The autonomous subject recognises the objective truth-value of her judgements *because they correspond to a norm that she recognises as authoritative*. Hence

---

[80] Again it may be objected that this is not what Kant really thinks, and that the outcomes of the Kantian CI are no less constructed (and to that extent non-alienating) than those of the IDP. In reply, we can say that the versions of US implicit in the CI and IDP are not different in kind; both are constructed, but the IDP version's construction is deliberately gradual and incomplete. Thus it is supposed to yield the provisional certainty of the Kantian version while alleviating what Rawls calls the 'burdens of judgement'.

[81] Gentile expresses the same point in *Religione:* 'Without [a] duty that is fundamental to all [the other] duties, we would be able to apprehend the others as, at most, simple notions: strange, flavourless notions, without positive significance or the capacity to hold our interest. But we would never know such notions to impose real obligations on our desire[s]. We would apprehend them as voices not directed at us. [...] [The subject would] remain outside and above the world in which this conversation is taking place' [90–1].

to be autonomous is to be able to justify and defend one's judgements in this fashion. *Autarchy* emphasises self-*sufficiency* as well as self-*government*. The autarchic subject need only feel certain about the judgements she makes, submitting to no authority other than her own. It is not necessary for her to be able to provide a robust defence of the reasons underpinning them.

Using different terminology, Stefan Bird-Pollan has challenged Korsgaard on grounds similar to those on which Gentile challenges Kant. It is unclear, writes Bird-Pollan, exactly what the autonomous construction of reason entails. He proposes two possible though contradictory readings of what Korsgaard is doing. One he calls 'the strong autonomy thesis', which holds that 'we will according to the principle of respecting all rational beings.' He contrasts this with the 'weak autonomy thesis[, which] merely states that we can determine ourselves according to principles we come up with'.[82] The strong version appears better fitted to what Kant has in mind, since it reduces the significance of principles improvised to fit the individual subject's current and contingent inclinations. Applying the weak autonomy thesis to reason in general, it is possible for S to invent any sort of explanation or rationalisation for her ideas. These need not satisfy any kind of outside scrutiny to count as rational. The strong thesis presses her to eliminate mad or otherwise bad reasons from her attempts at justification. If she is thinking *rationally*, she must present, or at least try to present, reasons that (would) make sense to another rational being.[83]

The strong autonomy thesis is designed to solve the problem of the incommensurability of persons' reasons. It follows from Korsgaard's (and Kant's and Gentile's) rejection of moral realism that no act has value in itself. Hence, as Bird-Pollan explains, 'my desire to sleep in on Sunday morning after a late night of drinking is not in any way "more privileged" as a principle of action than your desire to have me drive you to the airport early that day.'[84] If, as the weak autonomy thesis suggests, autonomy consisted only of acting on reasons S happens to value at the time, the question of *what is the right thing to do* would be unanswerable on anything but a subject-by-subject basis. Bird-Pollan

---

[82] Stefan Bird-Pollan (2011) 'Some Normative Implications of Korsgaard's Theory of the Intersubjectivity of Reason', *Metaphilosophy*, 42 (4), pp. 376–80 [376–7].

[83] It should be noted that this seems obviously circular. If I test the rationality of my judgement against what another rational person would judge, have I not presupposed some criterion of rationality by which I can meaningfully say that the other person is rational? An explanation of how we might escape the charge of circularity is given in Chapter 7, herein.

[84] Bird-Pollan (2011) [377].

claims that Korsgaard appears to endorse the strong and weak autonomy theses at different times, and that these theses make incompatible demands of S: either she is autonomous in the full (strong) Kantian understanding of the word, testing maxims against the Universal Law Formula and, if they pass muster, imposing them on herself; or in the weaker, 'immanent', more contingency-sensitive understanding, but never able to attain a privileged standpoint from which one set of reasons could be seen to be objectively better or worse than another.

Bird-Pollan proposes an explicitly Hegelian solution to Korsgaard's problem. He claims that she must deny the distinction between the strong and weak theses, and endorses 'the idea that reason has the inherent tendency to clarify itself through the interaction between subjects and objects', together with 'the idea of *provisional* universal willing'.[85] He goes on:

> This conception would allow for the development of reason through interaction. It would permit us to learn from our mistakes and improve the universality of our reflection. The essential point, then, is that norms are constructed communally and the more people self-consciously engage in this construction, the more these people are able to interact smoothly and justly. This suggests a gradual increase of the accuracy in our provisional universalising process.[86]

Here Bird-Pollan has very obviously (though, I assume, unintentionally) situated Korsgaard on Gentilean ground. The IDP is designed to address exactly this need; every step in the procedure is a move toward some abstractly conceived endpoint (genuine objectivity) that S knows she will not and cannot ever reach. To test one's reasons against those of other people is, provided that one is prepared to follow where one's best and most rational thinking leads, always a step toward a better, more complete justification for whatever view or action one proposes to hold or perform. In the context of the IDP, then, to abandon Kantian autonomy for autarchy does not signal the abandonment of principle in favour of contingency. Instead it is to unburden Kantian autonomy of its most implausible feature—the appeal to universality *per se*—and embrace the next best thing, namely the *idea* of universality whose concrete expressions will always be provisional and changeable, but ultimately justified through concrete thinking.[87]

---

[85] Bird-Pollan (2011) [379]; emphasis added.
[86] Bird-Pollan (2011) [379–80].
[87] It is worth noting in passing that Bird-Pollan (and, if he is right, also Korsgaard) do not conceive of 'other people' in the same unconventional way as they are imagined in the IDP.

The autonomy/autarchy distinction, though subtle, is more than a matter of words. Implicit in Kant's account of the autonomous subject is the assumption that the principles of reason to which one refers are insensitive to the contingent characteristics of the referring subject. An attempt to apply reason can reflect those principles more or less accurately. There is, as some philosophers put it, an Archimedean point from which the facts of reason can be seen. If Gentile really is describing an autarchic subject, judgements can be tested according to a wider variety of criteria. There is no assumption of a complete and permanent plan of reason, nor of formal principles such as the Universal Law Formula, to which any judgement *must* conform. Instead, if S's thought really is to remain homogeneous, reason must be able to shift with the development of *pensiero pensante*.

At this point it should be clear that Kant would agree with my assessment of Gentile's moral theory as laid out in Part I. If the standard by which value claims are tested — in other words, the yardstick for goodness — is the will of some particular agent, be this Benito Mussolini or God, S's conformity to that standard cannot be autonomous. She would not be 'legislating' her own actions.[88] While Gentile is less inclined to use the distinctively Kantian language of autonomy and heteronomy, they share the basic contention that beliefs, values and motivations cannot be 'conditioned' or 'determined' by anything other than the spirit of which they are constituent parts.[89]

6. Re-constructing Gentilean moral theory

Before concluding, it is worth adding some remarks on what Gentile *does* think worth retaining from the CI. He believes, crucially, that it cannot yield maxims independently. The temptation to try is common to 'hasty critics' of Kant's formalism. By interpreting Kant's work even 'more rigidly' than Kant himself did, such critics keep the CI from being anything but a formal procedure. To specify its content in advance as 'a law that is a pre-condition of the act of willing' would be 'fatal to liberty' and to 'moral life itself'.[90] The CI's role is not to furnish subjects with a test of a proposed action's moral goodness, but instead

---

[88] Schneewind (1992) [316].
[89] *Logica 1* [98–9].
[90] *Religione* [89]. Note that 'a law that is a pre-condition of the act of willing' is translated from '*una legge presupposta all'atto del volere*', or literally 'a law presupposed to/by the act of willing'. The word 'presupposta' (or 'presupposto') is more flexible than its direct equivalent in English, covering facts, pre-conditions, basic assumptions, bases, starting-points and pre-requisites.

the basic idea of a universal duty to which all particular duties are subsidiary:

> Beyond all the single duties that we distinguish from each other, and before which we can sometimes stand perplexed, we have one, without which there would be no way to conceive any determined and particular duty: *the duty always to do our duty*.[91]

This single, immovable duty is required to make all other duties intelligible. Without it they would present themselves to S abstractly, as 'strange, flavourless notions', like commands given in a sermon to which one is not really paying attention.[92] For a given subject, as *pensiero pensante*, that duty is always present, although the specific imperative contained within it changes over time. To be clear: S is always bound by duty, which, understood formally, is the duty to do her duty; but *what she is duty-bound to do* is contingent on the circumstances in which she finds herself and the claims (or reasons) she recognises as authoritative at the time. She cannot have two simultaneous but incompatible duties. All but one of these must be abstractions. Claims that she *would* recognise as authoritative in the event that she found herself in different circumstances cannot by themselves generate duties *for her*. She should regard them as duties belonging to someone else. Real duties, by contrast, arise through the 'spontaneous generation of the heart', as S feels herself to be personally committed to them.[93]

The duty to think is not imposed from without; the truth does not present itself to thinkers wholesale and without their participation. They must identify, create and realise it, motivated by the will. This, like all thought, is ultimately a process of self-creation, and is for that reason 'essentially moral', and, as we have seen, partly compatible with a Kantian conception of autonomy.[94] S thinks about and ascribes value to an abstract world in which she better understands what is presently unknown to her. She then sets about realising the object of her will. But the concrete will — that is, the will possessed in the unfolding present, and tied inextricably to S's current act of self-realisation — cannot ever be realised completely. To reach the target that she sets for herself, to realise 'a supposedly absolute form of the good, satisfying all of [her …] moral aspirations', would entail the end of willing, and therefore the end of morality. As the activity of *realising* or striving to realise an end, the will would 'strip itself of any moral virtue, since there is no

---

[91] *Religione* [90]; emphasis added.
[92] *Religione* [91]. I have combined two of Gentile's analogies here.
[93] *Religione* [91–2].
[94] *Sommario 2* [46–7].

morality that is not movement, life, creation of [...] reality'.[95] The truly moral will is never fully satisfied; its concrete form outstrips any abstract will (that is: some target that S consciously sets herself) at the moment its realisation is commenced. It creates an imperfect world, and, by extension, a new form of itself — the will — within it.

The disparity between the world that is and the world that could (and should) be is what motivates and defines morally virtuous action. The search for the good is endless, for the target at which virtue aims is always moving and never to be reached. Striving after goodness entails not 'the impoverishment and straining of reality, but [its] enrichment and reinvigoration'. In contrast to the ancient (Aristotelian) idea of perfection, then, Gentile's subject attains 'perfection', understood as 'fullness of being', in the concrete actualisation of her will; or, in less abstruse language, perfection consists of self-consciously *doing* what one thinks is right, rather than in some state of affairs that results from that action. Goodness is identified not with a static form of perfection, but with the construction of value *in fieri*.[96]

To sum up: the will, Gentile claims, is fully integrated with the moral subject. 'I freely want', he writes, 'insofar as I neither detach myself from my desire as an effect of my activity; and nor does my desire detach itself from me.' If either is detached from the other, subject and effect become mere objects, empirical phenomena comprehensible only within a mechanical, realist metaphysics of causation. The action would be 'crystallised in its external effects' as *pensiero pensato*, and as such immune from moral scrutiny.[97] The only solution to this problem is to conceive of subject and action, intention and effect, as one continuous process — as the moral manifestation of the pure act of thinking.

7. Conclusion

After all that we have seen in this chapter, a clear and precise statement of the link between Gentilean and Kantian moral theory remains out of reach. Several of Gentile's objections to Kant are recognisably Hegelian in origin. The accusation of 'empty formalism', with its denial of the possibility of substantive *a priori* principles, is chief among these. For the past two hundred years, much of western moral (and political) philosophy has rested on the assumption that one must choose sides between the great Prussian thinkers: on one hand Kant, with his formal, rational, universal principles; and on the other Hegel, with his

---

[95] *Sommario* 2 [42].
[96] *Religione* [94].
[97] *Religione* [81–2].

emphasis on contingency, 'situatedness', change and particularity. O'Neill's and Korsgaard's efforts to 'immanentise' Kant have shown that the image of him and Hegel as polar opposites is something of a caricature. Such an understanding would, among other things, make the observation that Gentile (or anyone) falls *somewhere between the two* a platitude so obvious as to be almost entirely unhelpful.

Gentile's position is distinguished by his insistence that while Kant's system relies on a problematic dualism of phenomena and noumena, Hegel is less successful in escaping this fiction than is commonly imagined. Hegelian moral philosophy has a tendency to be under- or indeterminate, assigning entities to special roles and describing the dynamics between them in terms of a broad historical narrative. These concepts are suited to ethical questions on a correspondingly large scale. The ordinary moral question 'What ought I to do now?' is not readily answerable in these grand terms. By having his theory hinge on the act of thinking, which preserves concrete contingency and abstract rationality alike, Gentile is better able to manage these small questions. As I have presented it, the difficult task Gentile sets for himself is to retain a role for specially conceived abstractions, such as the universal subject, which keep the construction of morality from becoming merely subjective: there is an end in sight. At the same time he recognises that pure objectivity is unachievable; aspirations to it make morality into something unreal, its content arbitrary and detached from the life of any actual person.

My account of Gentilean constructivism still has some way to go. This chapter has salvaged the concrete subject from the purported abstraction of Kantian formalism, but we have not yet seen what the Gentilean view of autonomy (or autarchy) implies in practice. By retaining autonomy without universal law, there is, as ever with Gentile's philosophy, a risk that actual idealist moral theory will become one of 'monad[s] without windows, [each] possessor of a private world and of nought besides'.[98] If that were true, the prospects for actual idealist moral justifications of political action would look very bleak indeed. To resolve some of the outstanding ambiguities, we will need a clearer understanding of the dynamics of the IDP. On what grounds, exactly, can S distinguish a good reason from a bad one? That question, broadly conceived, is the focus of Chapter 7. Before we answer that, though, we must ask how this formal procedure can

---

[98] W.G. de Burgh (1929) 'Gentile's Philosophy of Spirit', *Journal of Philosophical Studies*, 4 (13), pp. 3–22 [7]. De Burgh refers to a difficulty faced by actual idealism generally, but the point has particular significance when applied to moral theory.

acquire content. How are we to account for the origins of S's values? For Gentile, *education* is the answer; but with it come further questions about the possibility of morals that are at once binding and freely constructed.

Chapter 6

The Construction of Value in Gentilean Education

The preceding chapter gave us the IDP's outline. We saw how the subject (S) presents her reasons to one or more hypothetical interlocutors who offer alternative reasons in an attempt to persuade S to alter her position. S winnows the various reasons on offer and thereby establishes *the best* reasons that she can coherently construct, perhaps using a composite of elements from other sources. The IDP differs from Kantian constructivist procedures in its insistence that we recognise S's central and necessary role in the reasoning process. This consideration leads to a special emphasis on S's *autonomy* and corresponding conceptions of *universality* and the *ends* at which moral actions are directed. At the end of the chapter we saw how Gentile reclaims the CI as a strictly formal and permanent law commanding all persons to do their duty, but unable to explain what, at any given moment, that duty requires.

Gentile's solution to the problem of his theory's lack of content reveals a new and distinctive aspect of his constructivism. He proposes to use education to bring about 'determined subjectivity'.[1] In this chapter I show how this plays out as a process of *institutional constructivism*, whereby the state, represented by a teacher, guides S as she constructs her own knowledge and values. Throughout the chapter I address reiterations of a major objection to Gentile's proposal: if the teacher leads S to construct her knowledge in a pre-determined way, there is no

---

1 *Sommario 1* [129]. Gentile uses this phrase when describing the ideal state of affairs in which the scholar identifies wholeheartedly with the teacher. He writes: 'the scholar [...], when he truly apprehends and shivers and vibrates in the instructor's word[s], feeling inside himself a voice that gushes from his own inner being, does not watch the instructor, seeing his glasses and beard, nor the chair on which he sits. Nor does he [the scholar] hear his [the instructor's] word[s] as the word[s] of another. [Instead,] he is wholly caught up in the flow of the lesson, as all of [these peripheral details are] re-absorbed and fused in his determined subjectivity' [128–9].

meaningful sense in which S remains the autonomous constructor of her own ideas. If her subjective experience is conditioned ('determined') in this way, she has no autonomy, and cannot, therefore, hold moral responsibility for her actions.

The chapter is structured as follows. At sub-heading #1 I summarise the role Gentile assigns to education and explain why this may raise problems for his account of the autonomous subject. Next I give a more detailed account of Gentile's vision of moral education, first (#2) in metaphysical terms, and second (#3) in terms of the political state's role in shaping a unified public consciousness. At #4 I offer several versions of the argument that Gentilean education amounts to the indoctrination of citizens, followed at #5 by replies to these, showing that Gentile recognises the dangers an overly prescriptive and restrictive education would carry for his conception of thought's freedom. At the end of the chapter (#6) I consider what these considerations imply for actual idealist moral and political theory as a whole, before reviewing the problems still to be addressed in Chapter 7 (#7).

1. Autonomy, indeterminacy and 'determined subjectivity'

We have already seen how the IDP could be applied by a single subject. This reflects the actual idealist view that reasoning, like any form of thinking, can be enacted only in the first person by the subject of *pensiero pensante*. This is true even if S refers to other empirical persons, imagining herself as one of them in order to assess what she would do or think if she were in their position. For others' claims (reasons) to be intelligible to her, S must re-think and so reconstruct them for herself. Although S aspires to view her reasons from the standpoint of an impersonal *universal subject* (US), the lack of substantive *a priori* moral norms means she can never be certain that her judgement has truly universal and therefore inter-personal application. The range and force of a US's[2] claims depends upon the extent to which other subjects recognise the authority of its reasons. Hence S can use the IDP to identify and refine good reasons in order to construct moral duties applicable to her, but not (necessarily) to other people who may or may not share the relevant beliefs and values.

---

[2] I acknowledge that the idea of 'a universal subject' (among other universal subjects) seems jarring. My point is simply that actual idealism's rigorously subjective standpoint prevents us from saying that *my* conception of the US is the only conception there is. It is as universal and objective as I can make it, but it is not universal and objective independently of my (subjective) input.

If this were the whole story, the IDP would not have disarmed the accusation that actual idealism leaves S unable to make meaningful claims about value except insofar as she contingently *happens to affirm them* from moment to moment. There would be no possibility of the IDP's authoritative inter-subjective application. Gentile's explicitly political solution to this problem is to educate people so they share a common set of basic beliefs and values while identifying themselves as fellow contributors to and members of something larger than themselves: namely, the state. Thus persons' constructions of morality are given some of their content in advance. This maximises the likelihood of all recognising good reasons as authoritative, or, in the language of the IDP, of them coming to construct universal subjects with enough mutual similarity to make moral disagreements unlikely and resolvable. This opens the way for orderly and maximally beneficial social cooperation. Gentile argues that such an arrangement secures the liberty of individual and state alike. A correctly designed programme of moral education brings about 'determined subjectivity', in which S's free and autonomous will is guaranteed despite another subject (the teacher) having determined its object.

To defend this last claim, Gentile must face the objection that such a prescriptive education would effectively scotch the autonomy, liberty and equality of thinkers subject to it, and instead offer autonomy and liberty to only the person or persons who decide the educational programme's content, and equality only insofar as all subjects (apart from that privileged elite) are equally disenfranchised. Since the authority of autonomous thought applies only to the subject for whom that thought is concrete *pensiero pensante,* it is hard to see how the promotion of any specific values could be justified from an appropriately impersonal standpoint.

This problem is not exclusive to Gentile. Indeed, it is one that all deeply anti-realist constructivist moral theories must face. How can persons make claims on each other when they each construct morality for themselves; and if that construction is in any way conditioned, can the subject really be said to be its author? For example: as we saw in the previous chapter, despite Korsgaard's insistence that she describes a constructivism that runs 'all the way down', she imagines S constructing a hierarchy of 'practical identities' and the values that go with them. S may reject some of her values, like those attached to a role with which she no longer identifies. But this identification or rejection relies on further value claims; it is possible only because she already considers some other values worth retaining at the expense of others — that is, to be valuable. *These* values are not themselves constructed by S. Korsgaard is content to accept that there are certain values, beliefs and identities that persons hold without having consciously chosen them, perhaps as a result of their upbringing and circumstances. They are 'given' to them. S's constructive role is to review and subsequently endorse or abandon some (but not all) of these given values and identities at a later time.

Christopher Gowans has argued that Korsgaard's account of the 'given' makes her constructivist project incoherent. She cannot say that 'our identities are both given to us *and* constructed by us' without determining the outcomes of construction and so making them at best partly attributable to the subject. In other words, Korsgaard's attempts to explain the link between given and constructed values lead her to adopt a 'rather uncritical passivity' before those that she just happens to have.[3] The business of construction begins only when those values are already entrenched. As such it is not the autonomous subject but *they*, or the given's *sources*, that determine morality's content. Korsgaard's motivation for trying to marry universalism and contingency is clear: she means to address the shortfalls of Kant's declared moral theory, which treats its subject as a high-minded abstraction quite unlike any of the actual persons to whom said theory is supposed to apply. But she finds herself touting a theory unable to deliver what it promises without taking certain unconstructed features of personal identity for granted.[4] To describe the issue more formally, we might say:

> *If* subject S constructs value V on the basis of assumptions A, *and*
>
> Subject T constructs assumptions A, *then*
>
> Subject T constructs value V.[5]

If T constructs V in advance, there is nothing left for S to do. S's alleged autonomy depends upon the intervention of T. Therefore, S is not autonomous. Here Korsgaard's difficulties closely resemble Gentile's, but with one crucial difference. On Korsgaard's account, T need be a subject only in the broadest sense. It may alternatively be a culture, a constitution, a routine or any number of other things that determines what S takes to be valuable. In this respect Korsgaard accommodates the idea of *social construction*, in which the construction of norms is not

---

[3] Gowans (2002) [556]; emphasis added.
[4] Gowans (2002) [555-6].
[5] We can describe this argument using propositional logic. Let us say that $\{P_1:$ 'S constructs V using A'$\}$, $\{P_2:$ 'T constructs A'$\}$, and $\{P_3:$ 'T constructs V'$\}$. Hence: $(P_1 \& P_2) \supset P_3$.

(necessarily) attributable to any specifiable person. A purely social T need not satisfy any rational criteria for its constructed values to have force. We cannot blame something as messy and complex as a cultural tradition for failing to test the coherence and comprehensiveness of the values it promotes.

Gentile cannot accept the idea of *mere* social construction, for that would make received beliefs and identities into presuppositions, so infringing thought's autonomy. He thinks he can escape Korsgaard's bind by identifying T with a person, namely, the teacher responsible for S's education. This argument for rigorously directed education as a means to bolster individual autonomy might seem perverse. However, Gentile is acutely conscious of the risks that prescriptive, doctrinaire socialisation carries for his moral theory.[6] His solution to this problem — of describing the construction of citizens as something other than indoctrination — connects the moral and political elements of his theory, offering insights into his vision of the state and what criteria it must meet in order to have real moral authority.

2. Gentile's phenomenology of education

'The problem of education', writes Gentile, is 'the problem of man's formation'.[7] In actual idealist theory this can be understood literally according to its unconventional conception of the subject. Education is not a process of imparting information, or knowledge, to a passive or fully formed person. Rather, the acquisition of knowledge is a process in which S actively participates and is thereby changed, developed, realised, *constructed*. The most salient questions for us are: how is it possible for someone (a teacher) to *educate* another subject (S); and when this occurs, does S still construct *herself* in the way Gentile believes necessary for the resultant beliefs to have concrete value? A concrete conception of education, which for Gentile is the only real form it can take, must account fully for the process of construction and how it is brought about through the joint enterprise of pupil (identified

---

[6] In *Diritto* [74], for example, Gentile writes: 'A society that perfectly unifies spiritual diversity [within itself], leaving no trace of variety, is a society that has come apart on the inside, starved of any spiritual energy. Strictly speaking, it is already dead.' This passage exemplifies Gentile's commitment to what he later called 'the moment of otherness' in society. His ideal total state is characterised not by rigid conformity, but instead by wide participation, evaluation and criticism in conditions of solidarity. This point is well argued by Alessandro Amato (2011) [211-15].

[7] *Sommario 1* [116]. Note that these phrases occur in reverse order, as 'the problem of man's formation, which is the problem of education...'

here with S) and teacher.[8] In what follows I offer an outline of this relationship before drawing out its deeper moral and political implications at the next sub-heading.

The teacher's principal task is to situate persons in relation to each other, and further with 'the whole of what we call nature', understood broadly to mean *the world in which S finds herself*. In this way, with the teacher enabling or equipping S to understand herself in self-conscious relation to the world around her, she is given her 'spiritual being'. S's knowledge and understanding, together with her increased competence in articulating these as sophisticated and mutually coherent ideas, grant her access to culture, history and society, as well as the natural world, at a deeper level than is possible through experience alone.[9] No individual can realise her full potential without support from others; but more than using them as instrumental means to achieve full self-realisation, the Gentilean individual incorporates the social system within her identity. Where persons recognise each other as members of and contributors to a shared collective identity, they can more easily comprehend and respond to others' moral claims. Straightforward conflicts of interest and fundamentally contradictory or incommensurable reasons are less likely under these circumstances, though not ruled out. With widely recognised laws and civic responsibilities, a mutually intelligible language (so persons can understand each other), each person is situated in a wider social milieu. In Hegelian language, this is the basis of *reciprocal relationship;* S is morally bound to others so long as she recognises them as moral agents and they likewise recognise her.

The suggestion of holism reflects Gentile's belief that all thinking is imbued with a moral character. As we saw earlier, he insists that facts and values are inseparable, since 'there is no fact that is not the establishment of a value'.[10] We cannot cut the tie between truth and the affirmation of it, nor with its implications for the self-conscious thinker conceiving of herself as simultaneously 'the [person] that is and the [person] that ought to be'.[11] It would be a mistake to imagine that moral education can be 'differentiat[ed]' from the other areas of study, so that pupils are instructed *how to be good* much as they are instructed how to be good biologists or mathematicians or speakers of French. Gentile insists that these are part and parcel of the same process.[12]

---

[8] Note that, in the IDP, the roles of pupil and teacher might be occupied by the same person.
[9] *Sommario 1* [184–5].
[10] *Sommario 1* [118]; see also *Educazione* [137]; Bigongiari translation [137–8].
[11] *Sommario 1* [114–5].
[12] *Sommario 1* [117].

The claim that facts and values are not concretely separable does not tell us much about what kind of education Gentile recommends. There is a danger that his objections to abstract differentiation of moral and non-moral education will lead us nowhere. What, then, is he prescribing? Certainly he rules out a conception of moral education for which moralising takes place solely in ethics seminars, referring to unlikely and abstract examples. Rather, it imbues the entire relationship between pupil and teacher. It is not a mechanical process by which the raw material of an uneducated person is transformed into a morally upstanding citizen. That would contradict the conception of education as the 'realisation of ideality', a process of 'formation' identified with the 'development that is life'.[13] The realisation of goodness consists in action and process, rather than the life of a person abstractly conceived as possessing a permanent quality of goodness, virtue or similar. The value of moral life cannot be meaningfully separated from the living of it.

This last observation puts Gentile in opposition to Rousseau, who understands the aim of education as the realisation of the inherent goodness of human nature. Gentile, of course, doubts that this kind of essentialism can be meaningfully upheld. Education for him is 'the actual generation of the spirit, the whole position and resolution of its content, [and] its living history'.[14] It is, in sum, 'the creation of a world'.[15] It makes no sense to talk about cultivating good or bad moral qualities while they are only presupposed, unnoticed or unrealised, for the obvious reason that we cannot make substantive claims about an unknown and isolated property. However, we *can* afford to talk about formal requirements such as the one for *liberty*. Another major outcome of education, and especially moral education,[16] is that the educated subject should be freer and more autonomous than she would have been without it. Liberty, understood as S's self-realisation in the act of thought, requires that pupils are equipped to identify incoherence and eliminate false propositions from their beliefs. As an autonomous moral subject, S cannot depend on some outside source to supply her aims and values. She must construct her world for herself. In obtaining

---

[13] *Sommario 1* [198–9].
[14] *Sommario 1* [220].
[15] *Sommario 1* [220–1].
[16] By this I mean education that refers to questions of value, how to be good, practical reason and so forth; not an education that possesses moral attributes in and of itself.

and subsequently exercising the ability to judge truth claims, she comes to educate and thereby create herself.[17]

This does not mean that Gentile conceives of individuals educating themselves without direct input from others, like the paragon of self-sufficiency that is Rousseau's Émile.[18] The roles of the teacher and the school are referred to repeatedly in Gentile's work. The meaning of his reference to the pupil's 'self-creation' is unclear. If education is a process enacted by two parties, the teacher and the pupil, in what sense is the pupil's spirit *creating itself*? Or to put it another way: how can we know who is responsible for the creation of the resultant spirit? Of course, the actual idealist conception of the self as an act synthesising subject and object demands that, in a sense, anything that a person thinks (notices) be attributed to that person. Insofar as S thinks, she creates the stuff of her consciousness. In some cases, such as when someone has an original idea, this is self-evident. Other cases are more resistant to such labelling. When two people discuss a problem and arrive jointly at a conclusion, having each suggested propositions that the other accepts, is it still true that each is the sole author of the changes to her own spirit, or self, as it emerges from the discussion?

I think that the most plausible Gentilean answer to this question is as follows. Persons must think (articulate) and ascribe value to propositions for themselves. But this does not rule out the possibility of a second person presenting propositions to the first, or else showing the first person which ideas she might find most plausible or coherently thinkable given what she already thinks. Drawing on the IDP, we might say that a person can educate herself without the need for any other (empirical) person. For S to read Hobbes' *Leviathan*, for example, is, provided that she gives it sufficient attention, effectively to engage Hobbes in conversation. While she cannot respond to Hobbes — or, at least, cannot hope to read Hobbes' replies to any such comments — the dialogical process is borne out as she accepts or rejects Hobbes' claims,

---

[17] *Sommario 1* [143]: 'Why does the spirit educate itself, form itself, make itself? [...] If we remember that the spirit is self-creation, [we see that] this question contains its own answer. The spirit makes itself because it is nothing other than self-creation.'

[18] While I have not the space for a detailed discussion of Rousseau, it is worth noting that the model for Rousseau's Émile is Robinson Crusoe. See Judith N. Shklar (1976) *Freedom and Independence* [65]. Descartes, too, places a premium on the education of the self, rather than by another person: see 'Discourse on Method', in Cottingham et al. (eds.) *The Philosophical Writings of Descartes* (Volume 1) [124–6]. The same cannot be said of Gentile, although he would say that Crusoe's business in educating himself is more like conventional inter-personal education than is commonly imagined.

or else strives to grasp Hobbes' meaning, even when at first this seems obscure. There is a sense in which Hobbes is educating S, and another in which S is educating herself by speaking to herself in Hobbes' voice. The second sense is key, for the engaged reader not only re-thinks Hobbes' words verbatim, but also re-interprets and re-phrases them in order to understand them better. The same is true of a pupil as she learns from her teacher; education is meaningless unless the pupil is actively engaged in evaluating, understanding and realising the content of the lesson.

3. Education and the state

So far I have described Gentile's *metaphysics* of education, set out in the *Sommario di pedagogia* (1913 and 1914) and, to a lesser extent, the *Riforma dell'educazione* (1920). These ideas are consistent with the actual idealist conception of the person. Indeed, it is in the *Sommario* that Gentile first offers a systematic account of his epistemology and philosophy of mind, which together constitute this conception. Although these ideas are (arguably) only the 'dry bones' of the more elaborate theory of *Atto puro* and the *Logica*,[19] they are foundational to his later work, going largely unchanged amid the development and embellishment of the theory. It is notable that Gentile's distinctive conceptions of freedom, autonomy and authority all arise in a work about *education*, and are subsequently transferred to other theoretical contexts (politics, ethics) without substantive change. It strongly suggests, but does not quite prove, that Gentile modelled much of his social and political thought on what goes on in the classroom. In his early work, he tends to attach education to society rather than the state.[20] Despite the shift in emphasis that occurred after 1922, this link between education and politics survived the society-state transition, and as A. James Gregor notes, Gentile viewed the state as 'essentially a teacher'. Gregor distinguishes this conception from those of other Fascists, not least Mussolini, for whom the state was instead 'a disciplinarian'.[21]

---

[19] 'Dry bones' is H.S. Harris's description in his introduction to *Genesis* [20]. Elsewhere, in his (1960) *The Social Philosophy of Giovanni Gentile*, Harris emphasises that a substantive shift occurs in 1931's *Filosofia dell'arte*, in which a greater role is assigned to *feeling* [224n].

[20] In *Sommario 1* [142], for example, he claims that 'as a matter of necessity, society [...] must provide its members with an education.' It should be noted that there is not a hard distinction between the 'society' period and 'state' period. There are plenty of references to the state even in pre-actualist works like 'Programmi e libertà', in (1908) *Scuola e filosofia*, Palermo: Sandron, pp. 63–67 [66, for example].

[21] A. James Gregor (1969) *The Ideology of Fascism*, Toronto: The Free Press [129].

The characterisation of the state as teacher makes Gentile's educational theory begin to look newly sinister. The role of the school in ensuring that citizens 'want what the state wants [them] to want' becomes fully apparent. It is worth quoting from *Origini e dottrina del fascismo* (Origins and Doctrine of Fascism), in which Gentile really does appear to advocate some kind of state indoctrination, at some length:

> The Fascist state is [... a] popular state, and is in that sense [the] democratic state *par excellence*. The relationship between the state and, rather than [just] this or that citizen, each citizen who has the right to call himself such, is so intimate [...] that the state exists inasmuch and just so long as the citizen makes it exist.[22] So its formation is the formation of [a shared] consciousness by the people,[23] which is to say, by the masses in whose [collective] power the state's power consists. That is why the [Fascist] Party, and all the institutions of propaganda and education corresponding to Fascism's political and moral ideals, need to work at ensuring that the thought and will of one man, *il Duce*, becomes the thought and will of the masses. Hence the vast problem to which [the Party] devotes itself: to squeeze all the people, beginning with the little children, into the Party and the institutions it has created.[24]

Passages like this show Gentile's equation of authority and liberty at its most vulnerable to dismissal as Fascist apologia. To defend it, we must dig deeper to see what it means for the teacher to embody authority in the way Gentile thinks necessary to complement the liberty of the pupil.

The teacher is responsible for finding effective ways to communicate the abstract content of the lesson to the pupil. In Hegelian language, education consists in the realisation of a single spiritual (mental) process by the pupil and the teacher at once. The pupil strives to understand the teacher's lesson while the teacher tries to present it in a way that the pupil will understand. Through this slow-dance of the spirit they achieve *spiritual unity*. The aim of education is for them—to use a different metaphor—to converge on a single position, unified by a thought or idea, and aware of their commonality in doing so. Although the educational process is directed toward this specific end, the teacher

---

[22] Original Italian: '*...lo Stato esiste in quanto e per quanto lo fa esistere il cittadino*'. Thanks to Fabio Vighi for his advice on the translation of this passage in November 2012.

[23] Original Italian: '*Quindi la sua formazione è formazione della coscienza dei singoli, e cioè della massa[...]*'

[24] *Origini* [268]. For an alternative English translation, see Gentile w/A. James Gregor (ed., trans.) (2007) *Origins and Doctrine of Fascism*, Brunswick, NJ: Transaction [28-9]. A shorter version appears in Gentile (1928) 'The Philosophic Basis of Fascism', *Foreign Affairs: an American Quarterly*, pp. 290-304 [302-3].

must be sensitive to the pupil's particular needs, strengths and weaknesses. A pupil is not free or autonomous if she is expected to remember and repeat information without understanding it, or to follow rules without identifying with them and the ends they are intended to safeguard. The teacher's authority is not a limit on the pupil's liberty; rather, it is the pupil's autonomous recognition of the teacher as authoritative that makes him so.

Despite this caveat, the teacher undoubtedly retains considerable power to mould the pupil's identity to some predetermined form. He can, by more or less direct means, create and specify the pupil's will and its object. This is plain enough when Gentile writes:

> To educate [a pupil] is to act upon [her] mind, and therefore not to leave her to her own devices. [The teacher] cultivates interests that [the pupil] would not otherwise feel; points her toward a destination whose value she would not appreciate on her own; [and] pushes her along the path when she lacks the will to go on. In short he gives [her] a little of [himself,] and so fashions her into a creature with a character, a mind, [and] a will.[25]

We may infer from this passage that Gentile perceives the pupil as a malleable object whose consciousness and identity are largely[26] under the teacher's control. This would further imply that the appearance of education as a process of *self*-construction is an illusion, or at least that it describes the process from only the pupil's subjective point of view. But Gentile anticipates these concerns when a page later he writes:

> The mind of the teacher oscillates between the zealous desire to watch over the pupil, guiding her development along the best, fastest and most secure path; and the fear of starving fertile seeds, of presumptuously restricting the spontaneous life of the spirit and its personal impulses, or

---

[25] *Educazione* [41]; Bigongiari translation [37]. I use the female pronoun for the pupil and the male pronoun for the teacher. This is to ensure that it is always clear to whom Gentile refers. While the difference is not always explicit in Italian, Gentile tends to use male pronouns for generic persons. Note Bigongiari's less literal translation of the same passage: '[T]eaching implies an action exercised on another mind, and education cannot therefore result in the relinquishment and abandonment of the pupil. The teacher must awaken interests that without him would lie dormant. He must direct the learner towards an end which he would be unable to estimate properly if left alone, and must help him to overcome the otherwise [in]surmountable obstacles that beset his progress. He must, in short, transfuse into the pupil something of himself, and out of his own spiritual substance create elements of the pupil's character, mind, and will.'

[26] I've retreated to this position because Gentile refers to the teacher contributing 'a little of himself' to the pupil's character, mind and will.

of forcing [her to wear] a garment not fitted to her, [like] a [stifling] lead cape.[27]

Here Gentile acknowledges the importance of the pupil's active role in the educative process. He acknowledges that mechanistic indoctrination, insofar as it forces the mind to develop to a particular end, threatens to stifle individual potential—the 'spontaneous life of the spirit'. But again it is clear that Gentile wants to promote the free and active development of the individual *within* the sheer confines of a codified social and political order. He considers these aims complementary. The school becomes a miniature self-contained world, with rules, expectations and a shared moral code.[28] These extend to the rules and maxims with which pupils are expected to comply in the classroom —be kind, act fairly, do not fight, do not steal, etc.—and further to the structures of authority and obligation, dominance and deference, that define social life. More than an analogue for society at large, the school *is* the pupil's society. The resemblance between the teacher's authority (over the pupil) and the state's authority (over the citizen) is no coincidence. The two are the same; the teacher *is the state* for the pupil subject to his authority.

Gentile argues that the 'grave problem' of the pupil's autonomy can be resolved through the 'reconciliation of the *maestro's* authority with the pupil's liberty'.[29] The pupil's recognition of the teacher's authority is integral to the relationship between them. This requires that, in the pupil's estimation, the teacher belong to 'the highest grades of human value', deserving the same kind of 'religious reverence' as her priest and parents. The relationship is even one of *love*, manifest in 'spiritual expansion and devotion',[30] requiring the commitment and mutual recognition of each participant's role in constituting a unified spiritual

---

[27] *Educazione* [42]; Bigongiari translation [38]. This idea has precedents in Gentile's philosophy of education that predates his actual idealism. See Gentile's 1902 essay, 'L'unità della scuola media e la libertà degli studi', in *Scuola*, pp. 77–114 [91]. Note that in my translation of this passage I have inserted 'stifling' where Gentile writes '*mortifera*' (deadly). I choose 'stifling' to emphasise the unwieldiness of the garment rather than its poisonous properties.

[28] This conception of the school has clear parallels with Herbart's vision of the school as 'a miniature world, to be regulated by the same system of moral ideas as that which obtains in society'. See his (1913) *Outlines of Educational Doctrine,* London: Macmillan [12]. (Note that this line may come from the annotator rather than Herbart himself.)

[29] Gentile (1908) 'L'unità della scuola media e la libertà degli studi' [110].

[30] *Sommario 1* [175–7].

act.³¹ Teacher and pupil have different roles in the performance of this act. The teacher does not teach himself in the same way that he teaches her, and neither does the pupil teach the teacher. There is a clear analogy between Gentile's conception of the teacher–pupil relation and Hegel's conception of lordship and bondage, or master and slave, in the fifth chapter of the *Phenomenology*. At first the pupil, like the slave, must submit to the teacher, or master, who is dominant. As she learns to think, the pupil begins to see how much she does not yet know or understand. She subsequently recognises the teacher's authority, and strives to match it by self-consciously engaging with what is being taught. Thus the division between teacher and pupil, master and slave, is gradually bridged, and the two are united as joint and equal contributors to a single thought.³²

The resolution into full self-consciousness is only a target. There is no guarantee that it will ever be achieved. Much of the educational process occurs with the participants contributing unequally, one as recognised authority over the other, subservient member, who still tries to attain the liberty and autonomy necessary to resolve the distinction between herself and the teacher. Gentile's claim that liberty implies authority is a familiar tenet of the doctrine of positive liberty, famously articulated by Isaiah Berlin. Positive liberty is enabling freedom, or the provision of means to the realisation of persons' aims. This is distinct from negative liberty, or freedom from external restrictions on persons' actions. In his original description of the two concepts, Berlin warns that reliance on the positive concept of liberty can mean that persons are free to live only 'one prescribed form of life'.³³

This can be put more simply. Liberty does not imply an unlimited range of options. Liberty *per se* is an empty abstraction; to be meaningful it must be the freedom to do *something*. A subject with a wide range of choices but no power to choose decisively between them, or whose intentions are at the mercy of fortune (if she is prone to sudden and unpredictable changes of heart, say), is not free. The range of perceived options at least partly defines what the subject wants, wills and values.

---

31 Since I have mentioned *love*, it is worth taking note of Hegel's view that (as Judith N. Shklar interprets him) in 'the final act, the erotic act, the [spirit's] equivalent of reproduction [...] the ego recreat[es] itself fully in order truly to know itself. [...] In mutual recognition men acknowledge their identity and overtly know each other as one "we"'. See Shklar (1976) [59].

32 This is obviously a brief and simple summary of Hegel's description of lordship and bondage in Hegel w/Miller (trans.) (1977) [111–19; §178–96].

33 Isaiah Berlin (2002) 'Two Concepts of Liberty', in Henry Hardy (ed.) *Liberty*, Oxford: Oxford University Press, pp. 166–217 (essay originally published 1958) [177–81; quotation 178].

This ties with Gentile's conception of *character* and *civil courage*, according to which one must exercise 'steady fidelity to one's own conscience', and 'bear witness [...] to the truth recognised in one's own mind'.[34] That S could have been a different person, or at least could have ended up with different interests, beliefs and commitments if some features of her life had been different, is not a reason to abandon what she *is* and believes herself to be. So again: freedom is only freedom when S recognises it as such. The range of available options may be very small indeed. But provided that S's will squares with what is available, she is no less free than if we were to add to those options any number of extra possibilities that she does not want to pursue.

An example will clarify Gentile's meaning. For someone to be (positively) free to become an expert violinist, say, she will need access to at least a violin, perhaps a competent and knowledgeable teacher, supportive friends and family members, the time and space to practise and so forth. Even if her friends, tutors, family members and wider social environment are rigidly oriented toward this one specific outcome, she is undoubtedly free to pursue it. Indeed, she has considerable advantages over would-be violinists who lack these facilities. But these factors are liberating only insofar as the pupil aspires to be a violinist. If she wants to live a life in which violins do not feature in any way whatsoever—she finds practice a tiresome strain on her real aim of maintaining the callous-free hands requisite to becoming a hand model—then the encouragement of others and the quality of the available equipment and facilities give her no kind of benefit. It is tempting to conclude that while this unwilling violinist is free to pursue that specified career, she is not free in the sense of being autonomous; she does not identify herself as a violinist, and unless she changes her mind, the freedom she has to pursue the end has no concrete value for her.

In state and school alike, the optimal configuration of liberty and authority results in the overlap of the relevant parties' wills. The citizen who wants what the state wants her to want is likely to find that the opportunities afforded her correspond closely with her intentions and desires, assuming that the state brings it about that she is given what she wants. While there are certain things that the law prevents her from doing, she does not want to do them, so her liberty is, in an important sense, secure. Similarly, the state whose citizens want what it wants really is 'the democratic state *par excellence*', since all of its citizens,

---

[34] *Genesi* [31]; Harris translation [95–6]. 'Conscience' and 'mind' are used to translate repeated instances of the Italian word *coscienza*. In this I follow Harris. See the footnote in Chapter 3, section #2i, herein.

rather than just the outspoken or politically active holders of the most popular view, affirm the state's will, and find it in their interests to support it wholeheartedly. In this way the total state can avoid the kinds of deep and intractable disagreement that characterise less prescriptive, more liberal states.[35]

4. Three objections to Gentilean education

Gentile's defence of a self-consciously prescriptive educational programme (hereafter GE, for 'Gentilean education') can be dismissed very easily as a disingenuous attempt to disguise authority as liberty and suppression as assent.[36] Since subjects/citizens want what they want because this has been explicitly or implicitly prescribed for them, or, perhaps more worryingly, because they have been taught to believe that some external entity has authoritative insight into what they really want (but might not, as mere individuals, know that they want), it looks doubtful that any meaningful account of education as *self-construction* can be sustained. This gives us the *Indoctrination Objection* (hereafter *IO*) to GE. IO holds that in the state Gentile describes, citizens are nothing but products of a system of indoctrination, which is both impermissible and somehow distinguishable from a legitimate form of moral education. Gentile's political and educational theory contradicts his moral theory, rendering his system of thought incoherent and leaving him open to attack as unprincipled and intellectually dishonest.

Indoctrination can be defined in a variety of ways, so I shall treat IO as an umbrella term covering three subsidiary objections. While linked, each of these prioritises a different specific conception of what indoctrination means and why it is to be rejected. For IO to succeed, it must at least partially explain, if only negatively, what an authentic moral

---

[35] Obviously these claims are deeply contentious. To be clear: these are *Gentile's* reasons in favour of the total state, and are reported here without endorsement. They will be challenged in the next sub-section.

[36] Hannah Arendt describes such manoeuvres as characteristic of totalitarian regimes in general. They succeed in 'dominating and terrorising human beings from within' [325]. 'By pressing men against each other', she writes, 'total terror destroys the space between them; compared to the condition within its iron band, even the desert of tyranny, insofar as it is still some kind of space, appears like a guarantee of freedom. Totalitarian government does not just curtail liberties or abolish essential freedoms; nor does it, at least to our limited knowledge, succeed in eradicating the love for freedom from the hearts of man. It destroys the one essential prerequisite of all freedom which is simply the capacity of motion which cannot exist without space' [466]. See her (1962) *The Origins of Totalitarianism*, New York: Meridian.

education would look like. Otherwise there is a risk that any (moral) education must involve indoctrination, with the result that moral objections to GE lead nowhere. These three versions refer, respectively, to the claim that GE is indoctrination because it involves imparting *false beliefs* or operates with insufficient *regard for truth* ('the Falsity Objection'); because it involves the manipulation of pupils, whereby they are treated as means to the teacher's ends ('the Manipulation Objection'); and because its content is arbitrary, having no justified authority over the existing values and moral conceptions that persons might possess ('the Coercion Objection').

4i. The Falsity Objection

The Falsity Objection has it that beliefs imparted through indoctrination are false, whereas those imparted via a legitimate form of education are (at least potentially) true. We might say that an indoctrinator intentionally causes the pupil to hold dubious or false beliefs about nationality, responsibility and so forth, *while aware that these beliefs do not have the support of the best reasons*. GE misleads pupils into believing that they are all subject to some identifiable authority (the state) that they would not recognise if equipped with true beliefs.[37]

This claim is hard to sustain with reference to value education (a term that I shall use broadly to mean any kind of education that causes or encourages persons to adopt beliefs or commitments with explicit normative components). It is not clear in what sense it could be true or false that, as a matter of fact, 'Marie owes more to her native France than to Nepal, which she regards as her "spiritual home".' Nor is it certain by what criteria we could justify even the descriptive claim that Marie is meaningfully French rather than Nepalese. Even if this claim refers to a loosely defined set of further, verifiable claims—referring to where Marie lives, which language she speaks and in what kind of documentation her existence is recorded—the Falsity Objection cannot show conclusively that claims attached to organically arising social conventions are truer than those brought about through deliberate social engineering. So understood, the Falsity Objection would be unable to gain a purchase on the normative beliefs that GE means to inculcate.

We can reinforce the Falsity Objection against such replies by having it say not that indoctrination trades in *false* claims, but instead that its claims are presented in such a way that rational assessment of their truth-value is impossible. The following definition, from Thomas

---

[37] The Fascist regime's notoriously cavalier attitude toward truth and falsity supports this view.

F. Green, draws a fairly typical distinction between indoctrination and what the author calls 'instruction':

> In indoctrinating, the conversation of instruction is employed only in order that fairly specific and pre-determined beliefs may be set. Conflicting evidence and troublesome objections must be withheld because there is no purpose of inquiry. The conversation of instruction is adopted without its intent, without the "due regard for truth" so essential to instruction. [... T]he intent of indoctrination is to lead people to hold beliefs as though they were arrived at by inquiry, and yet to hold them independently of any subsequent inquiry.[38]

This is not quite the same as the claim that beliefs acquired via indoctrination are always false. It entails no contradiction with Green's definition for a teacher to indoctrinate a pupil with true beliefs. What matters is the route by which she is led to arrive at her conclusions. An uncontroversial claim, such as 'Sicily is south of Italy', can be learned by rote, through the study of maps and history books or by travelling. The same conclusion is likely to emerge whichever method is used, but only in the latter cases, where Sicily's location is something other than an article of faith, can the belief be shown to have the support of a coherent set of further beliefs. Demonstration of the reasons why the pupil should believe the proposition is prerequisite to the 'due regard for truth' that distinguishes indoctrination from genuine instruction.[39]

A sceptical worry arises. Since claims about nationality and civic or moral responsibility cannot be conclusively proven,[40] must they always be treated as beliefs conveyed through indoctrination—that is, without due regard for truth? If so, any attempt to cause persons to hold beliefs about nationality, say, involves indoctrination, and should therefore be abandoned.[41] The problem with this conclusion is that, in maintaining that no moral claim can be proven, it rules out any possibility of any such claim being legitimate; none can *possibly* pass the truth-regarding

---

[38] Thomas F. Green (1972) 'Indoctrination and Beliefs', in I.A. Snook (ed.) *Concepts of Indoctrination: Philosophical Essays*, London: Routledge and Kegan Paul, pp. 20–36 [34–5].

[39] Note that Gentile denies that there can be a hard distinction between education and instruction. See *Sommario 1* [223–40, and esp. 239].

[40] It may be objected that we have compelling reasons to live our lives some ways rather than others, and that this is all morality is about: there is no reason for us to go in search of free-standing moral particles, say, like the 'morons' Ronald Dworkin dismisses in his book *Justice for Hedgehogs*. But even then we face a serious (and, many sceptics think, insurmountable) difficulty in extending the claim 'there is morality' to 'person P actually possesses moral obligation M'.

[41] To be clear: it should be abandoned because it is nonsensical, not because it is morally wrong (which would contradict the premise).

test. The resultant position may suit a deeply sceptical theory, but is not much good for our purposes if our intention is to distinguish legitimate from illegitimate forms of education.

How can we bring it about that Marie (or S) holds specific beliefs and a certain social identity without infringing her autonomy and freedom to exercise due regard for truth? As I have said, the claim that Marie is French cannot be conclusively proven (nor disproven) as a matter of fact. Even if, as suggested above, Marie's alleged Frenchness is provisionally accepted as a convenient social convention attached to her language, location and documentation, we face a further difficulty in attaching to her any specifically normative claim, such as 'Marie, as a French person, ought to care about France and the people belonging to it.' We might think that Marie should come to this conclusion more-or-less spontaneously, partly because so much of what she knows is conventionally understood to be French, and what a person cares about and feels deeply committed to is usually what that person knows best. Could it be that a legitimate moral education reserves the issue of S's *identification* with values to be inculcated through undirected socialisation? If Marie is in France and surrounded by people who feel bound to each other as sharers of a common national identity, of which they take Marie to be a fellow holder, she will have difficulty in puncturing this idea of community by simply expressing scepticism about the meaning of Frenchness. The teacher could educate S about relevant topics that *do* bear truth-regarding scrutiny, such as language, history, politics and moral philosophy, but leave her to make the last step to the conclusion that she possesses a nationality and attendant responsibilities. S's move between *knowing about* a language, a culture, a system of norms and values and a certain group of close associates, and *identifying* herself with those things as integral parts of her extended spiritual personality, is one that she makes independently of the teacher. In this way, by thinking of herself as bearer of a particular social identity and responsibilities, S thereby *makes it true* that she possesses these qualities.

This solution implies that a legitimate, autonomy-preserving education requires the teacher to restrict his input to laying out the materials with which S constructs her moral self-conception. He goes only so far as to specify *what* she will construct, while avoiding responsibility for the resultant construction. The difference between the two is a matter of words. It is assumed that the pupil remains autonomous so long as the teacher takes care not to make any positive claims about S's moral responsibilities, identity and so forth, even if he consciously drives her toward a specified outcome. This conclusion is absurd. Suppose S asks the teacher directly: 'You say that most people here identify themselves as French, and believe themselves bound by French laws and the principles that underpin them. Are they right to think so? Am *I* French? Are *you*?' Mindful of offering a reply that he cannot defend, the teacher could shrug his shoulders, or ask a question in reply: 'What do *you* think?' But this is no answer. It suggests that S's identification with the role described for her is optional; she could just as well conclude that claims about nationality and normativity are arbitrary nonsense. Indeed, this is the opposite of what the laying out of that role was intended to achieve. By conceding that the question of whether or not S identifies with it is up to her, the teacher forfeits the operation at its most delicate and decisive moment. This whole solution relies on it never occurring to S to ask this question, having found its answer already settled in her mind after a lifetime of indirect socialisation.

4ii. The Manipulation Objection

The Manipulation Objection refers not to the truth-value of the beliefs S comes to hold, but instead to the *intention* of the teacher who causes S to hold them. The pupil is caused to hold specified beliefs in order to further some end. It suits the interests (or preferences) of the teacher, or some third party (such as the state), for S to hold them. Whether or not she has good reasons for doing so is immaterial. Indeed, harking back to the Falsity Objection's idea of 'due regard for truth', it is precisely the point of indoctrination that S should not be able to recognise and assess the reasons for holding these determined beliefs.[42] They are articles of faith that she affirms because she does not know what else she could believe or on what grounds she could justify the exchange of her current beliefs for different ones.

This objection is compatible with the one before. Consciously lying to S is obviously an example of manipulation, as this leads her to a belief that the teacher knows she does not, in fact, have good reason to hold. But the teacher need not disbelieve the proposition that S is caused to affirm in order for the process to be manipulative. He could cause S to hold true beliefs for bad reasons, or on the basis of false, incomplete or otherwise misleading information. For example: suppose my young daughter refuses to brush her teeth before bed, and I truthfully tell her, 'You know, I once read a story about a monster who ate

---

[42] Colin Wringe, for example, writes that 'the difference between the democratic teacher and the anti-democratic indoctrinator [is that] the indoctrinator is [...] concerned to instil certain substantive beliefs *in such a way that they will not later be questioned or changed*.' See Wringe (1984) *Democracy, Schooling and Political Education*, London: George Allen & Unwin [35]; emphasis added.

children who didn't have clean teeth.' In saying so I have the specific intention of causing her to do what I want—which is something I assume she has good reason to do in any case. My statement is true, although it is expressed with the expectation that the child will understand it one way (that is: as a cautionary tale about the link between dental hygiene and the risk of being eaten by a monster) and I another (as a means to have her brush her teeth, and, perhaps, to keep myself amused). I am cultivating in the child a habit that she will later have reason to endorse, but offering incomplete or misleading sets of true claims in order to do so.[43] So: if our pupil comes to hold a true belief, and this belief is the same one at which she would have arrived via another, sounder route, what does it matter how the ideas are transmitted?

Some help is offered in Gideon Yafee's recent article on the concept of indoctrination. In relating the following example, I shall refer to the teacher as *T*, and the pupil as *S*.[44] Yafee identifies two kinds of manipulation by which T can 'get [S] to do what she [T] wants [S] to do'. The first is characterised by T 'get[ting] her way by leading [S] to ignore those aims and wants with which [S] identif[ies] and do as she [T] wants', while in the second, T 'perniciously works on [S] to alter what [he] identif[ies] with so that it conforms with what she [T] wants [S] to care about'. Yafee claims to be more 'frightened' by the latter than the former, noting that

> The second kind of manipulation has lasting effects that the first does not. In the first case, [S] can look back on [his] conduct later and see that [he] had no reason of [his] own to do as [he] did, while in the second, the fact that [S was] being used is, in effect, concealed from [him]: [he] will see [him]self later—and [he] won't be mistaken—as having had reasons of [his] own for doing as [he] did.

---

[43] To extend that example: we can probably agree that I would be abusing my parental authority if I were to invoke spurious monster-based fables every time I want my daughter to behave and think in a way I have prescribed, even if at no point do I lie or prompt her to do something I do not think she would endorse if presented with the relevant facts. To reinforce the example, we might further suppose that her bedtime has passed, she has been drinking sugary soft drinks, and she is too young to be moved by true accounts of the effects such chemicals can have on unbrushed teeth.

[44] Note that the genders of these participants are different from those used throughout most of the present book. As Yafee relates his example, he is the victim of a female manipulator. I replace first-person references with a male pronoun and retain the third-person female pronoun for the manipulator.

'If I have to choose,' Yafee concludes, 'I would rather be a pawn than a toady.'[45] Why would he object more to being manipulated into acting as a 'toady' than a 'pawn'—a response he assumes most people would share? After all, Toady-S does not have to contend with the kind of dissonance imposed on Pawn-S, who, by contrast, is at least potentially conscious that what he is doing is in tension with his actual aims and wants. Although Pawn-S is not free to do as he wants, he is at least free to resent this lack of freedom. Toady-S's actions square with his aims and wants, if only because T has caused them to do so. As such, Toady-S really did have 'reasons of [his] own' for doing what he did at the time he did it. If later he comes to his senses and re-adopts those aims and wants that he had before T caused him to change them, he will doubtlessly perceive his T-caused actions as misguided mistakes, or at least actions that, given his renewed aims and wants, he should not have performed. But this would be true however the change in actions and wants occurred. It is perfectly ordinary to change one's mind about what is valuable or worth doing, and there is no reason to assume that S's non-T-given aims are themselves any more justifiable or long-standing than the ones that temporarily replaced them. The factor determining whether T's intervention is legitimate is whether the T-given aims *withstand reflection*.[46]

Recall my earlier description of a teacher who fosters S's social, cultural and political identity without at any point forcing it upon her as an article of faith. Thus he might preserve S's autonomy while effectively specifying what she will autonomously choose. The problem with this is that it assumes the teacher's ignorance of the likely consequences of his actions. Undoubtedly the teacher has assisted in the process of socialisation that we may reasonably expect to occur anyway, as a consequence of the pupil's situation within a particular social context. If it occurs to the teacher that a pupil loaded with knowledge of some particular culture, and surrounded by people who claim to belong to it and to subscribe to a broadly shared system of values, is likely to identify herself with that same culture and value system, does the teacher then possess the *intention* to cause the pupil to hold dubious beliefs? I do not see how we can say for certain either way. A teacher *might* have unscrupulous motives and try to bring it about that a pupil holds beliefs that are false or at least suspect, in that she (the pupil) has no more reason for holding them than for holding one or more other, incompatible beliefs. But supposing it is granted that the pupil will

---

[45] Gideon Yafee (2003) 'Indoctrination, Coercion and Freedom of Will', *Philosophy and Phenomenological Research*, 67 (2), pp. 335–56 [338].

[46] A fuller account of what this entails is given in Chapter 7, herein.

acquire a nationality, which, much like her name, is neither deducible nor provable, the teacher might then say, by way of justification: 'The pupil will incorporate this nationality into her self-consciousness as a result of her upbringing and ordinary social development. Her education will give her access to culture, shared values and norms, and a language, so admitting her into a rich social identity which she can share with her peers.'[47] Thus he can present reasons for so educating the pupil that do not rely on free-standing and suspect value claims (e.g. 'Marie ought to identify herself as French') but instead value claims that correspond to truth claims ('Marie identifies herself as French, so she should be educated to make the most of that identity').

4iii. The Coercion Objection

Another variant of IO holds that this kind of education, unlike legitimate varieties, entails the coercion of S.[48] Obvious ways in which education could be coercive include mandatory submission to restrictive oaths, prohibitively harsh punishments for expressions of dissenting views, or constraints on with whom pupils may associate. (In a wider political context, these would account for the detention of political prisoners or prohibitions on public meetings.) Less directly, coercion might consist of restrictions on what pupils are permitted to read, view or hear (that is: censorship or media control). While Gentile opposes the idea of a police state,[49] his remark about 'propaganda and education'[50] suggests that this second kind of coercion is not ruled out. Pupils could be indirectly forced to hold specified beliefs by depriving them of access to alternatives, or else because they are overwhelmed by evidence — which I interpret broadly to include propaganda and rhetoric, as well as logically sound arguments and demonstrations — for the belief specified by the teacher.

To assess the force of this objection, we need a clearer understanding of why coercion is to be rejected in the context of education. There are undoubtedly cases in which coercion is not morally amiss, even in the context of the classroom. If pupils are restrained from fighting or similarly dangerous or disruptive activities, for example,

---

[47] This resembles the kind of hypothetical agreement discussed in Chapter 7, sub-section #3i herein.
[48] Yafee (2003) [*passim*].
[49] *Genesi* [124–5]. Gentile's concerns about police states have been discussed in Chapter 4, sub-section #4 herein.
[50] This phrase occurs in *Origini*, in a passage already quoted in this chapter (sub-section #3). The specific remarks that led to him being characterised as '*il filosofo del manganello*' (the philosopher of the blackjack) should not be overlooked, although there he refers to the state and not to the school.

they are in a sense being coerced. The same is true of threats of punishment for misbehaviour or even the simple expectation that pupils be in specific places at specific times. But this would happen in practically any tenable and orderly classroom, regardless of how doctrinaire or liberal the education programme might be. There is no evidence to suggest that GE would be any more than ordinarily strict or harsh in its punishments. If it is to be criticised for its coercion, the fault must be found in the theory itself.

It can be argued that GE is coercive in that it leads (or forces) pupils to hold pre-determined beliefs, as the previous two objections claimed. To this the Coercion Objection adds that those pupils are also *prevented from holding beliefs that they might* (legitimately)[51] *have held otherwise.* As the Manipulation Objection claimed, GE masks some options from pupils in order to ensure that they choose (construct) beliefs in the way the teacher desires. Thus they are deprived of a range of options, and tacitly of the freedom to choose. With respect to moral beliefs, this is hardly exclusive to doctrinaire, illiberal education systems. D.O. Hebb, for example, argues that

> [a] liberal, democratic, moral education sets out, rightly, to *remove* freedom of choice from a child's mind in moral questions. [...] Imposing ideas we agree with is OK, and necessary too. Education is in a bad way if a boy on reaching maturity has to sit down and argue out the question before deciding whether race prejudice is a good thing, or cruelty to animals, or fascist governments, or "Watergating" — or if a girl leaving home has still to figure out whether a career in shoplifting or prostitution would be a good idea. Impose ideas? Try to limit freedom of choice? Of course we do, all of us.[52]

On Hebb's account, an educational programme may legitimately exclude options like these and impose others. But since he refers to a 'liberal, democratic moral education', the denial and imposition of options cannot be so prescriptive as to deny pupils any choice whatsoever — otherwise it would not be liberal, and it would lack the plurality of views necessary to make democratic politics meaningful. How, then, is Hebb able to specify that racism, animal cruelty and so on are wrong? If the reason is simply that they are not 'ideas we agree with', then he is vulnerable to charges of partiality. By the same logic, GE could have any content whatsoever, provided that 'we' — the repre-

---

[51] I add 'legitimately' because *any* education prevents persons from holding certain beliefs. The assumption here is that pupils could 'legitimately' have thought otherwise, meaning that what GE causes them to think is in no way privileged above these neglected alternatives.

[52] D.O. Hebb (1974) 'What Psychology is About', *American Psychologist,* 29 (2), pp. 71–9 [72].

sentatives of the state, perhaps—agree with it. A stronger argument may be that a programme that makes no impositions, and permits persons to develop moral beliefs favouring racism and animal cruelty, allows the acceptance of beliefs that persons have no good reasons to hold. We cannot expect people to recognise themselves as morally bound to laws underpinned by good reasons while their personal beliefs are groundless and arbitrary.[53] A rationally justifiable system of authority demands at least a basic level of rationality and mutual comprehensibility among its subjects.

5. Replies to the Objections

In this sub-section I offer Gentilean replies to IO as a whole. In doing so I attempt to establish the extent to which GE can yield the content of Gentilean moral theory without distorting its form.

It is plain that Gentile cannot endorse an education system that disregards the value of truth. We have already seen that his theory of truth relies on both S's affirmation of a proposition and that proposition's coherence with other beliefs. For S to arrive at a belief without knowing *why* she holds it would satisfy only the first of these requirements. It may be that later she comes to see why her belief is justified, but until that occurs—until she is able to provide a structure upon which that belief can rest—the proposition cannot rightly be called true. Moreover, to acquire a belief through indoctrination is not to act freely. Unless S can justify this belief to herself, subjecting it to critical scrutiny through the IDP, she is unable to revise or reject it at any later time. It becomes an assumption, an abstract proposition with its truth-value already given.

This reply partly addresses the Manipulation Objection. The extent to which persons may be legitimately 'manipulated' is severely limited by the requirement for beliefs to have the support of reasons. However, this does not counter the claim that to impose specific values is to use persons as means to an end.[54] GE certainly has an end in view: namely,

---

[53] This is not to suggest that the choice is between wholesale rational paternalism and out-and-out relativism. There is no reason to assume that people who have *some* rationally grounded beliefs and others that are arbitrary cannot live together in a stable community. What matters is that, unless *some* demands are made about what they believe, they can believe *anything*, including groundless claims about, say, a hierarchy of races. This would disable any attempt to have them reach agreement in moral matters.

[54] To elaborate: these values, which are inculcated deliberately, are the state's means of creating order. The problem is that what leads them to behave in an orderly fashion is a set of values that are shared but, at least at the outset, externally imposed, and whose content is ultimately arbitrary.

the unity of spirit through which the pupil can attain autonomy. Within the social microcosm of the classroom, the teacher does not personally stand to gain much from pupils' compliance. Certainly disciplined and engaged pupils are easier to manage, and as such easier to instruct in the skills requisite to autonomous mastery of the subject at hand. There is nothing obviously sinister about making a five-year-old do what she is told *because she is a member of the class,* and *all members of the class are required to obey the rules,* provided that this dependency does not hinder her development later when she is better equipped to reason for herself. The teacher imposes his authority so as to clear away children's undesirable tendencies (recalcitrance, laziness, unwillingness or inability to communicate with others, disrespect, ignorance) and replace them with desirable ones (including, aside from the opposites of those listed previously, sound judgement and self-control) before the former can become ingrained to the hindrance of the latter. A child with these positive qualities will make the teacher's job easier, of course, but this is not the chief end at which enforced discipline is aimed. Rather, if it is to have any value, the teacher does it for the child's ultimate benefit.

Transplanted to a political context, this theory looks rather different. Rather than a child identifying herself as a member of the class and, by extension, one obliged and expected to obey the rules and respect the teacher's authority, a citizen educated in this way is expected to identify herself with the state, and to obey its laws and its assumed authority. Hence the citizen attains a sort of autonomy, just as the pupil does; but it is a special kind of autonomy, in that all members of society direct themselves towards compatible ends. This brings about order, social cohesion and the greatest possible correlation between what citizens want and what they are positively free and able to achieve.

I doubt that we can dismiss GE as a poorly disguised licence to dominate. Adrian Lyttelton writes that Gentile actively opposed the idea of 'direct political indoctrination' of the mechanical and systematic variety. What he wanted, Lyttelton writes, was 'spontaneous discipline', with citizens submitting their wills entirely and voluntarily to the state while simultaneously thinking, acting and creating the world around them.[55] Gentile's educated citizen is not a mindless drone, driven to hold pre-conceived ideas and habits by the removal of alternatives and (perhaps) a lingering threat of state violence. Rather, she is free to do what she wants to do provided that this remains within carefully arranged moral and legal confines. The ability to think freely and

---

[55] Adrian Lyttelton (2004) *The Seizure of Power: Italian Fascism in Power, 1919–1945* (revised ddition), New York: Routledge [341].

critically is paramount within Gentile's idealist system as a whole. It is only by applying reason carefully and correctly that a person may realise her full potential as a thinking being.[56]

It can be objected that order, cohesion and positive liberty are only secondary aims, and that what Gentile really wants is a placid and compliant population over whom a specific political elite—the mysterious *uomo fascista*, or *il Duce*—can exercise total control, without the need to accommodate prior social conventions and norms. I cannot conclusively disprove this claim, of course, since I have no privileged access to Gentile's true intentions. However, assuming a reasonable degree of correspondence between what he wrote and what he thought, in his defence I can say this: the central tenets of actual idealism are at odds with this reading. Gentile conceives of legitimate moral claims as those generated by free and reflective agents. As such, persons have responsibility for co-ordinating their own lives and assessing the laws they employ in doing so. Actual idealism's starting position, set deep in the act of thinking, must rank highly among the possible conceptions of the person best suited to safeguarding the autonomy of the individual subject. In short: if Gentile really did intend his educational theory as a licence to dominate, he made the task needlessly difficult for himself.

It is also clear that Gentile opposes coercive education that would obstruct the pupil's ability to think, or to reconcile her thoughts with her actions.[57] There is no reason to assume that forced compliance, whereby the pupil's behaviour is tightly controlled, implies that the pupil *thinks* what her teacher wants her to think. Even if the forced compliance were so comprehensive and relentless that she lost the ability to think critically (an idea commonly invoked in discussions of so-called 'brainwashing')[58] she would be deprived of the liberty

---

[56] Recent theorists have defended education's powers to increase autonomy while reducing basic (negative) freedom. See, for example, Johannes Giesinger (2010) 'Free Will and Autonomy', *Journal of the Philosophy of Education*, 44 (4), pp. 515–28 [525]; and, for a version concocting similar conclusions using more Kant and less education, Sarah Buss (2005) 'Valuing Autonomy and Respecting Persons: Manipulation, Seduction and the Basis of Moral Constraints', *Ethics*, 115 (2), pp. 195–235 [226-33].

[57] At least this is true of his philosophical work. It is well established that Gentile endorsed, or at least failed to prevent, the introduction of mandatory oaths of allegiance in the Italian education system. See e.g. Harris (1960) [197].

[58] E.F. O'Doherty (1963) 'Brainwashing', *Studies: an Irish Quarterly Review*, 52 (205), pp. 1–15 [esp. 13-15].

necessary for any affirmation to have moral significance. 'The spontaneous life of the spirit' would be fatally stifled.

The practical implications of Gentile's view can be seen in his recommendations for policy reform. In an early educational work, he stipulates how religion should be taught in school, trying to reconcile his nascent actual idealism with the Catholicism with which the vast majority of Italians — the audience for his desired reforms — identified themselves. Gentile acknowledged that the discipline of philosophy takes time and effort to understand, and for many (perhaps most) people, it will not seem intuitively obvious or easy to grasp. Small children, for example, are likely to lack the skills necessary to reason out their beliefs. A full appreciation of the moral and practical reasons not to steal or set light to cars, say, is beyond the child's grasp. Some people may never be able or inclined to tackle such demanding ideas. But morality is not only for moral philosophers; we cannot wait for persons to become autonomous before teaching them how to exercise their autonomy. Religion offers a solution to these problems. Children may be taught to hold the right beliefs (for now let us confine these to moral convictions, such as 'stealing is wrong') for reasons that are at once easily grasped and, on further examination, potentially specious (e.g. 'because God is watching you and He disapproves of theft'). For this to be legitimate, it must be assumed that those same conclusions can later be endorsed after rational and disciplined reflection. The original reasons given serve as a short-cut for those not yet able to make sense of the truer and more demanding ones, which may be taken up later when subjects are equipped for the task. On first approach, though, as Harris puts it, 'the pupil's liberty is in the teacher's keeping.'[59]

The strongest version of IO that can reasonably be mounted against GE argues that the early stages constitute a sort of well-intentioned indoctrination, intended to inculcate a set of values, commitments and/ or beliefs *par provision* until they can be examined and subsequently accepted by a better-informed, self-conscious and autonomous subject. Obviously of great importance are the stages that follow. The pupil must, after this thoroughly determined beginning, be taught to take charge of her own thinking, in order that the re-examination and assessment of her received opinions can result in their vindication.

---

[59] Harris (1960) [quotation 86; see also 68–71]. I was going to draw a comparison between these ideas and Plato's 'noble lie', but annoyingly Harris has beaten me to it [95].

6. Re-appraising Gentilean education

The preceding objections and replies offer a clearer impression of GE and the moral and political theories with which it is linked. Especially striking is the conception of the free and autonomous subject that emerges from this discussion, as well as the conception of political equality that goes with it. In this sub-section I draw out some of the implications of these ideas, showing how GE refines the Gentilean vision of morally authoritative political institutions.

6i. Gentilean education and political theory

Education is one area in which Gentile's moral theory has a direct political application. The political state has a role to play beyond the metaphysical business of the IDP. Its role is explicitly practical, setting curricula and determining what is taught to whom. We may ask: given what we know about Gentilean moral theory, what is the most convincing way to characterise the role of the state in the construction of the circumstances of moral reasoning? Is its proper role to engage directly in 'soulcraft', shaping individuals and imposing on them preconceived values and beliefs;[60] or instead to teach people how to live alongside others while thinking and acting as autonomous moral agents?[61]

Let us examine the case for each side. I have already cited Gentile's claim that 'as a citizen, I want what I want: but, when I look more closely [*quando si va a vedere*], what I want coincides exactly with what the state wants me to want.'[62] On Gentile's unusual conception of the will's relation to knowledge, to share the state's will is also to share at least some of the substantive beliefs underwriting that will. (Since the state, *qua* abstract entity, cannot strictly hold beliefs, it must be assumed that both its beliefs and its will are inferable from its doctrinal statements or laws.) The state's power to change citizens' wills is limited by the necessity of their thinking. Gregor has argued that while the Gentilean state undoubtedly holds very considerable powers to shape the individual's 'moral world', it

---

[60] I take the term 'soulcraft' from the liberal education theorist Eamonn Callan, and especially his book (1997) *Creating Citizens*, Oxford: Clarendon Press. He defines it 'as the moulding of citizens according to some traditional standard of human excellence' [4].

[61] I am grateful to Peri Roberts for bringing these questions to my attention in June 2012.

[62] *Educazione* [33]. In Bigongiari's translation [29], this passage is rendered thus: 'as a citizen, [I] have [...] a will of my own; but [...] upon further investigation my will is found to coincide exactly with the will of the state, and I want anything only in so far as the state wants me to want it.'

> assumes moral significance only when the individual is *persuaded* or persuades himself that the state is *his* state. Only then does the state become a moral reality for the individual [... However, 'p]ersuasion' and 'consent' are terms that can only be appropriately applied in contexts where intellectual freedom obtains. Men are persuaded to consent without coercion *only by good reasons* [... accessed via] an appeal to reason and human sentiment.[63]

This is a reasonable précis of Gentile's basic position. It does not answer our question, however. To illustrate, suppose for now that the state *can* provide persuasive arguments to support its substantive claims. At no point does it present as true any claim that is demonstrably false. There is still considerable scope for variation in how the state employs its 'good reasons' in practice. It could be that the state, citing marginally better reasons for preferring one end rather than another, acts against the wishes of people who disagree, and perhaps care very deeply that the present state of affairs should continue. The persons likely to be affected by a given policy cannot be expected to change their minds as if by fiat whenever the state announces its position on some controversial issue. The state does not control its citizens' lives directly, and it cannot do their thinking for them. As mentioned in previous chapters, it cannot judge every possible point of disagreement in advance. Indeed, if we remember that it exists chiefly as a metaphor, it becomes plain that the state cannot possibly hold a monopoly on good reasons prior to any person constructing these. That is: any appeal to the state's good reasons must at some stage collapse into the good reasons of an actual thinking subject who is something other than a metaphor.

Gregor's 'good reasons' formulation also fails to explain what stance the state may legitimately take on beliefs whose content is largely arbitrary or under ordinary circumstances taken as true because of convention and indirect forces of socialisation. Beliefs—even treasured beliefs—are not always reached via the best available arguments. As such it is unclear what the state could legitimately cite as universally recognisable or otherwise objectively good reasons to make citizens identify themselves principally as Italians rather than Sicilians or Florentines, say. This problem is compounded if we consider what would make a state's reasons in favour of this policy demonstrably better than reasons existing people might offer in favour of their Florentine or Sicilian self-conceptions. This leaves open deeply contentious questions of whether good reasons should be understood as

---

[63] Gregor (1969) [225–6].

those grounded in value or expediency, justice or the common good, and still further metaphysical questions of what reason entails.

I do not propose to settle these issues here. I point them out only to show how deep the problems run. What matters for our purposes is that Gentile does not offer a substantive solution either. His theory does not give rise to a comprehensive policy programme, but instead a set of strictly formal considerations for any thinker engaged in designing one. It does us no good to follow Gentile's rigorous strategy if we then fudge more substantive conclusions than his theory allows. It is notable that he prefaces his comments on 'the fundamental antinomy of education' — that is, the clash between the ideas that education is supposed to augment its recipient's freedom, and that it destroys its recipient's freedom by forcing compliance — with the following proviso:

> A warning in advance: my solution does not eliminate all difficulties. It is not a key that opens all doors. [...] Education's value is in the problems that arise from it, and for these we can never hope to find a solution that would free us from having to think.[64]

This does not mean that the state's proper role in educating citizens is indeterminate or arbitrary. Another way to characterise the state's educative role is to say that it should teach people *how to live together*, rather than imposing on them a comprehensive conception of value. This is a closer fit with recent liberal responses to the question of paternalism in education, where it is commonly assumed that there is value in maintaining pluralism, though not necessarily boundless pluralism, for its own sake. It seems that a policy designed to accommodate every possible extension of pluralism, including deeply irrational, internally contradictory and other-denying doctrines, would deprive the state of any basis on which to justify its actions. If it is disabled to that extent, it cannot meaningfully exist, for the idea of the state as an authoritative entity relies upon its members' recognition of it as such.

Individuals need not be iterations of the same person in order to live together. The state cannot control the fact that persons have different life experiences, which may contribute to identity-formation in ways that the state cannot predict or act against. For state education to rob

---

[64] *Educazione* [42]. Bigongiari's translation is less literal, but maybe clearer: 'I must at the very outset utter an emphatic word of warning. My solution does not remove all difficulties; it cannot be used as a key to open all doors. For as I have repeatedly stated, the value of education consists in the persistence of the problems, ever solved and yet ever clamouring for a new solution, so that we may never feel released from the obligation of thinking' [38].

citizens of their ability to disagree with it, each other, or established conventions, would saddle the state — or rather, those persons representing it — with implausibly extensive responsibilities. The state would need a full array of facts and reasons at the point of its creation.[65] To find out on what basis we might design a Gentilean scheme of social co-operation in which persons can live together, we must refer to special kinds of construction designed to produce firm outcomes despite constructors' different (and not always negotiable) beliefs. That will be one of my tasks in the next chapter.

6ii. Gentilean Education and the IDP

I now return to the IDP to see what the educational theories so far described can reveal about Gentile's model of practical reason. This can be achieved at two levels. The first is strictly metaphysical, while the second refers to the more commonsensical business of what a teacher may legitimately teach.

There can be no doubt that the teacher and the socius fulfil the same moral role. The pupil refers to the teacher when she wants to know what to do. At first she submits wholly to the teacher's authority, as she is not yet equipped to test the coherence of the reasons presented to her. Later she can expect the teacher to supply an answer supported by reasons that she (the pupil) can understand. If she is unconvinced by the reasons offered, she may challenge or reject them. But integral to the relationship between pupil and teacher is that they recognise and respect each other as thinking beings; the pupil may not arbitrarily reject the teacher's reasons, but if she can show those reasons to be flawed, the teacher must try to better them. Through this joint endeavour, together with a shared recognition of the value of *truth*, pupil and teacher do not compromise their respective arguments in the sense of meeting half-way; rather, they both move toward a common destination, however distant this is from either's starting point. They aspire to that *spiritual unity* in which there is only one concrete subject. The same applies to the way in which the autonomous subject refers to the socius in order to identify the best reasons for action. The difference is that the socius is internal rather than external. However, it can still be challenged, contradicted and altered, but only if S genuinely believes that she can offer better reasons for thinking or doing something other than what the socius prescribes. If S is to remain an active participant in moral life, she must ultimately satisfy the socius, coming to identify it with US, which represents the truth.

---

[65] This possibility has already been discussed in Chapter 3, sub-section #4i, where I called it the *Regress Problem*.

For this chapter, one pressing question remains. Can Gentile coherently argue for a constructivist moral theory based on S's autonomy and liberty at the same time as a political and educational theory whose central concern is 'man's formation'? On the evidence we have seen, and in light of the formal restrictions on the power of educators and states to specify the content of persons' values, I think he can. This will not convince all critics, of course. The objection that existing values would be effectively crowded out by the externally imposed set, and that existing values ought to be respected *because subjects already consider them to be valuable,* cannot be conclusively countered on its own terms. But that objection amounts to a general endorsement of the status quo; it only assumes that existing values are more worthy of retention than their alternatives. Nor does this give us reasons to think an S holding organically arising, traditional values, say, is any more *autonomous* or *free* than if she held another, artificially devised set. They are effectively *given* to her in either case, although clearly much depends on how they are presented. Gentile's version, premised on the IDP, accepts the arbitrariness of value while insisting on the subordination of any belief to reasoned thought. In other words, S may review and reject her values according to the reasons she has for holding them; and although she can never be certain that her assessment of reasons does not itself rely on controversial value claims, she must try to justify her values using the best standards she can devise. Once again, this task can never be completed, but any thinker who recognises the authority of her own thought is compelled to engage in it. The question of how S might go about this task is one of those addressed in the next chapter.

7. Conclusion

We have seen how Gentile reconciles two ideas: first, that values are transmitted between persons and through cultures, and, second, that moral subjects are autonomous constructors of their own values. This leaves unresolved the question of exactly what those values should be. Intractable conflicts of value are not wholly ruled out. We have not yet seen a Gentilean decision procedure for resolving problems where parties are at odds over what to do. While individuals continue to live their own lives, they cannot become iterations of the same person. Even the most extensively socialised individuals must retain the power to disagree with each other. Owing to their separateness, they cannot share a single, unified and equally transparent conception of value using which they make identical judgements with perfect consistency. If they did, moral theory would be a descriptive exercise with no power to determine what anyone really ought to do. But if society is to function in an orderly and stable fashion, and is to accommodate the possibility of internal change,[66] it must have some orienting assumptions in place. Rationally justified laws, for example, guarantee the state's moral demands of its citizens against the caprices of the changing personnel charged with administering them. The model for this process of rational justification is the IDP.

---

[66] By 'internal change' I mean that persons' values may alter, perhaps dramatically, over time. These changes may affect some people within society in different ways and/or to different extents than others. That I call this change 'internal' does not exclude the possibility of people arriving in society from the outside: emigration and immigration are themes that Gentile addresses rarely, and then without much departing from the assumption that states constitute closed societies.

Chapter 7

Dialogical Constructivism and the Idea of Agreement

So far in Part II we have seen that Gentile endorses the Kantian conception of reason as a process by which the subject (S) strives to give her judgements universal and therefore objective status. He aims to do away with any transcendent elements in Kant's ethics, modelling actual idealist moral theory instead upon the metaphor of the internal dialogue by which S reviews and evaluates her reasons for thought and action. We have also seen how Gentile's theory of education fits together with his constructivist moral doctrine. S is at once a product of her society and an autonomous agent responsible for her own constitution. Appropriately configured, these simultaneous constructions need not conflict.

This chapter explicates the IDP's mechanism and shows how it functions as a practicable constructivist device. To begin, I argue that the metaphor of dialogue is the model best suited to moral reasoning as Gentilean constructivism conceives of it (sub-heading #1). I then explain how, even if the dialogue is strictly an internal procedure, it enables S to refine her subjective beliefs into objective claims. Drawing especially on the work of Donald Davidson, I introduce two formal principles to guide S's conduct when applying the procedure (#2). Next I ask *how* S interacts with the socius (A). I examine the cases for verificationist and falsificationist versions of the IDP, finding that it is compatible with both, but that the latter is the most useful for drawing firm conclusions (#3). In the last substantive part of the chapter I explain the relationship between the IDP's interlocutors and real, 'external' people that S might encounter. I show that while Gentilean constructivism is primarily a meta-ethical doctrine, it carries some substantive implications for the moral status of others and, by extension, how S may legitimately behave toward them (#4). I conclude with a brief summary of the IDP's purpose and function as developed in this chapter and the two that preceded it (#5).

1. Justifying dialogue

Before elaborating the fine details of the IDP, we must first establish the status of the dialogical metaphor at its heart. Metaphors necessarily represent their objects in imperfect or incomplete ways, accentuating certain characteristics at the expense of others. It may be that the metaphor of dialogue is no more than an optional literary device by which reasoning can be depicted, and that other ways of doing so would bring out features that are obscured or distorted in this version. To see whether this is true, let us ask: *How do the IDP's specifically dialogical features affect its function and outcome? Could the same conception of reason be re-stated without the metaphor of dialogue?*

Here it is useful to review the main similarities and differences between the Gentilean and Kantian versions of constructivism. Gentile and Kant both acknowledge that the fact of S being a finite, particular subject, thinking particular thoughts in a context that she does not always fully comprehend, denies her direct access to a purely objective world of things in themselves. They also recognise that to abandon the idea of objectivity altogether, and settle instead for unanchored subjectivity, is to give up on serious inquiry. To make sense of objective reasons despite the impossibility of direct access to them, S must refer to other people, be they real or hypothetical, to find out what they (would) think about whatever problem she faces.[1] The standards of objectivity are imposed by a test of universality, which amounts to a test of whether the judgement would be reached by rational persons assaying the relevant issue from their own points of view. These other people are rational, and their reasons to that extent worth taking into account, if S can recognise that they have good reasons for thinking as they do.

This formula—call it the *anti-realist formula*—is obviously circular. It appears that, in order to determine which persons are rational providers of reasons, S needs some prior standard of rationality. She needs to beg the question for the answer. It is always possible that she, and any or all of the other people to whom she refers, are deeply mistaken about reasons. A serious error at the outset could lead her astray as she tries to establish grounds for objective inquiry. The justificatory process

---

[1] Compare O'Neill's account of Kant: '[Kant says] a thinker "reflects upon his own judgement from a universal standpoint." However, this universal standpoint is no pre[-]established Archimedian standpoint of reason; rather it is one that the thinker constitutes "by shifting his ground to the standpoint of others." The reflexive and this-worldly character of a vindication of reason is here apparent: Reasoned thinking is governed not by transcendent standards but by the effort to orient one's thinking in ways that do not preclude its accessibility to others' (1989) [26].

is, in principle, endless. Kant, along with some of his constructivist interpreters, brings this to a halt by affirming the existence of a single external world and a plurality of persons in it, their thoughts structured to fit the cognitive architecture common to any and every conceivable rational being. Gentile does not deny outright that an external world exists, but argues instead that nothing about the world (or a cognitive architecture that would give rise to purely objective reasons) can be said, and still less known, unless it is mediated by S as she thinks in the continuously unfurling present. Responsibility for the construction of truths is shifted squarely onto S, rather than S and a plurality of other persons who live in and refer to the same world. If the IDP is a doctrine of inter-subjectivity, it is one that grants a peculiarly central role to the one concrete subject.[2] However, this is ultimately an issue of terminology that need not detain us here.[3] Suffice it to say that thinking is all S has to distinguish good reasons from bad ones, so by her own lights she must do the very best thinking she can.

Gentile thinks it is possible to accept the circularity of the anti-realist formula without surrendering the aim of objectivity. An important corollary of this view is that the process of construction, the work of reason, can never be finally completed; knowledge of the truth is something S acquires and loses on the shifting sands of doubt and its perpetual resolution. The metaphor of dialogue enables us to model the open-endedness of this process. Moral reasoning, like reasoning of any kind, requires S to assay the merits of claims that she does not at the outset know to be true. If she always had unmediated, unshakeable certainty in all matters, she would have no need to apply reason.[4] She

---

[2] Here it is tempting to add that S has responsibility for the construction of truths *within her own phenomenological ambit,* or *the world as she understands it,* or *the totality of her knowledge,* or however we style it. However, this addition would be redundant, since on Gentile's account, *there is no standpoint beyond S.* We are all S to ourselves.

[3] If the IDP is an inter-subjective procedure, it represents an unconventional branch of inter-subjectivity in which one concrete subject (S) has a uniquely prominent role, and the others with whom S interacts are understood as abstract entities that exist only inasmuch as S understands them. In this respect, to call the IDP 'inter-subjective' is misleading rather than straightforwardly inaccurate. Some other term like *social subjectivism* may better express its distinctiveness, but again this term might be thought to suggest that Gentile thinks that a social entity (e.g. a group, a society) is a subject. As discussed in previous chapters, he sometimes *suggests* this, but only as a metaphor.

[4] This is not to say that her beliefs would always be true. She might be deeply deluded. What matters is that she believes them to be true and can see no

would have certainty not as the result of having dispelled doubt through careful reflection, but because alternatives do not occur to her; the facts, as far as she can see, consistently conform to her beliefs and expectations. Such a thinker would be highly unusual, though not wholly inconceivable. S might live a closely regulated and unproblematic life in which all decisions are made by others behind the scenes. Circumstances in which she needs to think could be carefully limited in order to prevent doubt from entering her mind. But since actual and at least minimally autonomous subjects typically live alongside others under conditions that are *not* so artificially regulated, reason comes into play whenever S faces a number of options for belief or action, and acknowledges that, viewed from different perspectives, there might be reasons in favour of each. Conscious that she occupies just one of several possible points of view, S is compelled to address the alternatives in order to make sense of an objective world. Thus, recognising her own finitude and the role of reasoning in overcoming it, she is thrown into 'dialogue' with real or merely possible occupiers of those other points of view.[5]

We have seen already that reasoning involves the reconciliation of two abstract parts of S's extended personality. One is her ego, representing what she wants *for herself*, and what she *now thinks*. The other is the socius, or A, which is, or at least grants her access to, her conscience.[6] This reconciliation does not occur without S's conscious intervention. The familiar feeling of regret at having behaved selfishly or against one's better judgement, or in spite of one's *better self*, is testament to this. S can know what reason commands only if she actually, actively thinks, subjecting her own ideas to scrutiny as though they were presented to her by someone else, and the ideas of others (if only hypothetical others) to scrutiny as though they were her own. S arrives at a reasoned conclusion by considering and responding to a range of

---

reason—or, more radically, has no conception of the possibility that there could be a reason—for her to doubt them.

5   This is well expressed by Fred D'Agostino (1993) 'Transcendence and Conversation: Two Conceptions of Objectivity', *American Philosophical Quarterly*, 30 (2), pp. 87–108 [89]: '[I]t follows necessarily and from the bare fact of our *being* oriented to the world that there are a plurality of alternative ways in which we *might* have been oriented. If there is *any* perspective on the world, then there are, necessarily, a *plurality* of alternatives to it. This much is obvious from reflection alone—at least on the assumption of our (relative) finitude in relation to the world.'

6   In questions of theoretical reason, which are not, according to most theories apart from Gentile's, morally significant, the 'conscience' might be substituted by 'S's rational self'.

alternatives to the view she ultimately affirms. In this respect the reasoning process resembles a conversation. Yet it may be objected that the uncompromisingly subject-centred position of thought in actual idealism means that there can be no *real dialogue* whatsoever, since S must be the final arbiter in questions of truth concerning the world that she constructs. Even if S speaks to other empirical people, they present her with reasons only insofar as she recognises them to do so. Being *like* a conversation in some limited respect, we might say, is not enough to justify the use of dialogue as the basis for the whole procedure.

This objection can, I think, be answered. While it seems paradoxical to claim that it is only by addressing the reasons of others that S can properly situate herself in her autonomously constructed world, careful consideration of Gentile's theory shows this paradox to be specious. Unless S has a conception of what *someone else* would or might think about the judgement she is making, even if that second person is an imaginary version of herself and different only in that the alter-ego has settled on an answer to the question S is still considering, S has no standards by which to judge whether her current thoughts are the ones she ought to think.[7] Questions of their value *would not arise*. From moment to moment, S would simply think whatever she thinks, unable to conceive of what *another person would think* (but S herself does not currently think) in the way necessary for her to view her thoughts from the critical distance that objectivity requires.[8] Such distancing occurs whenever S conceives of herself both as an agent thinking in the present and a person with a past and a future (or several possible futures). As S evaluates these imagined alter-egos, herself as she once was and as she will (or could) be, she alters her present convictions and attitudes toward the world around her. Thus she effectively changes something of herself and casts moral judgement on the world as something to be conserved or revised, condemned or condoned. Recognising that this change is an act is the cornerstone of moral thought as Gentile conceives of it. To think otherwise is to be swept along on the outpouring of historical contingency, passively accepting the world as it is and declining to bear part of the responsibility for it.

Despite these grand claims, dialogical thought is remarkably ordinary, and can be seen in persons' most routine reflections. Suppose, for example, that S, writing an account of some historical event, notices

---

[7] Once again I am using 'to think' as a catch-all term that could be extended to beliefs, actions and so forth.

[8] This again reflects Gentile's notion of the way concrete thought is 'imprisoned' in abstract thought, already cited in Chapter 2, herein. As before, see Fabio Gorani (1995) 'Logo concreto e logo astratto nel pensiero di Giovanni Gentile', *Idee*, 28–9, pp. 139–60 [152].

that one of her sentences contains a word that could be understood in several ways. Unless she means to exploit the ambiguity for some other purpose — perhaps as a means to amuse or confuse the reader — she is moved to choose a different word, or else to alter the structure of the sentence, by the thought that its meaning would (or could) appear unclear to a second person, *even though the intended meaning is perfectly obvious to her*. Thus she anticipates and accommodates others' ignorance of her thoughts. To do that she must also have an idea, however inexact, of what they *do* know and think, and of what she could have thought if she had read the same sentence without privileged knowledge of the author's (her) intentions when writing it. She can estimate what they might think because she is a thinker herself, capable of abstracting from and thus objectifying her own thinking.[9]

Dialogue can also be invoked when S does not possess privileged knowledge. Suppose she faces some emergency in which she does not know how to proceed; a friend suddenly falls ill and S is the only person to hand, but she is ignorant of medicine and too panic-stricken to be sure she is thinking clearly and rationally. To determine what she ought to do, she may ask herself how someone else would respond to this situation. Lacking outside help, S cannot conjure a full account of what an experienced paramedic would do, for example, because the relevant information is unavailable to her. She must work with what she has. Her imaginary alter-ego could be a relevant *model* for conduct, as specific as a trusted person who has told her how he acted in similar circumstances, or as general as someone she credits with qualities like decisiveness, composure and common sense.[10]

---

[9] The same principle applies even to mundane tasks like writing shopping lists. S might know *now* what she intends to buy, but she is aware that at some future time she may forget. She imagines her future self appealing to her present self for help, and in response she writes the list. She is using an imagined dialogue to anticipate and address possible errors other people, including versions of herself, might make.

[10] This would also cover people who, faced with a dilemma, turn to the Bible to see what Jesus or some similarly worthy figure would do. They do not seek to understand *why* what Jesus did is the right thing to do; they assume instead that if he did it, it *must* have been so, and must also be the right thing for them. (Thanks to Michael Baxter for suggesting this example in November 2012.) Note also that in *Religione*, Gentile describes the role of heroic examples in moral thinking. The fact that somebody is known to have behaved in a certain way when faced with a certain problem is of no moral significance while S remains a 'passive spectator' on his actions. There is a reason to emulate that person only when S actively identifies him as a model of good conduct, and links his actions with her own. S must feel

These examples show that, while it is a metaphor, the internal dialogue models the ordinary thinking of individual subjects. In some cases the dialogical exchange is more obvious than in others, and S may view many decisions in terms of reasons *simpliciter* without having them expounded by specific agents, imaginary or otherwise.[11] But such reasons can be cast in a suitably constructed dialogue in a way that place-holding reasons of the kind described above — reasons that S only incompletely understands and *assumes* to be valid in the absence of more detailed information — cannot be cast so easily in a strictly rational procedure. Under ideal conditions, a dialogue between fully informed and perfectly rational interlocutors will yield the same conclusion as a purely rational formula applied to the same facts, but since actual persons are not guaranteed to be fully informed and perfectly rational (or, as actual idealism conceives of it, *their constructor*, S, is not), they cannot view the construction as though from the outside while it is still in progress. They must reason as well as they can with the resources available to them, remaining all the while sensitive to any new considerations that arise. In this respect the open-endedness of the dialogue is a manifest strength: it is phenomenologically accurate and workable in plausibly non-ideal conditions. It is fully compatible with conventional rational thinking, but flexible enough to accommodate working assumptions, best estimates and uncertainty in both its workings and its outcomes. The challenge for the rest of this chapter is to show that, despite its open-endedness, the IDP can systematically discipline S's thinking.

2. Internalism and the real world

My version of the IDP so far lacks a detailed account of how the procedure is to be concluded. It also lacks any clear explanation of how the IDP might be used to decide between actions jointly undertaken by

---

her heroes sharing in her struggles and anxieties, reflecting her actions 'like [a] mirror of [her] own person' [91–2].

[11] Take crossword puzzles, for example. It is likely that, where several words could fit a clue's specifications, the solver works out the most plausible answer without any kind of personification taking place. But the crossword solver could ask herself which of several answers the crossword setter would be most likely to use. Say there is an obvious solution to the crossword question in the solver's esoteric regional dialect, but she knows that the setter is probably not from that region — or, at least, that the setter would know that much of his audience would be excluded if he used such an exclusive term. Hence the solver imagines herself as the crossword setter, who (she speculates) would not share her sense of which words most obviously match a given clue.

persons with diverse values and commitments. As noted previously, Gentilean constructivism admits only one concrete subject, so other persons' claims can only become concrete when enacted as *pensiero pensante*. Inter-personal or (more accurately) inter-subjective acts are strictly impossible. But, as Gentile's use of the internal dialogue so vividly shows, the idea of other people remains a persistent feature of socialised subjects' actual thinking. S can imagine points of view other than her own, and although to her these are abstract to the extent that they contradict her own views, they are capable of affecting her and giving her reasons to think something other than what she presently thinks. She feels the weight of others' claims upon her, and thinks of herself as a person among other persons, situated in a shared reality, even if she acknowledges that she cannot truly know subjective experiences other than her own.

This last point is important. It might be thought that Gentile's theory is one of radical internalism, claiming that everything is thought, everything is contained in S, and claims about anything outside S are necessarily abstract or untenable. But the view of Gentile as a thoroughgoing internalist is, I think, mistaken. It presupposes his endorsement of the 'ghost in the machine' myth attributed to Descartes and various other thinkers (chiefly idealists) who conceive of mind and matter in dualistic terms.[12] The IDP's 'internal' location is a metaphor. Strictly there is no brain or body or mind inside which it can take place. While Gentile certainly identifies himself as an idealist, his theory does not entail the strong metaphysical claim that objects of experience are 'made of thought', nor that we can only perceive the 'ideas' of them. Instead he holds we can know the world only by thinking about it, since without thinking, we would be unable to know anything whatsoever, rendering truth claims not only nonsensical but impossible. His claim that subject and object are dialectically linked must not be reduced to a dubious metaphysical claim about the truth of the whole, the oneness of being, or similar. There is no contradiction in the idea that we think of ourselves as belonging to an external world while necessarily positing it in the act of thought.

Donald Davidson has propounded a relevantly similar theory concerning the role of 'triangulation', enacted by two speakers with reference to a single object, as the basis for a plausible conception of objectivity.[13] In contrast to Gentile's theory, Davidson's is explicitly

---

12   Again, this is covered in lucid fashion by Gilbert Ryle (1990) [13–25].
13   Davidson wrote in the analytic tradition, and, as far as I am aware, never expressed any interest in or even knowledge of Gentile. Nor did he dedicate much work to moral theory. His chief interests were the philosophy of mind

externalist. When he refers to 'the second person' he means a *real* second person; he does not seem to take seriously the idea that a single (empirical) person can speak for both sides of a conversation.[14] Nor does he go so far as Gentile in claiming that the world *does not exist* except insofar as it is conceived or thought about. Where Gentile refers to thought or thinking, Davidson tends to refer to language and concepts. Of course, these are not mutually exclusive. Davidson insists that 'languages [are not] separable from souls; speaking a language is not a trait a man can lose while retaining the power of thought.'[15] Much depends on how we conceive of the act of thinking that Gentile describes. We might ask: for Gentile, *what is it to think that P?* Is it to express P as part of a sentence, with the form '[I think that] P'? If so — and I think this is at least a plausible interpretation — the difference between Gentile's thinking and Davidson's speaking becomes trivial. Acts such as willing, believing and holding obligations can be re-cast as Davidson-style 'evaluative attitudes',[16] or as general dispositions to think that P, where P refers to the value of certain states of affairs or kinds of action.

2i. Triangulation and objectivity

Davidson insists that theories like Gentile's result from 'run[ning] together two problems', namely, the problem of knowledge, or of how beliefs are justified; and the 'conceptually prior' issue of how 'the concept of an objective reality' arose in the first instance.[17] I gestured in this direction back in Chapter 2, when I identified the Being There Problem.[18] As I described it, the problem is one of understanding where claims' contents originate, or, alternatively, why subjects think what they think, even when they would rather think otherwise. I noted that this problem risks exposing Gentile's idea of thought's creative and constructive capacities as 'an amplified sort of noticing'. In more formal language, this can be called a problem of *indeterminacy*: since an object's

---

and theories of knowledge, meaning and truth. It is for his insights into these that I take up his work.

[14] Davidson (2004b) 'The Second Person', in *Subjective, Intersubjective, Objective*, Oxford: Oxford University Press, pp. 107–21 [107 and 115n11].

[15] Davidson (1984) 'On the Very Idea of a Conceptual Scheme', in *Inquiries into Truth and Interpretation*, Oxford: Oxford University Press, pp. 183–98 [185].

[16] Davidson (2004a) 'The Emergence of Thought', in *Subjective, Intersubjective, Objective*, Oxford: Oxford University Press, pp. 123–34 [125]; see also Gentile's *Sommario 1* [60–1].

[17] Davidson (1995) 'The Problem of Objectivity', in *Problems of Rationality*, Oxford: Oxford University Press, pp. 3–18 [4].

[18] See Chapter 2, sub-section #4ii, herein.

position in thought is S's first interaction with it, we cannot account fully for how that thought came to be. It makes no sense to refer to the 'origin' of the thought, since that presupposes an unknown position from which the thought may originate, and this is, by definition, outside the ambit of knowledge. In his systematic works, Gentile seems content to accept that the problem is insoluble, since the commonsensical idea of an objective reality is untenable. But as Davidson points out, without an account of an objective reality, there are no grounds on which to say that claims are true or false. Correspondingly, if there were no truths that could persist and be shared by a plurality of possible subjects, the IDP would have no purpose.

Davidson proposes to use the idea of 'triangulation' to open the way for a concept of objectivity in judgements. He writes that 'the objectivity which thought and language demand depends on the mutual and simultaneous responses of two or more creatures to common distal stimuli and to one another's responses.' Triangulation consists of the 'three-way relation among two speakers and a common world'. It is by this process that content is 'bestowed' on language.[19] By speaking, the subject (first person) recognises a second person as party to a shared external world; these three components, the first person, second person and reference point, constitute the 'triangle'.[20] Davidson's aim here is to show how linguistic communication and the ascription of meaning are possible. But at the end of this essay he adds:

> Belief, intention, and the other propositional attitudes are all social in that they are states a creature cannot be in without having the concept of inter-subjective truth, and this is a concept one cannot have without sharing, and knowing that one shares, a world, and a way of thinking about the world, with someone else.[21]

These concluding remarks do not signal a radical departure from Davidson's earlier interest in language. He is simply gesturing toward some areas on which a claim about the inter-subjectivity of language, or meaning, could gain a purchase. While Gentile's IDP, at least as I have presented it, is not about defining the concept or necessary conditions of language, it plainly relies on something like the triangulation procedure that Davidson describes. Truth claims, being claims, are linguistic constructs, and thinkers' attempts to appraise them involve re-stating their contents in different words to see if, after review from a

---

[19] These introductory remarks come from Donald Davidson (2004) *Subjective, Intersubjective, Objective,* Oxford: Oxford University Press [xv].
[20] Davidson (2004b) 'The Second Person', in *Subjective, Intersubjective, Objective,* Oxford: Oxford University Press, pp. 107–21 [120].
[21] Davidson (2004b) 'The Second Person' [121].

variety of perspectives and taking into account different ways of articulating or expressing the same idea, they still make sense. If the socius (A) were conceived as something distinct from S, and unable to refer meaningfully to the objects to which S refers, the whole premise of the IDP would come apart. A could never provide reasons for S to alter her starting assumptions, since A's claims would be irrelevant to S's object of judgement. Subject and socius would be mutually unintelligible.

Davidson assumes, rather like Kant, that the world must be conceived in a certain way. Unlike Kant, though, he does not found this on a theory of mind, but instead on a theory of meaning and interpretation. '[D]ifferent points of view make sense,' he writes, 'but only if there is a common co-ordinate system on which to plot them.'[22] Full-blown conceptual relativism would make communication impossible, but, importantly, any 'common co-ordinate scheme' need be shared only in a general and loose way, subject to the push and pull from differences in interpretation, belief and so forth. We cannot say for certain that 'all speakers of language' share 'a common scheme and ontology'. What this *does* rule out is the idea of an 'uninterpreted reality', existing wholly separate from anything we might say or think about it.[23]

The above remarks contain points of overlap and divergence with actual idealism. Gentile cannot endorse Davidson's theory in quite the way he presents it, since it assumes a readiness to speak of a single object viewed from several empirical persons' subjective points of view. Davidson lacks Gentile's metaphysical baggage, and of course uses different terminology to express his ideas. However, Davidson's point about the impossibility of an 'uninterpreted reality' is close to Gentile's about the absurdity of the doctrine of transcendence. For us to 'interpret' reality (in Davidson's language) is surely for us to 'think' it (Gentile's); it is in saying something about an object, if only to oneself, that one 'realises' the object as a concept. The idea that this claim must be comprehensible to other people is compatible with Gentile's identification of truth and universality, which is, in a sense, the primary motivation for the IDP. To make truth claims about an object requires us to present the claim to another person, even if that second person is only imagined. Those (real or imagined) persons may disagree with our judgements, but in order to expose us as mistaken they must present their reasons in terms that we can understand, and which refer to what we must assume to be a shared, objective world.

---

[22] Davidson (1984) '...Conceptual Scheme' [184].
[23] Davidson (1984) '...Conceptual Scheme' [198].

2ii. Two principles for the IDP

Davidson's way of drawing out the implications of the active nature of thinking can help us understand the workings of the dialogical process. It does us no good to be overly literal when conceiving of the IDP. If I am puzzling over a problem of what I ought to do, and ask myself 'How would Plato answer this question?', I should not be perturbed by the fact that the real Plato would be unable to offer me any comprehensible answer whatever, for the very mundane reasons that I speak a language he could not possibly have known, and I cannot speak ancient Greek. My imaginary Plato, in the IDP, speaks English. I must assume that although I know his arguments only in the words of his translators, there is a world that, despite a two-and-a-half-thousand-year divide, he and I share. His ideas are not only the words in which they are expressed. If they were, they would be erased in the course of translation and re-interpretation. They also have content, and refer to objects—that is, co-ordinates in a system, rather than objects in themselves—that I must assume I can meaningfully re-construct along the same lines as they were intended. As Davidson puts it, the 'method' underlying the idea of the conceptual scheme is 'to make meaningful disagreement possible'. This, he continues, 'depends entirely on a foundation—*some* foundation—in agreement'. Thus 'charity is forced on us; [...] if we want to understand others, we must count them right in most matters.'[24]

Coupling this idea of charity with Davidson's arguments about the necessity of a shared world, then applying both to the Gentilean IDP, we can say that the claims other people make of S, or otherwise present to her for inspection and assessment, must be assumed to have a basis in a world or set of co-ordinates that she also shares. Triangulation is useless to S if she fences off all beliefs contrary to her own as incommensurable with and therefore irrelevant to them, being matters of opinion that are true for their holders but not for her. This works both ways: she cannot hold firmly to her beliefs and censor or ignore dissenters without trying to re-articulate her ideas in terms that they might understand. The IDP forces S to re-state, re-assess and either re-affirm or modify her beliefs in light of superior reasons. Otherwise actual thinking, *pensiero pensante*, would become shackled to *pensiero pensato*, and its constructive capacity, or its capacity to make objective truth claims, would be disabled. It does not matter whether these interlocutors are real (external) or hypothetical, since as providers of reasons these groups are exactly equivalent. A reason offered by another person and understood by S is no different to one that occurs to

---

[24] Davidson (1984) '...Conceptual Scheme' [196–7].

her without their intervention. S's awareness of the fact that another person is real may provide an *additional* reason for or against some course of action. What makes the reason count is not the fact that this person has (or has not) expressed it, but instead that it strikes S as something she cannot afford to ignore while maintaining her faith in her own thinking.[25]

In light of the above observations, we can usefully add to the IDP's design a general *Charity Principle*. This principle stipulates that S must grant A (or, more abstractly, opposing views) a degree of interpretive charity comparable with what she expects others to grant her. She must make a reasonable attempt to justify her claims, or to articulate the relevant claims of others, in terms comprehensible from points of view other than that of the proposing party. This is closely tied with the idea of 'followability' taken from O'Neill and discussed in Chapter 5. No claim can be granted objective status unless it sustains reasonable scrutiny under the principle's conditions. Under this formulation of the Charity Principle, S must decide what degree of interpretive charity is to be granted to interlocutors' claims, how much she (S) expects to receive in turn, and what counts as 'reasonable scrutiny'. Plainly these cannot extend indefinitely, or the IDP's intended endpoint of making (tentatively) objective judgements would never be reached.

One important corollary of the Charity Principle is the idea that S and A (the interlocutor/s) are assumed to be equals in some significant respect. Call this the *Equality Principle*. This principle is not taken as a fact about the actual persons who hold, or are imagined to hold, certain views. It is not a claim about any independent moral fact. Rather, it is an orienting assumption that subjects must make in order for the IDP to supply even nominally objective conclusions. As mentioned before, for S to rule out a range of actual or possible positions *without subjecting them to rational scrutiny* is anathema to the idea of objective judgement. Other people are equal insofar as they attempt to describe the same objective world. Of course, their claims are not equally true, and their supporting arguments are not (necessarily) equally valid. But they must be treated equally at the beginning of the reasoning process.

The Equality and Charity Principles are closely related, and each helps to clarify the purpose of the other and of the IDP as a whole. The IDP may be thought of as a procedure for the abstraction and objecti-

---

[25] This is well illustrated in *Sommario 1* [131]: 'A Chinese [person] will be able to explain clearly to me — I who do not speak Chinese — the most interesting points of wisdom [*una sapienza*] about the forms of life most conducive to my happiness; but, since our activities (our spiritual moments) do not coincide, [her] lesson is not a lesson for me, and has no value. It is not spirit.'

fication of S's actual or concrete thinking. It enables S to present her own reasons and thoughts as though they belonged to someone else. In doing this she gives each of those others a status equal to her own and to each other, ignoring the necessary qualitative difference between her subjective concrete thought and the abstractions in whose terms she thinks. In a surprising and oblique way, the requirement for S to view other people as avatars of reasons actually drives her to grant them a substantive moral status. Now that S is made equal and equivalent to them — she has, as I have put it before, presented herself as a person among persons — she must treat them as she expects to be treated. Thus charity is, as Davidson put it, forced upon her; she cannot knowingly represent another person *uncharitably* because by doing so she would license uncharitable treatment of herself. (These ideas owe much to the Golden Rule, to which I return at the end of the chapter.)[26]

3. Agreement and the IDP

We now have a reasonably clear picture of the IDP's purpose and structure. The procedure models and formalises the reasoning process by which S refines subjective into objective reasons for thought and action. S may consciously employ the IDP when she faces any problem whose solution is not immediately obvious. Alternatively she may use it to check claims that she already assumes to be true. The procedure's principal aim is not to attain purely objective reasons, for those would rely on a false conception of the *logos,* and would not count as reasons for any actual subject. Instead the aim is to place S in relation to an objective world, showing her to be a person among persons with whom she shares common reference points. Only through the recognition of this commonality — obvious, perhaps, to everyone but philosophers — can S make meaningful truth claims about facts and values.

I have also described the endpoint of the procedure. The IDP is (provisionally) completed when S identifies a set of reasons with the universal subject (US), meaning that she (S) thinks she has ruled out 'the possibility that other subjects, or the same subject under different circumstances, would think differently' about the judgement she is making.[27] After this S must 'make [her]self agree'[28] with US, reconciling her concrete thinking with the conclusions to which her reasoning has taken her. Otherwise the conclusion has only abstract value, and S's

---

[26] This chapter, sub-section #4ii.
[27] *Logica 1* [46]. This has been cited already in Chapter 2, sub-section #4, herein.
[28] *Logica 1* [97]. I gave a fuller version of this passage in Chapter 5, sub-section #1i, herein.

concrete thought is incoherent insofar as it contradicts the reasoned conclusion: she has recognised that she does not think what she has the most reason to think. In order to make her beliefs coherent, she must adjust the affected beliefs. But since S remains a *thinking subject*, this still occurs within a complex of grounding assumptions and values already held. There is no guarantee that any two subjects thinking through IDPs will settle on the same conclusion. It is only when a relevant problem or question arises that their differing assumptions need to be challenged.[29]

This account still lacks a clear explanation of the IDP's intermediate stages between S's identification of the need for objective justification and the articulation of US's reasons. How is S to progress through the dialogue? How are interlocutors to be selected, and by what process does S determine that a given reason or selection of reasons (A) is superior to and more objectively justifiable than one that she presently affirms? I contend that these questions can be answered by reference to the idea of agreement. However, this agreement must be carefully designed if it is to be compatible with the IDP as I have so far presented it. The principal difficulty is that S is the only one of the IDP's participants capable of changing its position while retaining a continuous identity. The socius, or A, represents a position that may be occupied by any one of an indefinite number of interlocutors. Any change to the reasons presented by A entails the replacement of one interlocutor with another. It is not necessary for the reasons presented by a series of A-interlocutors to be mutually coherent. The procedure's outcome should be the same regardless of the order in which interlocutors are consulted; the order is determined only by the interlocutor's reasons' relevance to the position S currently holds.[30] Since the content of A's reasons is specified by S, there cannot be any meaningful agreement between them; indeed, the only formal criterion that A must meet is that its reasons *are not identical* to S's, since otherwise they would have nothing to say to one another. Agreement between any A and S is coincidental, even ephemeral, to the point of meaninglessness.

The impossibility of genuine agreement between A and S shows that IDP cannot be a *contractarian* procedure. Nonetheless it remains a *constructivist* procedure. The differences between these are not always obvious, especially since several prominent advocates of the latter

---

[29] There is an obvious analogy between this thought and Rawls' idea of 'the burdens of judgement', described in *Political Liberalism*.

[30] A minor clarification: A's objections are relevant to particular positions that S may adopt. It does S no good to consider an objection that is unconnected to what she currently thinks.

invoke contracts or contract-like procedures in their theories.[31] But there are contractarian doctrines, such as John Locke's, that rest on moral realist premises (e.g. that property is a natural, God-given right). There are also constructivist doctrines that abstract any contract-like procedures to such an extent that disagreement is impossible, or only one (hypothetical) participant is required. (The first stage of John Rawls' constructivist doctrine, laid out in *A Theory of Justice*, has sometimes been characterised in this way.) The two differ in the relative weighting of actual and hypothetical agreements. Contractarians typically prioritise agreements that persons have or could actually have made; constructivists prioritise those that persons, or their idealised representatives, *would* have made if they had the opportunity to do so. Thus the constructivist can derive moral claims about persons who could never really have agreed—two people who are deeply, stubbornly unreasonable and prone to defining their own beliefs as those most opposed to each other's, for example.

3i. Hypothetical agreements and constructivism

Constructivists very often employ the idea of agreement without any actual agreement taking place. One popular method is to invoke a *hypothetical agreement* whereby the legitimacy of a claim is tested against standards to which persons *would* agree if they had the opportunity to do so. If this were a case of working out to what terms actual persons would agree, hypothetical agreement would be, at best, an accurate replica of actual agreement; it would be no more determinate than that. S would need perfect knowledge of the real interlocutors to whom she refers, and their weaknesses (stupidity, ignorance, prejudice, corruption and so forth) would play out in their absence. The question of just which persons should be included in the dialogue would go unsolved, and hypothetical dialogue would yield no more agreement than the real thing. In order that hypothetical agreements can settle upon firm conclusions, constructivists typically introduce artificial elements fitted to idealised choice situations so that a limited number of conclusions, and perhaps only *one* conclusion, is possible. Interlocutors, or parties to the agreement, might be imagined with special characteristics that real persons do not (necessarily) possess: perfect

---

[31] For an interesting discussion of the ways in which some authors (Rawls, Scanlon) claim to offer theories that are both contractarian and constructivist, see Onora O'Neill (2003b) 'Constructivism vs. Contractualism', *Ratio*, 15, pp. 319–31. For an example of a paper explicitly articulating a doctrine belonging to both camps, see Ronald Milo (1995) 'Contractarian Constructivism', *Journal of Philosophy*, 92 (4), pp. 181–204.

rationality, absence of bias, knowledge or ignorance of their own or other interlocutors' circumstances and so on.[32] Thus it is possible to rule out certain reasons as illegitimate, and ideally to increase the likelihood of interlocutors' convergence on a single conclusion — even if this is one they would never have reached if they had tried to reach an agreement with all their contingent characteristics in play.[33]

Against such determinate kinds of hypothetical agreements is the concern that idealisation will 'alienate us from the conclusions drawn from the theory'.[34] I take this to mean that hypothetical agreements are entered not by any real person, but by persons' idealised avatars, which are like real persons plus or minus problematic characteristics or operating in contrived and counterfactual circumstances. There can be no definitive account of what features should be added or excluded, and it is possible that real persons will object that their reasons are artificially 'bleached out' in order to bring about the appearance of unanimous agreement.[35] (The procedure for obtaining agreement may rely on controversial assumptions about whether it is rational to act on one's own interests or in the interests of one's family, for example. A real person who holds an opposing view of rationality may demur that the procedure is unduly biased against her.) If this is right, given their strange origins, hypothetically derived agreements would lack purchase on real persons' lives. As Thomas Hill explains, they 'would be arbitrary and so [their] results would have no moral force'.[36] This would also be true of the IDP if S were entitled to select or exclude any

---

[32] John Rawls employs such agreements in his account of Kantian constructivism, as well as his own theory (the original position as presented in *A Theory of Justice*) based on the same. He designs his procedure so its conclusion would be accepted by any 'fully reasonable rational (and informed) person', *even if no such person exists.* See Rawls (2000) 'Moral Constructivism', in Barbara Herman (ed.) *Lectures on the History of Moral Philosophy*, Cambridge, MA: Harvard University Press, pp. 235–52 [244].

[33] This is well put by O'Neill (1989) [206–10].

[34] This objection has a long pedigree, and appears under different guises in works by, among others, Joseph de Maistre, G.W.F. Hegel and Jean Hampton. My quotation comes from Thomas E. Hill Jr. (2001) 'Hypothetical Consent in Kantian Constructivism', *Social Philosophy and Policy*, 18, pp. 300–29. Note that Hill *does not* think that idealisations necessarily lead to this kind of alienation. He adds that 'hypothetical consent is not merely a weak practical substitute for actual consent in particular cases where actual consent should be the standard' [305].

[35] Many critics have pointed this out, but I take the phrase from Simon Blackburn (1999) 'Am I Right?' (Review of T.M. Scanlon's *What We Owe to Each Other*), *New York Times*, 21/02/1999, [Online], http://www.nytimes.com/books/99/02/21/reviews/990221.21blact.html [Accessed 16/07/2012].

[36] Hill (2001) [305].

A that she pleases. This would allow that the procedure's outcome is a direct result of S's partial preferences as she consciously or unconsciously forces the dialogue toward a pre-determined destination. Such a procedure would fail to satisfy Gentile's test of universality.

It seems that, if the IDP does rely on a kind of hypothetical agreement, we have a choice between a procedure that is (potentially) partial, and therefore unable to attain the universality required for judgements about reasons to hold for persons who do not already hold the relevant beliefs; or one that is artificially impartial, but alienated from the lives of real people and/or (potentially) biased toward certain outcomes as a result of controversial assumptions made in order to even out partial considerations.[37] How to escape this dilemma? Given actual idealism's conception of truth, we cannot reject artificiality wholesale if without it we could never attain even provisionally universal and objective judgements. Although Gentile's theory hinges on a method of immanence and not transcendence, S remains able to use abstract thought to orient and evaluate her current, concrete thinking. Abstract artificiality is not ruled out. What matters is that S accepts that there are *good reasons* to refer to such abstractions rather than what she just happens to think.

The need for abstraction arises whenever S acknowledges that she might be wrong, or that she might later change her mind. She wants her judgements to have the support of reasons that she expects she will still be able to endorse in the future. She enters a hypothetical agreement with (at least) imagined versions of herself; she agrees, in effect, to allow her judgement to be guided by good reasons (i.e. those best suited to universal recognition) and not merely the reasons that now occur to her. So while persons may disagree about what rationality entails, no one would say that the best way to choose principles is to have an irrational person decide. While persons are in many respects unequal, it would be difficult to formulate a general rule to determine which persons ought to have more or less say in the decision procedure. This offers further support to the Equality Principle described earlier. Claims about the moral equality of interlocutors need not reflect any strong metaphysical or moral claim about real persons except so far as they are (potential) reason-bearing thinkers. Similarly, to argue from an artificially contrived position of impartiality avoids the deeply controversial problem of ordering persons' partial claims in any kind of pre-determined hierarchy.

---

[37] Some of the latter concerns were raised in the discussion of the Universal Law Formula in Chapter 5, sub-section #3, herein.

3ii. Verification and the IDP

S and A's hypothetical agreement to submit to the commands of reason may be considered an extension of the agreement between S and US at the end of the IDP. But the procedure's intermediate stages are still inadequately defined. What use can the idea of agreement have for a procedure defined by disagreement? One use, already hinted at in my discussion of the triangulation model of reasoning, is the assumption that *other people agree with us about most things*. Disagreement is significant only where broad and general agreement obtains. S distinguishes a stream of unconnected thoughts from reasoning by reference to what other people would think. If S believes that her sequence of thoughts could be followed by other people who are sufficiently intelligent and informed of the relevant considerations, or by an ideally rational agent, she may legitimately describe the sequence as a *reasoned* one. This positive conception of the IDP's role is analogous to the epistemological principle of *verification:* a claim has greater truth-value if it can be verified, which, with respect to constructed moral claims, entails its (probable) affirmation by other rational persons in like circumstances.

Consider how the IDP might be used as a verification procedure. This interpretation is most useful in instances when S enters the dialogue already fairly confident that she has the right answer to whatever question she has asked. To bolster her confidence, she can present the argument to hypothetical interlocutors in order to confirm that, as far as she can judge, they would have good reason to accept her conclusion.[38] She may be aware that the interlocutors she can imagine do not represent all the arguments there are. The best she can hope for is general *coherence* with the claim contained in her conclusion: the interlocutors cannot abandon their positions and adopt that of S, but at least they are broadly in agreement with her about the most relevant claims. That coherence test entails verification in that presenting claims to an interlocutor involves offering compelling reasons to accept those claims and articulating them in terms the interlocutor would understand. This verificationist version of the IDP is especially useful when S has determined that a particular A has special authority on some issue, perhaps

---

[38] Two points. First, there is a difference between thinking that the interlocutors 'would have good reason' to accept a conclusion and thinking that those same people (if the interlocutors are identified with actual persons) *would* endorse it. Second, subjects can make judgements like this in a wholly self-deceptive way; they say, 'I'm sure [such-and-such] will agree with me!' having forgotten or being ignorant of some fact about the second person that weighs against this claim.

because its reasons represent the consensus of acknowledged experts. (If my doctor tells me that my health would noticeably improve if I halved my intake of cigarettes, I take the fact that he is a doctor to be a reason to believe him. I need not know all the relevant facts about the effects of cigarettes in order for this to count as a reason for me.)[39]

This account of the IDP leaves it vulnerable to the charge of conservative bias or 'parochialism'.[40] Even if S attempts to consider the reasons that persons other than she would offer, her 'process of correction' relies upon 'a prior framework of accepted judgements about reasons'—that is, an existing set of coherent beliefs that she assumes to be true and shared, or sharable, by other rational persons—and so leads to 'a complacent re-affirmation of whatever [she] happen[s] to think'.[41] The range of positions represented in the dialogue does not cover all the possible arguments there are. S can never be certain that there is not an as-yet-unconsidered argument that would conclusively trump all those she has considered. If S is insufficiently imaginative or informed of the facts and possible argumentative positions relevant to the question under scrutiny, and is aware of only a small number of alternatives to her starting assumptions (if she has any), it is unlikely that her conclusions will fall far from the positions she considers. Lacking access to the broad range of interpretive positions required for the dialogue to gain its own momentum, as it were, S is for now restricted to a conservative range of conclusions.

To the charge of conservative bias Gentile (or I) can reply that the IDP does not represent a one-off event for fixing all subsequent judgements. Rather, it represents the best reasoning S can presently manage, rooting out partial, controversial and faulty claims as best she can, given the limits of her knowledge and understanding. The process can

---

[39] To elaborate upon that example: what matters is that I am not party to the considerations behind the doctor's judgement. Reasons can count without me having full knowledge of all the relevant facts; I simply take it on faith that my doctor, whom I have no cause to doubt, knows more about the facts than I do.

[40] 'Parochialism' is D'Agostino's word: 'Those judgements are objective which could be justified to a suitably general audience. Surely, it is not enough, if we are to claim objectivity, merely to have confronted other perspectives and found common cause, in any variety of ways, with their advocates. [...] It will not always be enough, to minimise the risk of parochialism, simply to strike some conversational agreement with the proponents of other perspectives' (1993) [101].

[41] T.M. Scanlon raises these objections to 'coherence theor[ies] of reasons for action', and particularly John Rawls' conception of reflective equilibrium. See Scanlon (1998) *What We Owe to Each Other*, Cambridge, MA: Belknap Press [70].

and must be re-enacted over and over in light of new considerations and changing events. Indeed, it is never entirely completed. We speak of separate dialogues for the sake of convenience, but really there is *one dialogue* that continuously unfolds in line with actual thought. S is not committed to the wholesale endorsement of any claim put forward at the beginning of the procedure. The dynamic of constant adjustment and re-appraisal, or what Fred D'Agostino calls 'reflectivity', is central to the idea of the IDP as a dialogue, rather than the rational selection of one among several pre-conceived options.[42]

A further difficulty emerges from the charge of conservatism. I mentioned before that a subject who was ill-informed, unimaginative or confused might struggle to give the IDP much momentum. By that I meant that if S were unable clearly to articulate her reasons for holding the view she means to defend, the range of possible conclusions would be limited by the small number of coherent and appropriately configured[43] opposing views she considers. Under these circumstances, it may be plausibly objected that to ascribe objective status to any claim is absurdly premature. After all, S may recognise the inadequacy of her materials, and know that for now, any conclusion she reaches cannot be much more than her best estimate. But this is still a qualified estimate; and provided that it is kept available to be re-thought, re-appraised and adjusted in the course of *pensiero pensante*, it is the truest claim she can justifiably make. Gentilean objectivity does not presuppose correspondence with a transcendent realm of facts, but instead maximal coherence with the best thought S can muster.

3iii. Falsification and the IDP

The IDP's strengths are more clearly displayed if it is understood as a procedure by which S tries to find persuasive reasons to think that her present beliefs *are not* justifiable. This avoids the basic problem of the necessary differences between S and A. What is now at issue is not whether most people would agree with S's judgement, even if this agreement can be at best approximate, but instead whether *any* A can provide widely acceptable reasons to doubt that S's claims, and the reasons that support them, are justifiable. This gives greater prominence to the actual idealist conception of value (goodness and truth) as constructions of a self-conscious subject who at once affirms them and

---

[42] D'Agostino (1993) [101].
[43] By 'appropriately configured' I mean that the opposing A-views should be designed so as to challenge S in the most effective ways possible. If S lacks a clear idea of what she thinks and why she thinks it, she will not be able to identify or articulate correspondingly detailed objections.

denies their opposites. In simpler, less Hegelian language, this means that for a claim to be actively and meaningfully recognised as *true*, S must also conceive of what its truthfulness rules out. Similarly a moral claim must be non-arbitrarily selected from a range of options, with S finding good reasons in favour of choosing it. Since in the IDP it is not possible for A to resemble S exactly, S may more fruitfully consider a range of reasons *against* her continuing to support whichever claims about truth or reasons she presently affirms. S can have confidence in reasons that are defensible against the widest possible range of objections.

Just as the positive, agreement-based conception of the IDP is analogous with the principle of verification, so the negative conception is analogous with falsification. A claim is objectively true if there are no widely acceptable reasons for rejecting it. In moral theory, this negative conception is characterised by tests of whether an action would be *wrong* and not whether it would be *right*. Of all the recent Anglo-American constructivists, T.M. Scanlon is best known for advocating such a principle. He argues that an action is wrong 'if its performance under the circumstances would be disallowed by any set of principles for the general regulation of behaviour that no one could reasonably reject as a basis for informed, unforced general agreement'.[44] This principle differs from the kinds of hypothetical agreement described previously in that it avoids any appeal to kingdom-of-ends-style idealisation. The aim is to establish the absence of any clinching objection rather than universal agreement; this determines that an act (or thought, or reason) is not wrong, rather than certainly right. In terms of the IDP, all that is required is for some A to present S with a compelling (reasonable, followable) reason to think that her action should be rejected. For example, it could be that A identifies an instance of incoherence in S's beliefs, meaning that what S now proposes to do or consider objectively justifiable is inconsistent with something she already recognises as true. As suggested in my discussion of Davidson, such inconsistencies may only become apparent after S has rehearsed a variety of different interpretations of the act she proposes to perform. Again she is compelled to adjust her beliefs and reasons to bring about the greatest possible coherence. The specific content of this coherent set is determined by S's conception of what other people would think about her judgement. For a claim to count as a reason for S, it must *compel her to act upon it*. Just as noticing that one holds two mutually contradictory beliefs provides a reason to reconsider which (if either) is

---

[44] Scanlon (1998) [153].

true and which is not, the identification of reasons as reasons is integral to the dynamic of self-correcting, self-conscious *pensiero pensante*.

This version of the IDP once again demonstrates the procedure's plausible phenomenological basis. Abstraction is required only as S surveys a range of objections that others might make. She distinguishes relevant from irrelevant objections using standards that she recognises in her own thinking: they are objections that she could imagine herself making if she were someone else. At no point does she abandon her subjective standpoint, which can, after all, encompass both concrete and abstract thought. Thus, to use another metaphor, the IDP enables S to turn over her reasons and examine them from a variety of different angles, seeing how they would look from other perspectives without changing her own position.

4. Inter-personal applications of the IDP

There is another way in which the IDP might be used to derive some kind of agreement. This is as a model of inter-personal agreement, on which theme I have touched only in passing so far. As mentioned, the IDP cannot be called a convential inter-subjective procedure because in it there is only one concrete subject who constructs the other interlocutors for herself. S can imagine, with good reason, that other persons are subject to their own IDPs, but she, as concrete subject, cannot be party to any IDP other than her own. This problem stands even if she thinks of herself, in a commonsensical way, as one subject among others. I mean to argue that, despite this apparent problem, the procedure may still be used to generate genuine inter-subjective reasons.

4i. 'Stacking' and objectivity

While S cannot be directly party to other persons' thoughts and subjective experiences, nothing in Gentile's doctrine excludes the possibility of her referring indirectly to them, or to their attempts at achieving objectivity in their judgements. She can ask other people what they think about a given problem, and what conclusions they have reached after due consideration. Thus those other people can be re-admitted to S's IDP, offering (presumably) stronger and more sophisticated arguments in favour of their chosen positions than they did when the S first considered what they might argue. One salient difference between these interlocutors and those conceived as personal, partial and so forth, is that those who have engaged in an IDP procedure, or rigorous reasoning, can try to present their arguments in impersonal and (tentatively) objective terms. Both S and interlocutor are referring to the same abstract object, namely, an objective truth supported by a complex of reasons to which both have access. Both are trying to articulate *good reasons*, or reasons for *both of them*, rather than reasons that are merely *theirs*.[45] Thus there is scope, at least, for a solution to the problem of the incommensurability of different subjects' reasons. Once subjects agree on a shared (or sharable) conception of objective truth, grounded on good reasons, they can construct new features of a (shared) reality on behalf of persons to whom they have not directly referred, and justify its content on an impersonal basis. This kind of objectivity does not refer to some unattainable, transcendent object, of course. It is instead the best impression of objectivity that subjects can construct from the best thinking they can manage. It may be replaced by better reasons at some later time, but for *now*, in the ever-unfurling present, it serves as a workable model of objective truth.[46]

Figure #4 models an inter-personal application of the IDP. Two subjects, Sa and Sb, each conduct the process as before (IDPs #1 and #2). Each then presents the other with her conclusions, *viz.* the reasons attached to the US as she conceives of it. This enables each (Sa in this diagram) to run through the procedure again, having 'stacked' the other's strongest reasons (USa and USb, respectively) as the first pair of interlocutors, in the positions formerly occupied by PS and A_1. Thus it is possible to attain a higher level of objectivity than before (USc).

---

[45] I owe this useful distinction to Peri Roberts.

[46] There is a clear parallel between this version of the IDP and Rawls' 'reflective equilibrium'. Although the IDP is designed to minimise the risk of subjects' alienation from the results of their investigations, it does not rule out the possibility that such alienation with occur. It may be that S's conception of reason in its pre-procedural comprehensive doctrine is at odds with the impersonal reasons that emerge from the IDP. For such a subject, the 'burdens of judgement' (Rawls' phrase) may be unbearable. She may then struggle to reconcile herself with what she has demonstrably good reason to accept, or (irrationally) reject any moral or political demands premised on those reasons. It is even possible that many, most or all persons in society share this response. If this were to occur, the prospects for a persisting, stable and orderly society, built on coherent and widely recognised principles, look doubtful. The claims emerging from the IDP would have only abstract value. See Rawls (1980) 'Kantian Constructivism in Moral Theory', *Journal of Philosophy*, 77 (9), pp. 515–72.

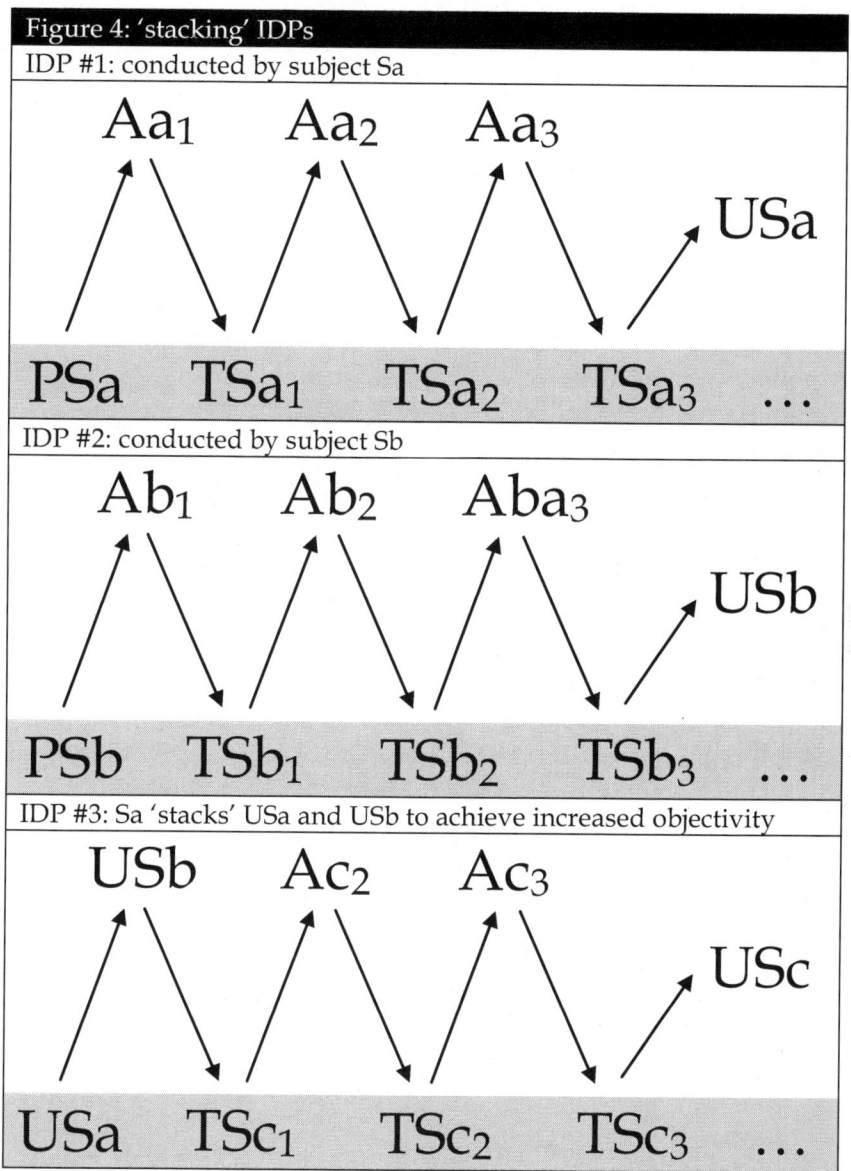

As hinted in previous chapters, the idea of *constructed objectivity* is a major theme in several Kantian philosophers' works. Most notable of these authors is John Rawls, who intends his original position thought experiment to generate principles of justice, which might be thought of as meta-ethical principles for the governance of subsequent agreements. On Rawls' view, the principles do not impinge on persons' substantive beliefs or 'comprehensive conceptions' of the good life. The agreement taking place behind the veil of ignorance is meant to answer only one narrowly defined question, namely, what principles would best define just social institutions. If similar conclusions can be drawn out of the Gentilean IDP, it may be possible to wrest authority out of the grip of some arbitrary figure (*viz.* the socius as the *uomo fascista*) and to locate stronger orienting principles for the design of society. This would give rise to a distinction between what Rawls calls 'the right and the good', or between 'a political conception of justice and a comprehensive religious, philosophical, or moral doctrine'. Rawls' political conception of justice 'is formulated not in terms of any comprehensive doctrine but in terms of certain fundamental intuitive ideas viewed as latent in the public political culture of a democratic society'.[47]

Gentile does not address these distinctions directly, at least in the sense that he does not define 'the right' (*il diritto*) and 'the good' (*il bene*) in the same way as Rawls. In Italian the term '*diritto*' has a broader meaning than the English term 'right', and covers right in the various senses of propriety, entitlement (e.g. a legal right) and, less familiar in English, the whole gamut of legal culture.[48] As such the word, when referred to as an abstract noun, carries a stronger legal connotation than the English words 'right' and 'justice', which can also be used to refer to moral entitlements or configurations of normative claims without any specifically judicial implications. However, there is enough material in his *Filosofia del diritto* to re-construct a plausible account of how Gentile would characterise the relation between the right and the good in terms commensurable with the Rawlsian-Kantian version sketched above.

Goodness, as we have seen, consists in the value assigned by S to some end or object. It is the product of S's act of willing some state of affairs into existence. In order to be will, rather than velleity, claims underwriting it must pass coherence tests according to S's conception of her own character and the beliefs she holds. The reasons for holding a given set of values may be wholly personal, contingent or loosely conceived. The right (*diritto*) extends this conception of goodness by subjecting it to more rigorous tests from an increasingly impersonal (though never completely objective) standpoint. Reasons given in its favour are *good reasons* in the sense that they are strong, widely applicable, and would be judged as such by persons at a wide range of hypothetical standpoints.[49]

---

[47] Rawls (1988) 'The Priority of Right and Ideas of the Good', *Philosophy and Public Affairs,* 17 (4), pp. 251–76 [252].

[48] See Chapter 4, sub-section #1, herein in which I note that Harris translates *Filosofia del diritto* as *Philosophy of Law*.

[49] This is a reasonably charitable interpretation of Gentile's meaning. See *Diritto* [67 and 73–5].

On Gentile's account, then, the right and the good are not independent categories of value. They are dialectically linked: one is a refined and depersonalised extension of the other. This does not mean that, through the IDP, S's conception of goodness is replaced by a conception of right. The two exist simultaneously, just as S exists (abstractly) as ego and (concretely) as universal *pensiero pensante*. In other words, S remains a person among other persons, and need not permanently erase her particular and contingent characteristics in order to imagine what she would think without them. She may revise or abandon certain of her values and dispositions in light of insights gained from her constructed impersonal standpoint. But her powers to do so need not, and indeed *cannot*, be limitless. Otherwise she would be lost in the abstraction of the kingdom of ends, 'breath[ing] the pure air of moral life' without having any real life to lead. Were there no opposition, no 'disvalue' (*disvalore*) and no possibility of change, there could be no value and no binding moral claims. There are reasons that are good for S and others that are good for both S and interlocutors with other points of view. The range of relevant interlocutors can be extended indefinitely, but the procedure cannot yield permanent foundations for all possible persons without being brought prematurely to a halt by means of some abstraction that disregards the contingency and finitude of actual thinking.

4ii. Persons and principles

A further major clarification is in order. It may yet be thought that Gentilean constructivism is exclusively concerned with meta-ethical problems, and particularly that of how it is possible for S to apply and be bound by moral claims when she is the only concrete subject in a universe of her own construction. We have seen that Gentile's method of immanence denies him some of the more obvious answers to this allegation. He cannot endorse any account of transcendent, freestanding, unconstructed moral facts. His understanding of transcendence means that this is also true of moral claims based on social convention or some other process occurring independently of S's thinking. Although there are good reasons to suppose that moral standards arise in this way—this is how a sociologist or anthropologist might account for them, for example—S must recognise and impose them upon herself if they are to be concrete and binding *for her*, rather than abstractions applicable only to merely possible persons. Another implication of the actual idealist method of immanence is that we *must* endorse a thoroughgoing constructivist theory about morality (and, for that matter, every kind of truth and knowledge). No other option is tenable. In that respect Gentilean constructivism may be thought of as a vindication of constructivism *per se,* and especially of the constructivist conception of objectivity as the product of a universalising procedure.

It is not clear that Gentilean constructivism can generate substantive solutions to any actual problem S might face. Strikingly absent from the theory is any decisive principle by which S can *test* whether a proposed action is justified. Kantian constructivism employs the categorical imperative as precisely such a test: maxims are either compatible with it, however its demand for universality is formulated, or not. We saw in Chapter 5 that Gentile must endorse *something like* the categorical imperative, although he is unable to endorse any of Kant's various formulations of this principle in quite the ways they are presented. Chapter 6 gave us an account of how we can make sense of the idea of moral claims that are at once constructed by S and some external source (the state, the teacher or society, which, viewed through the IDP, amount to the same thing), and the present chapter has extended that theory to show, if only formally, how S goes about distinguishing good (sharable, impartial, universal) reasons from bad (non-sharable, partial, particular) ones. But it is still left to S to recognise and respond to good reasons, so it may be objected that Gentilean constructivism cannot deliver what it promises. The purported universality of the IDP's conclusion is universal only among people with whom S already shares a set of substantive beliefs about reasons. If we concede this objection, but reply that *any claim to be rational must be underpinned by some such substantive beliefs*, it may be further objected that Gentilean constructivism appears practically indistinguishable from, and presents no objection to, the more radical Kantian constructivisms, like that of Onora O'Neill.[50]

Several questions arise. Does Gentilean constructivism give us such a test? What kinds of action, if any, does it *rule out*? Is there anything that S is categorically *not permitted* to do? To find an answer, let us consider Gentile's account of good and evil in *Genesi*. Among the stranger features of actual idealism is that it gives us an account of *goodness* but no strong account of *badness*. Evil is not different in kind from good, but is rather its absence; the relation between them is no different from that between falsity and truth, error and correctness.[51] Gentile sometimes

---

[50] Note that here I single out O'Neill because, unlike Rawls, Scanlon or Hill, she purports to be a constructivist 'all the way down' (Korsgaard's phrase) about both practical and theoretical reason. Although Gentile's moral theory bears a resemblance to Korsgaard's, especially in the central role it assigns to autonomy, the dialogical elements of the IDP place it closer to O'Neill, who uses the principle of 'followability' to similar effect.

[51] At this point it is worth recalling the *positivity* of Gentile's doctrine, which was discussed in Chapter 2, herein.

equates goodness with spiritual activity *per se,* which might be thought to rule out any possibility of wrong-doing.[52] If whatever S does is good by virtue of being done, and only the present is concretely real (and, by extension, available for moral evaluation), she cannot possibly do wrong.[53]

This conclusion rests on a mistaken conception of what Gentile means by his admittedly elusive concept of spiritual activity. The logic of the theory imposes some formal restrictions on what S may do. In particular, she must not behave *hypocritically* or *arbitrarily.* To act morally, she must subject her deeds to appropriate scrutiny, attempting always to square them with her moral convictions, even while these convictions may themselves be revised to ensure maximum coherence. This is one function of the IDP. S must not accept convenient assumptions as permanently or indisputably true; she must not be intellectually dishonest, for that would undermine the very idea of truth on which her beliefs and her 'faith in thinking' are founded. What matters above all is that S freely and consciously *chooses* her actions, participates in the betterment of the world, and takes responsibility for what she does.[54] These are all formal demands rooted in Gentile's coherence theory of truth, and concern S's orderly and systematic treatment of her own ideas and actions. The Equality and Charity Principles similarly urge S to treat the IDP's interlocutors equally and charitably *because they represent reasons*, not because they, or the persons on whom they are modelled, have independent moral status.

We have yet to answer the objection. Kantian constructivists may equally say that actions (or maxims) are assigned their moral value as they pass through the categorical imperative procedure. Gentile's claims that, first, the procedure must be applied while the action is

---

[52] In *Diritto* [67], for example, he writes that 'The good [...] is the value of the spirit in its dialectical actuality and [...] the real [*maggiore*] concreteness of spiritual reality. [...] The spiritual act is moral inasmuch as [it is the] realisation of the spirit; and the negation of morality cannot therefore be conceived as a real moment of the life of the spirit without coming into the concept of spiritual development.'

[53] In *Genesi,* Gentile writes that 'The truth is that evil, sin, guilt, like any error, is that anguished root from which life, in all its manifestations, grows; [it is] that nullity that plays havoc [*vaneggia,* raves] in the depths of the human soul when [someone] comes to a halt, pauses, and is uncertain of how to go on. Then, as it is well said, he loses heart, feels himself diminished, or dying inside. That is: his true life is diminished, and he yearns to escape this nullity and renew his grip on reality' [52-3]. Note that I have altered the structure of this sentence to clarify its meaning.

[54] *Genesi* [51–5, but especially 52]; Harris translation [116–20, but especially 117].

ongoing and, second, conclusions cannot be drawn with more than provisional certainty, are of trivial importance if the procedure yields no conclusions, being conducted in S's private internal world in isolation from other real persons.[55] It would be a disappointing outcome for this book if it turned out that any aspiring Gentilean constructivist must appeal to Kantian constructivism whenever she wants to know what to do. When all its superfluous features are cleared away, Gentilean moral theory would constitute a redundant justification of a Kantian theory—not quite Kant's, admittedly, but one in the Kantian mould—that supports itself perfectly well in any case.

I do not think that this sombre assessment can be right, but it is difficult to make confident claims about what Gentile's theory implies for the S-independent status of other, actual, external persons. Any such persons are necessarily beyond the ambit of moral inquiry, for any such inquiry, if it is to count, *is necessarily S's*. The political state can go some way toward solving this problem by defining the formal status of citizens in law, which would imply that if S identifies the political state with the transcendental state, she is morally committed to treating compatriots as the law requires. But even this is not a satisfactory reply to the objection, since after all, the state's laws are available for revision, and there is no guarantee that they will define the rights and responsibilities of citizens in a way that S considers rationally justifiable. Nor is there any guarantee that the persons with whom S interacts are her compatriots. While it may be denied that non-compatriots have any moral status, this would be starkly at odds with a moral theory premised on thinking. Anyone capable of thinking or otherwise behaving in a rational way may be represented in the IDP. Surely if other people have any moral status, it is because S perceives them as rational creatures (in the sense that they are capable of giving S *followable reasons*), not because, or at least not exclusively because, they think they belong to some particular political community. S may find compatriots' reasons more transparent and easily followable than those of non-compatriots, and the existence of shared institutions and cultural references—their greater familiarity, in short—means that S is better placed to anticipate their reasons. But in none of these cases do we need a jointly posited political entity to generate moral truths. Instead the key is mutual comprehensibility. Supposing S is a recent immigrant to a new state, say, it would be bizarre to assume that she understands her compatriots, who are strangers to her, better than she

---

[55] To be clear: the problem is (colloquially) that the IDP can never reliably *seal the deal*, which is not quite the same as saying that it can yield no conclusions whatsoever.

understands her old friends and family members in her original state. The relevant commonalities straddle national boundaries.[56]

The politicisation of the internal society takes us only so far. It is not yet a principle. Are any substantive demands inferable from the two principles governing S's management of the IDP? Consider first the Charity Principle, which, in the IDP, stipulates that S must grant interlocutors or opposing views a degree of interpretive charity comparable with what she expects them to grant her, and attempt to justify her claims, or to articulate the claims of others, in terms comprehensible from points of view other than her own.[57] This principle expresses the imperative for S to overcome her partial and particular nature in order to attain an appropriately 'impersonal' standpoint from which universal judgements, to which class all true moral judgements belong, can be cast.[58] Plainly my formulation of this principle owes much to Davidson and O'Neill, but it should not be forgotten that Gentile identifies the categorical imperative with the Christian command to 'love thy neighbour as thyself'.[59] These, he claims, are respectively modern and ancient expressions of the 'supreme ethical law', and as such are mutually equivalent. The significance of both, he thinks, is in the idea that the moral law is imposed by S upon herself: she views herself as one among others, and enters a reciprocal, moral relation to each of them, *even though she is the only concrete thinking subject*. To love her neighbour as herself, she must love herself as she does her neighbour. The two must be treated alike if their differences are to be resolved into

---

[56] Again, this is well illustrated by Gentile's description of Italian immigrants to the United States in *Educazione* [14]; Bigongiari translation [10]. This citation was given earlier in a footnote: see Chapter 3, sub-section #2i, herein.

[57] I have slightly altered the wording from my earlier account of the Charity Principle.

[58] *Sommario 2* [31n]: 'The true judgement (like the beautiful poem and the good action, and everything that expresses the life of the spirit, and for that reason [*perciò*] has a value) is always impersonal, not because it is not incarnate in a person (or rather, is not the incarnation of a person), but because thought in act is universal. It is true that truth has a value independent of the mortal man who discovers it, whereas it [truth] survives, [and is] immortal, all the more universally recognised so long as it is less tied to particular names [*nomi*] and cases; but it is also true that all this has a significance because it implies that the truth forever rises up again [*rigermoglia*: re-sprouts, re-grows, re-germinates] in the immortal spirit that makes itself author and guarantor of it.'

[59] King James Bible [Mark 12: 31]. This is arguably a version of the Golden Rule, which might be more simply expressed as 'do as you would be done by'; from this point forward, whenever I refer to 'the Golden Rule', I assume that either phrase can be understood by it.

a single universal spirit, united in the empire of impersonal reason.[60] This amounts to a further vindication of the Equality Principle.

With the Golden Rule as a guide, we can lead Gentilean constructivism out from its resolutely internal starting position and into the real world. S always has reason to treat others (or rather, *any other*; each thinking person imposes a separate claim upon her) in a way that she would want to be treated, given her understanding of how others think and how she differs from them.[61] Through the IDP she can appeal to more detailed and particular reasons in order to manage the problems of conflicting interests that have traditionally dogged such theories. A contrived example: if S sees that she has the opportunity to prevent some stranger from enduring an imminent meaningless and painful death, she plainly ought to do so. But if S sees that she has the opportunity to save one (though not both) of *two* strangers simultaneously facing the same fate, she faces a problem of justification: each potential victim has an equal claim to be saved, and the satisfaction of either entails the dissatisfaction (painful death) of the other. Under such circumstances, S must weigh up further reasons — the comparative risks involved in saving one rather than the other, the age and health of the potential victims, or any of countless others — in order to justify her ultimate decision. Unlike Kantian constructivism, there is no expectation that all the relevant facts will be considered. Instead S must act; unlike philosophers contemplating abstract examples, she does not have the luxuries of time and privileged knowledge.

A final point. Early in this chapter I stressed the 'open-endedness' of dialogical reasoning, and suggested, somewhat tentatively, that with regulations to keep the procedure from becoming hopelessly indeterminate, this could be a strength. The intervening discussion has revealed a further advantage of this open-ended method. One common objection to moral theories grounded in universality, objectivity and impartiality says that they stand to alienate subjects from their actual commitments. The levels of artifice and abstraction required to model these ideals make the relevant persons appear decidedly unreal. We have seen that S may run a reason through an indefinite number of stacked IDPs, making it progressively objective and impersonal. But since the IDP's endpoint is identified as S's *considered conviction*, it could be that increased impersonality and objectivity will make it more difficult or even impossible to accept. The procedure for cementing

---

[60] *Religione* [87–8].
[61] I include this last clause in anticipation of the objection that S may be a sadomasochist or suicidal. These facts do not (unless she genuinely thinks that all others share her inclinations) entitle her to inflict pain or kill people.

considered convictions could lead in the wrong direction, making it harder, not easier, for S to affirm the conclusions to which she is led. It is also unclear where this stacking process ought to end. If it could legitimately be brought to a halt after *any* number of re-iterations, would it not also be legitimate for S to stop it after just one, or even a cursory reference to a weak objection?

The former problem contains a solution to the latter. The procedure extends as far as is required for S to reach a considered verdict. If she reasons in isolation, making decisions that affect only her, she need only satisfy her own self-conscious objections. This does not mean that she may bring the procedure to a halt wherever she chooses. Indeed, by *choosing* to bring it to a premature conclusion with objections outstanding, she is consciously complicit in her own self-deception. She knows that the conclusion at which she has arrived is not (necessarily) the one that she ought to affirm, and she is not, until all the known objections are addressed, thinking as well as she can. Nonetheless, and as we have seen, the procedure's endpoint is at best provisional. It is true that S's deliberations with other people, modelled here on the 'stacking' of different persons' IDPs in a higher-level procedure, may bleach out features of S's reasons that made them especially attractive to her when she first considered them, and it may be that, if the IDP's interlocutors, including S, have beliefs so divergent and particular that they cannot be followed and affirmed by all the participants, then no good reasons will be reached. However, this does not mean that every application of the IDP is bound to lead to this justificatory dead end. Even for an individual subject, the scope of justification is limited by the terms that the relevant persons are able to accept. Hence the reasons binding a large group of persons or an institution may be different to those binding individual members or smaller subsets of those groups when viewed individually. A wider or narrower range of reasons may be taken into account as circumstances require.

5. Conclusion

As with construction in the real world, the assembly of a philosophical edifice begins dramatically. Ambitious claims are set out, old ideas are demolished, and bold new structures are put in place. The concluding stages are less spectacular, but of no less importance. As with the unglamorous but necessary tasks of sweeping up, painting walls and checking a building for structural integrity, this chapter has been concerned with fine correction and detail.

I began by justifying the use of a dialogical metaphor in place of a more conventional single-subject conception of thought. I argued that the IDP has several features that make it particularly well suited to the kinds of justification undertaken by the actual, finite subjects who face moral choices. Chief among these features is the dialogue's capacity to model the way in which S may draw judgements after viewing a set of reasons from a variety of abstract standpoints, including those of S herself, imagined in counterfactual circumstances or at another point in time. The dialogue also clearly models the way in which S conducts the reasoning process by asking herself questions and rehearsing prospective answers to them. This, I argued, counters the charge of indeterminacy that can be made against coherence theories of truth. Next I discussed the role of dialogue in making sense of an external world about which objective claims can be made. I argued that for dialogue to fulfil this role, S must assume that other people, including abstractly conceived interlocutors, agree with her most basic beliefs about the composition of the world. This observation yielded the Charity Principle and, extending on themes hinted at in previous chapters, the Equality Principle. Together these regulate the IDP and enable S to scrutinise candidate reasons in a reasonably impersonal and impartial manner.

The chapter's second half concerned the role of agreement in the IDP. I argued that it is most effective as a falsification procedure, since its participants cannot refer to the outside world from within the bounds of the dialogue. This gives rise to a conservative bias, certainly, but this is mitigated by the indefinite status of the procedure's conclusion, which can only ever be the best S can currently devise, but can never be enshrined as a permanent and necessary feature of all subsequent thought. Again it is by shifting between standpoints that S can test each set of reasons in the coherent set she currently affirms. I showed how the IDP allows S to open the critical distance required for her to scrutinise her beliefs in this way *without* requiring—or, at least, reducing the need for—the kind of abstraction that would cause her to become alienated from her conclusions. At the end of the chapter I discussed the way in which the IDP can be applied by multiple thinkers in order to achieve the high level of objectivity required to justify political and social action. This is achieved by 'stacking' the conclusions of individual subjects' IDPs. Thus the internal dialogue can be used to model the reasoning of groups or institutions that cannot think independently of the individual subjects that compose them.

One interesting corollary of this chapter is the thought that Gentilean constructivism might be able to operate in the context of political institutions other than the state, or even in the absence of any formal political institutions whatsoever. It certainly appears that Gentile took for granted that the empirical state prevailed, providing the firm authority, order and guidance needed for actions to be morally justified and carried out on behalf of a group. This assumption is understandable. Just as authors writing today often design their theories to fit the constellation of political institutions that currently exist, including but not restricted to states, Gentile wrote with a world of discrete states, and especially Italy, in mind. Nonetheless, I believe that he relies more heavily on this political conception of ethics than his moral theory requires, and his dismissal of the idea of a stateless or asocial person as an empiricist's fantasy in fact makes too little of his theory's potential to be applied to the less rigidly state-centred world in which we now live. What emerges very clearly from his political work is a deep anxiety about the fragility of order and its attendant benefits. It is in response to that that he insists on the need for the state to impose and safeguard order, rather than relying on it to arise organically. Given the turbulent politics of the period in which he lived, it should come as no surprise that someone so committed to the development of Italian national culture should have had such concerns. But those problems, historically interesting as they may be, need not concern us. Perhaps we now have the luxury to imagine our political and cultural institutions holding together without a steely and uncompromising authority figure tethering them to a common centre.

Let me put it plainly. Gentilean constructivism, at least as I construe it, does not presuppose the existence of any particular political institution. S may be a prominent politician or a lonely castaway, a democrat or a dictator—provided that she is a dictator who responds appropriately to reasons. For her to act as a moral agent, she must work always to reconcile herself with the demands imposed upon her by other people; she must try, in other words, to justify her thoughts and actions using the best reasons she can find. The possibility that she is *radically mistaken* about these reasons makes no sense from within her phenomenological ambit: the reasons are what she makes them. All that Gentilean constructivism requires, by way of institutions, is S's conception of herself as one person among others, and the path she follows through life as just one among many that she might have taken. That is the basis for Gentile's view of the person as a social animal, which in turn is the basis for his view of the person as a moral and philosophical animal, too. Only by conceiving of herself in this way can she distinguish herself as a free and autonomous agent, as the master of her own fate, rather than a passive subject of a 'blind fortune' over which she has no control.[62] To whatever political institutions, if any, she finds herself bound, she must try always to justify her actions (and theirs to her) as *good reasons*. Any action will prove more difficult to

---

[62] *Religione* [121].

justify when referring to people who deeply disagree with her beliefs about what reasoning entails.[63] But on the Gentilean account I have presented here, no one may be excluded out of hand from the scope of concern; the contingent facts of empirical politics do not dictate who is in and who is out of the transcendental state, of which there is only one for each of us. This point is obscured, I think mistakenly, by Gentile's insistence that the state, as political institution, constitutes the outer limit of an individual's social identity.

---

[63] I note in passing that this point seems to explain the persistence of the communitarian impulse in ethics: we cannot rely upon everyone thinking enough like us for them to accept the reasons we offer on their behalf, so we restrict the scope of concern, often along crude and arbitrary lines, to people who share with us some common ground, such as a language, a culture or a commitment to specific values.

Part III.
Giovanni Gentile and the State of Contemporary Constructivism

Chapter 8

Conclusion

In Chapter 1 I set myself three objectives. These were:

i. ...to discover not what Gentile's philosophy meant for him and his contemporaries, but what it could mean for us.

ii. ...to describe a kind of moral constructivism that stands as an alternative to the dominant Kantian variety; and

iii. ...to rehabilitate Gentile as a major moral and political philosopher whose ideas can be fruitfully applied to contemporary analytic normative theory.

I claimed that, while these aims could be achieved separately,[1] they were closely interconnected, so I would try to meet all three over the course of the book. At last I am in a position to gauge my success in doing so. To achieve this I will need to take a broad view of what has gone before. This chapter begins with a summary of the main arguments in Parts 1 and 2 (sub-heading #1). Over the remainder of the chapter I discuss the merits and shortcomings of the actual idealist moral theory I have presented. The major points covered, in order, are: a summary assessment of actual idealism, comparing what it promises with what it delivers, and finding that these are more modest (and less disparate) than its critics have often imagined (#2); an account of what Gentilean moral theory, as a radical variety of constructivism, can tell us about more moderate varieties (#3); and a final comment on how the moral theory here presented, which owes much to Gentile but does not really belong to him, represents a first step toward a selective rehabili-

---

[1] It could be that actual idealism is a distinctive variety of moral constructivism that fails on its own terms or relies on some historically contingent fact, such as the presence of an unusually efficient totalitarian administration, in order to work. In either case the theory would have nothing to say to us.

tation of actual idealism, which, carefully interpreted, offers a pertinent and original perspective on the practical problems of today (#4).

1. Overview of conclusions

I have tried to develop a version of Gentilean constructivism based on the internal dialogue. To do this I have supplemented Gentile's account of the dialogue with principles to increase the likelihood of the procedure generating consistent and significant results. Thus I hope to have promoted the internal dialogue from a metaphor into a workable constructivist device. The IDP can be understood as a tool for use in moral philosophy, enabling S to determine whether she has *good* ('universal') *reasons* to think some thought or perform some action. To have such reasons is to have moral responsibility for the thought or action. However, to think of the IDP exclusively as a moral device is misleading.

Actual idealism rejects the conventional hard distinction between normative and factual claims. It attempts to unite the two in the act of thinking. Gentile runs factual and moral claims together, arguing that, as viewed by S, they are both underpinned by values that she must work to realise. That rational persons value truth above falsity is what motivates them to scrutinise their beliefs in search of errors, and in doing so to assess those beliefs according to the strengths of their underlying justifications. That they value certain states of affairs is what motivates them to articulate the momentary manifestations of their continuous present acts as series of separate and abstract events, each backed by intentions or causes and resulting in consequences. These enable agents to decide what actions are best and most justifiable. The construction of morality, then, is an extension of something that rational, truth-seeking persons do in any case. Moral claims will never be meaningless while S continues to think and evaluate the world and the changes to it she, by her actions, brings about. For S to think without acting is for her to indulge in inconsequential, abstract velleity. Action without thought, or without S articulating the action in terms of ends, beliefs and values, is unreal. So understood, thinking and acting are part of the same inherently moral enterprise.

Gentile's justification for this unusual view, as I understand him, would be that normative claims are entirely familiar components of the way subjects think about their choices. The question of what it means to say that S has *a reason* to perform one action rather than another is notoriously difficult to answer without circularity, and Gentile never answers it directly. The difficulties of explaining it are counterbalanced by the ease of grasping it. There is no real mystery in the thought that S might have more or most reason to perform certain kinds of action and to avoid others, nor in the idea that her intentions and dispositions can change in light of due reflection. There are bad as well as good reasons for action; the two are distinguishable only after they have been *constructed* (or, perhaps, deconstructed and reconstructed) using an appropriately designed procedure. By coupling ought-claims with truth claims Gentile makes both available for rational tests within the IDP. The truth of an ought-claim does not result only from S's belief or will that it be true; it must also be shown to be *thinkable*. On Gentile's account of consciousness, this requires that it cohere with other beliefs and can sustain rational scrutiny from the artificial standpoint of a universal subject. These tests are not only ideal but *necessary* for any thinker hoping to make justified truth claims.

Chapter 3 showed that several of Gentile's works completed before the rise of Fascism, most notably *Fondamenti della filosofia del diritto* and the *Sistema di logica*, include hints about how the universal subject is to be constructed. In these he describes thinking as a dialogue between the S and an imaginary 'other' — the 'alter [ego]' or 'socius'. For the purposes of moral philosophy, which we can understand as the process of making judgements about what S ought and has most reason to do, the aim of this exercise is to refine S's personal and partial reasons into impersonal and impartial ones by examining claims from a range of actual and/or hypothetical perspectives different from the one she presently occupies. Gentile never lays out this process in a systematic fashion, and can, at first reading, be seen to describe a lightly rationalised theory of the conscience and how persons' thoughts are affected by the claims of other thinkers. But his earlier insistence on the *activity* of thinking, as opposed to complacent passivity, suggests that this cannot be the whole story. The conscience sometimes makes demands of us when we would rather it did not. If those demands are to have any *authority*, they need to be seen to give us *reasons* to act on them. Those reasons are constructed (or else found to be flawed) only as the conscience's demands are inspected and assigned their value in the course of the IDP.

Gentile's equation of the political state and the socius is not wholly implausible, but, as I argued in Chapter 4, it is incompatible with actual idealism's basic principle of the liberty of thought. In this respect I partly endorse Gennaro Sasso's characterisation of the link between the systematic, pre-Fascist works of actual idealism and the Fascist regime. Sasso probably overstates his case, though, as Alessandro Amato has recently shown. Amato maintains that actual idealism was realised in Fascism, but at the same time served as 'a moment of anti-Fascism', provoking the regime to respond to internal and external criticism in the endless unfurling of historical contingency.[2] While there is merit in this view, it does not square fully with Gentile's comments, which sometimes imply that the socius is simply *l'uomo fascista*, which is in turn a spiritualised avatar for Benito Mussolini. This fully Fascist rendering of the IDP proves self-defeating when we ask how Mussolini himself knows or determines what is the right thing to do. He cannot appeal to himself as though the best possible judgements were already available to him. We might be tempted to try a backward rationalisation for Gentile's whole-hearted endorsement of Mussolini, explaining it in Carl Schmitt's terms as a kind of decisionism: 'the state' must take a stance, and Mussolini has the advantage of already holding the power to turn his views into action. But this too would undermine the actual idealist premise of thinking as a free act. It would also imply that Gentile was a relativist about values. This is incompatible with his constructivism, as Part II's more elaborate version of the IDP goes to show.

Given my aims to present the IDP as a constructivist procedure that stands as an alternative to the dominant Kantian variety, and to show that the IDP can be fruitfully applied to contemporary normative analytic philosophy, I began Part II with a discussion of Gentile's view of Kant. He maintains that Kant fails to overcome the problem of transcendence, although he comes closer to achieving this than any previous philosopher. This means that Kant's constructivist project presupposes unconstructed elements that cannot be justified. These include his conception of universal reason as a fixed and permanent object corresponding to the cognitive architecture of rational beings. While Gentile refers to universal reason, he denies that this can be concretely conceived as a pure object. For him there is only thinking; reason itself is constructed, not discovered, and if we are to make sense of the idea of universal reason, we cannot attempt to do it *a priori*, having cut ourselves off from the object of our inquiries. Gentile finds similar fault with Kant's moral theory, and maintains that Kant can only deduce substantive principles or maxims by inserting presuppositions in his *a priori* scheme. With this argument, the foundations for Kant's categorical imperative procedure are undermined.

Gentile does not deny the attractiveness of Kant's aim to ground (moral) principles in universal reason. He merely disputes Kant's method of constructing those principles. In Chapter 6 I discussed his

---

[2] Part of this sentence is lifted from my review of Amato's book. See James Wakefield (2012) 'Alessandro Amato, *L'etica oltre lo Stato*' (review), *Intellectual History Review*, 22 (4), pp. 548–51 [551]. The quoted passages are from Alessandro Amato (2011) *L'etica oltre lo Stato: filosofia e politica in Giovanni Gentile*, Milan: Mimesis [215].

argument that if persons are to live together in a shared scheme of social co-operation, they need to be educated in such a way that their conceptions of reason are at least mutually intelligible. Here we can see that Gentile is less willing than Kant to assume that principles of universal reason are transparent to all thinkers at all times. He thinks that substantive principles must be taught before they can be critically assessed. Some people may never want or be able to subject their reasons to rational scrutiny, so for them, education provides a comprehensive and reasonably stable (if not static) worldview. But for reflective and conscientious thinkers, education supplies the means by which claims, including those arising in the course of that education, can be criticised and revised. This process is, and must be, endless. On Gentile's account, we can never justify the complacent acceptance of previous reasons as predicates of any future thought. If we were to do that, we would have unwittingly confused abstract *pensieri pensati* with concrete *pensiero pensante*. Of these, only the latter is real, necessary and binding.

Chapter 7 addressed overlapping themes of dialogue and agreement. My first task was to show that a dialogical conception of reason is both useful and recognisable as a model of the way in which thought ordinarily occurs. To test the certainty of beliefs S presently holds or thinks she might have reason to hold, she imagines what other people would or might say about the judgement she is making and to the reasons given in favour of her conclusion. Thus she distinguishes beliefs supported by good reasons from those supported by reasons that she *just happens to affirm*. For propositions to be true or false, S must assume herself to inhabit a shared world to which her claims refer. For a claim to be true for S requires that it also be true for other people, *even if they do not yet realise it.*

Since moral judgements are often made with imperfect knowledge of the relevant facts, consequences and the possible interpretations of these,[3] S can use the IDP in several different ways. One is to identify a range of reasons that other people might offer for and against a given judgement. This enables S to estimate, if only crudely, how extensive the subsequent dialogue will be. Deeply contentious questions, or those related to persons' partial and particular interests, will yield wider

---

[3] I say that S 'often' makes judgements with imperfect knowledge because it is possible that the judgement is deductively obvious, say, in which case its premises contain everything required for the inference to be made. Given actual idealism's unusual account of what counts as a moral judgement, even mathematical reasoning is included in the range of morally significant actions. Conventional moral decisions about action are rarely made with perfect knowledge of the relevant considerations, though.

ranges of different positions than those relying on fewer contested beliefs. S may base her judgement on the view held, or likely to be held, by all or most people that she considers authoritative within the relevant domain. A stronger version of the IDP works as a *falsification* device, with S rehearsing the most plausible objections to the claims she presents. This acts as a rigorous test of coherence, and while certain kinds of question cannot be answered fully by this method—empirical questions referring to *evidence*, for example—S may at least find weaknesses that call for further investigation to settle which answer most closely squares with the facts. Either method can be extended to incorporate the best conclusions reached in *other persons'* dialogues, with one conclusion 'stacked' against another. Thus bias is incrementally worked out of the process and its conclusions, giving way to more objective reasons.

2. Actual idealism assessed

In earlier chapters I noted that actual idealism has sometimes been interpreted as making implausibly bold claims about the relation between thought and the world. It may appear at first glance—and long thereafter, if many of Gentile's learned critics are anything to go by—that the doctrine's claims about the unconfined creative powers of thought lead to 'giddy visions of human omnipotence',[4] with logic (or thinking) imagined to be 'self-critical and autonomous and the lord of creation'.[5] It is a theory that, via subjectivism and a positive (though assuredly not positivist) conception of truth and reality, says anything is possible. Reality is wholly ours to create, construct and configure; evil is only error, and error exists only in the past. There is nothing but the ever-present act of thinking, and to posit anything outside that is folly. The hard sciences, for all they purport to have shown, have mistaken the nature of thought and reality itself. They offer us little but abstract conjectures. All is philosophy, for thinking is the engine of history, morality, life itself.

For some students of idealism, Gentile's great promises might prove an exciting and enticing prospect. So they seemed to his 'disciples'. His claims for actual idealism are more ambitious than even the wildest to appear in the works of Kant, Hegel and their followers, largely as a result of the doctrine's uncompromising and uncompromised principles: there is *nothing* beyond what is thinkable; there is *nothing* that is

---

[4] Harry Redner attributes this view of actual idealism to Gentile's followers. See Redner (1997) [33].

[5] George Boas (1926) 'Gentile and the Hegelian Invasion of Italy', *Journal of Philosophy*, 23 (7), pp. 184–8 [185].

not thought; thinking subjects are therefore *the creators of reality*. While other idealists situate thought in a system, Gentile claims that the system is subordinate to thinking. But for those unsympathetic to idealism, Gentile's promises show the doctrine to be a hollow façade of hyperbole concealing the more modest truth about thought, the persons who think it and the world they inhabit. Persons are anything but omnipotent. We are vulnerable creatures, thrown into situations we did not choose, and with limited powers to determine how our lives turn out. Thinking may solve conceptual problems, or problems with ideas, but it can do nothing about the brute facts that arise in experience. Discord, unhappiness and dissatisfaction are facts of the matter, and such facts cannot be changed by thinking alone. By way of poor substitute it can rationalise these away or else ignore them. To take refuge in an ivory tower of concepts is not to embrace some higher reality, but instead to abandon the only one there is. For all its creative powers, notes Roger Holmes, even Gentile's thought seems unable to construct a world in which water flows uphill. Nor can it make two plus two equal five or eradicate unhappiness and uncertainty. To attribute our apparent inability to achieve these ends to negative moments in thought's dialectic — to say that things are bound to get better as a result of changes to the facts or to our dispositions toward them — is at best wishful thinking and at worst a meaningless collection of words.

These contrasting accounts of actual idealism are caricatures of interpretations described in the preceding chapters.[6] Both, in their different ways, make the doctrine look rather silly. One says it claims far too much, and that it dismisses what has proven a reliable and useful body of knowledge, namely the hard sciences, as false. The other emphasises the persistence of the external world and the vanity of a doctrine that tries to deny or do without it. Neither view can be wholly and seriously maintained, but each contains some truth. Gentile really does make overambitious claims for actual idealism, and in identifying positivism, empiricism and realism as the chief obstacles to human progress, he very likely misdiagnosed the historical and political problems he faced. But his basic assertions about the construction of reality can be made without lapsing into the kinds of absurdity stressed in the second account. The notion that knowledge is constructed is not alien to the way thought is ordinarily discussed. Nor is it easily denied. It does not entail any further claim about the construction of the objects that are known or thought about. Anything that is not thought is left outside the ambit of knowledge. The existence of a world prior to

---

[6] ...and nowhere more so than in the discussion of the being/Being There problem in Chapter 2 (sub-section 4ii), herein.

thought is not part of a theory properly concerned with thinking. Stated as simply as this, actual idealism seems far removed from the bombastic speculation described above. Gentile need not, as one critic has put it, try to 'lift himself up by his own braces' by claiming both that there is a world and that we construct it.[7] His real aim is to show that we cannot know or understand or say anything meaningful about a non-constructed world without thinking about and so creating it. The issue of the non-constructed world's existence is revealed to be a canard, unanswerable without the intervention of a thinking subject, which would, of course, entail its construction.

3. Constructivism writ large

This brings me to the issue of actual idealist moral theory's status as a distinctive and radical variety of constructivism. It is constructivism *writ large*, without concessions to any form of realism. Reality's only necessary foundation is its basis in the act of thinking. As such, Gentile's doctrine can be called a constructivism that runs as near to 'all the way down' as is possible without becoming wholly unintelligible. His insistent claim that everything is constructed is not an empty exaggeration. When applied to nature and the empirical stuff of experience it may be thought to promise something it cannot deliver, but with respect to moral theory this concern may at least be bracketed. Moral theory is, of course, strictly theoretical; it does not describe a world of empirical objects. There can be no doubt that it is constructed *as theory*. Questions of its content's status, whether there are moral facts and so forth, are more controversial, but I cannot see how there can be absolute facts of the matter beyond deductively certain but hollow platitudes such as 'it is always immoral to perform immoral actions.' The *reasons* on which morality hinges, and which give it its rationale and authority, are not ready-made facts about the world. They are constructs designed to explain and order the values that we, as conscious agents possessing both concrete creative powers and abstract ideas of the past and possible futures, assign to the facts. A mechanical universe without consciousness would contain neither reasons nor values.

Gentile is unusual among advocates of constructivism in that his political ideas are explicitly state-centric and illiberal, even authoritarian, in character. The trend among recent (usually Kantian) constructivists has been to talk about politics in terms of 'scheme[s] of

---

[7] This idea, already cited in a footnote in Chapter 2, sub-section 4ii, comes from George de Santillana (1938) [369].

social cooperation'[8] in which justice, not order or authority, is the highest virtue. These theorists have generally found in favour of refined versions of liberalism for which the state may be an agent, but one with a carefully specified jurisdiction. Persons are understood as free and equal fellow participants in the scheme, and they each possess inalienable rights and responsibilities. It is from this conception that the other features of political constructivism follow. Pluralism is accepted as a fact that must be accommodated, since claims about moral facts are so deeply contested that, even if they were true, to act upon any one conception at the exclusion of others would be a kind of dogmatism. Laws are good laws, and therefore worth following, if they are compatible with the outcomes of a suitably designed procedure (suitably designed, that is, if it accommodates the view of the person just described). This provides a test of legitimate authority and political obligation. Few actual social schemes, if any, will conform perfectly to the principles derived from this procedure, but constructivism nevertheless offers an ideal on which the best and most just of these should model their policies.

Gentile's stated objections to liberalism are unpersuasive. This is partly because they respond to beliefs that few of today's liberals, if any, still hold.[9] But his underlying concerns about the arbitrariness of presuppositions give us better reasons to doubt recent constructivists' accounts of the necessary features of any just social scheme. At least in the way I have presented it, Gentilean moral constructivism endorses conceptions of liberty, equality and autonomy (or autarchy) broadly similar to those found in Kantian theory, but arrives at them from a separate starting position and subsequent route. This means that these conceptions' details are subtly different, and their political corollaries strikingly so. But Gentile's moral theory does not lead inexorably to Fascist totalitarianism. In fact it is compatible with a wide range of political configurations. What matters, ultimately, is that an institution's constituent members identify with it. Gentile's response to the fact of pluralism is to allow the state or the persons representing it to set about consciously determining or at least limiting with which associations people identify themselves. That those associations arise organically or as a result of social engineering is largely irrelevant to the question of whether the resultant moral beliefs can impose obligations on those party to them.

---

[8] This is Rawls' phrase. See his (1985) 'Justice as Fairness: Political, not Metaphysical', *Philosophy and Public Affairs*, 14 (3), pp. 223-51 [229].

[9] See Gentile's remarks on liberalism in chapter 10 of *Genesi*. He equates it with atomism and anarchy(!)

What Gentilean moral theory most starkly shows is that constructivism is not guaranteed to lead to any one benign conclusion. In response to the implausibility of substantive moral realism, constructivists offer a strictly formal alternative. But doing this gives them no special entitlement to specify what substantive beliefs and values may serve as the materials of construction, nor what conclusions a properly configured and applied procedure may reach. Designers of constructivist procedures must walk a tightrope between under- and overdetermination of outcomes. If too little is assumed at the beginning, the procedure's formal elements will be left in the hands of its protagonists. As a result it will be unable to produce firm, reliable and replicable results, since one person's version need not resemble any other's. If too much is assumed, the procedure will beg its own questions, issuing results that reinforce those same assumptions. The process of construction would eddy around a core of substantive presuppositions.

Kantian theorists assume more than they are entitled to in order to generate a benign and universal moral order. Gentile assumes less, though not, of course, so little as he claims. While I have argued that there are problems with the conception of the total state that Gentile advocates, his moral theory does not rule out such political orders altogether. Instead it calls for rigorous procedural justification of the state's demands, and implicitly rules out hierarchy and dogmatism. However, unless constructivist theory is larded with presuppositions about what is to count as valuable, there is no way to determine decisively and for all time what political actors, or moral agents of any kind, ought to do. Subjects face choices as varied as the changing circumstances in which they arise. If the method of immanence is the best we can hope to defend, moral decisions cannot be purely abstract choices between pre-defined sets of options, but between acts to which we must assign values as we go along. So value is something that is constructed and brought to the material—the brute facts before us—rather than found free-standing in the world. Procedures like the IDP are useful for laying bare the constructive business of thinking, but our awareness of the procedure's formal elements cannot by itself tell us to what conclusions it will lead. Actual thought, with its constant review, self-criticism and revision, is indispensable if actions are to have any value whatsoever.

4. Final remarks

To finish, it is worth stating again that the version of actual idealism presented in this book, and especially its second half, is *Gentilean* but not strictly *Gentile's*. In some respects my method is conspicuously different from his. I view the development of actual idealism as a reaction to and attempted correction of earlier philosophical systems, not some great leap forward in any grand developmental account of the history of ideas. I have not tried to offer a rounded picture of Gentile himself, with reference to his motives, influences and biography. Nor have I dedicated much space to the elaborate system in which he situated his moral theory. My largely ahistorical approach is evidence of this; according to Gentile's preferred method of reading historical texts, any proper interpretation of his work must account for the complexities of his life and times. Even if he would have disapproved of the method employed in this book, this is no reason to approach his work any differently. I have tried not to trace his every footstep, but instead to see where he set out to arrive and to chart the surest course by which, given the most defensible tenets of actual idealism, he might have reached that destination.

The task of philosophy is not only to understand theories as their originators understood them. After all, even they, like Gentile, may be prone to self-deception, confusion and similar human weaknesses. There are two separate roles for readers of philosophical texts: one as intellectual historians, concerned with when, why and how ideas came about; and another as philosophers proper, concerned with identifying the problems faced by real thinkers and finding the best possible solutions to them. Both are legitimate and independently valuable approaches to the same material, but they are mutually distinct activities. The controversy surrounding Gentile has led previous commentators to dedicate themselves to the first task at the exclusion of the second. But the latter has, in Gentile's terms, *concrete value*. The problems of today will lose none of their urgency while past ideas are treated exclusively as historical artefacts. Moral philosophy, in particular, must be able to offer insights into how we ought to live now. Otherwise it is nothing more than historical literature, made up of outmoded answers to questions we no longer need ask. This book represents a step toward a more perspicuous reading of actual idealism, motivated by the thought that at the heart of this strange and radical doctrine is something better attuned to the present climate of Anglo-American philosophy than has been previously appreciated.

The rehearsal, re-appraisal and refinement of past thought may never finally be finished, for the problems of philosophy manifest themselves in ever-changing ways. They do not arise out of nothing, but from our reflections on the real and immediate problems we encounter in life. Gentilean constructivism recognises the situatedness of thought, its 'absolute immanence' and the futility of trying to escape it. Yet it also recognises the importance of retaining a robust conception of truth as opposed to falsity. To embrace both these principles requires us to occupy an uncomfortable position, and it is tempting to lard the theory with transcendent features to give fallible subjects the impression of a clear target at which to direct their thoughts. But these transcendent features can only be included as presuppositions, and, despite their superficial appeal, they are not rigorously defensible from the standpoint of actual thinking. Constructivism, if it is to be more than well-intentioned guesswork, *must* embrace the contingent and provisional nature of truth and reality. Even if that is all we take from Gentile, we will have gained a new perspective on today's practical philosophy, and especially the foundations on which our existing philosophical constructions stand.

With this book I have attempted to elucidate and reinforce that distinctive Gentilean position. A fuller appreciation of the implications and applications of a constructivist theory rooted in actual thinking will demand references to questions that Gentile never considered and to debates that have arisen or substantially changed in the seven decades since his death. Those aims remain to be met in the future. For now, it is enough that this theory may at last be considered worthy of serious critical attention, granted the freedom to develop out of the shadow of its originator, and recognised as a variety of contemporary constructivism in its own right. We may justifiably reject Gentile's assassins' claim to have killed both the man and his ideas in April 1944. Our greater remove from the period enables us to view actual idealism with a clear-sightedness and selectivity that they, for whom Fascism was a real and immediate threat, did not have the luxury to exercise. It falls not to them but to us, armed not with weapons but with our powers of scrupulous critical thinking, to determine which ideas are worth reviving and which rightly belong to the past.

Bibliography and Appendix

1. List of works cited

1i. Works by Giovanni Gentile

Gentile, Giovanni (1904) 'Fenomeni e noumeni nella filosofia di Kant', *La Critica,* 2, pp. 417–22.

Gentile, Giovanni (1908) *Scuola e filosofia,* Palermo: Sandron.

Gentile, Giovanni (1920b) *La riforma dell'educazione,* Bari: Laterza.

[Gentile, Giovanni (1922a) *The Reform of Education,* New York: Harcourt, Brace and Company (translated by Dino Bigongiari).]

Gentile, Giovanni (1922b) 'Le ragioni del mio ateismo e la storia del cristianesimo', *Giornale critico della filosofia italiana,* 3, pp. 325–28.

Gentile, Giovanni (1922–3) *Sistema di logica come come teoria del conoscere,* Bari: Laterza (two volumes: first vol. originally 1917; second vol. originally 1923).

Gentile, Giovanni (1928) 'The Philosophic Basis of Fascism', *Foreign Affairs: An American Quarterly,* pp. 290–304.

Gentile, Giovanni (1933) *Introduzione alla filosofia,* Milan: Treves.

Gentile, Giovanni (1957) *Discorsi di religione,* Florence: Sansoni (fourth, expanded edition; originally 1920).

Gentile, Giovanni (1959–62) *Sommario di pedagogia come scienza filosofica,* Florence: Sansoni (two volumes; originally 1913–14).

Gentile, Giovanni (1963) *I problemi della scolastica e il pensiero Italiano,* Florence: Sansoni (originally 1912).

Gentile, Giovanni (1975) *Genesi e struttura della società,* Florence: Sansoni (originally 1946).

[Gentile, Giovanni (1960) *Genesis and Structure of Society,* Chicago: University of Illinois Press (edited and translated by H.S. Harris, from *Genesi e struttura della società,* above).]

Gentile, Giovanni (2003a) *I fondamenti della filosofia del diritto,* Florence: Le Lettere (originally 1916).

Gentile, Giovanni (2003b) 'L'atto del pensare come atto puro', in *La riforma della dialettica hegeliana,* Florence: Le Lettere, pp. 183-95 (this essay originally 1911; book originally 1913).

Gentile, Giovanni (2003c) *Teoria generale dello Spirito come atto puro,* Florence: Le Lettere (originally 1916).

[Gentile, Giovanni (1922) *The Theory of Mind as Pure Act,* London: Macmillan (translated by H. Wildon Carr, from *Teoria generale dello Spirito come atto puro,* above).]

Gentile, Giovanni (2004) 'Origini and dottrina del fascismo', in Renzo de Felice (ed.) *Autobiografia del fascismo,* Turin: Einaudi, pp. 247-71 (this essay originally 1927).

[Gentile, Giovanni (2007) *Origins and Doctrine of Fascism,* Brunswick, NJ: Transaction (translated and edited by A. James Gregor. This translation originally 2002).]

1ii. Works by other authors

Accame, Giano (2004) 'Gentile e la morte', in Roberto Chiarini (ed.) *Stato etico e manganello: Giovanni Gentile a sessant'anni dalla morte,* Venice: Marsilio, pp. 51-62.

Alcoff, Linda Martín (2001) 'The Case for Coherence', in Michael Patrick Lynch (ed.) *The Nature of Truth: Classic and Contemporary Perspectives,* Cambridge, MA: MIT Press, pp. 159-82.

Amato, Alessandro (2011) *L'etica oltre lo Stato: filosofia e politica in Giovanni Gentile,* Milan: Mimesis.

Aquinas, Thomas (1927) *The 'Summa Theologica' of Thomas Aquinas,* Part 2 (first part), second number, questions XLIV-LXXXIV, London: Thomas Baker (translated by the Fathers of the English Dominican Province. This translation originally 1912).

Arendt, Hannah (1962) *The Origins of Totalitarianism,.* New York: Meridian (originally 1948).

Ayer, A.J (1971) *Language, Truth and Logic,* London: Penguin (originally 1936).

Bagnoli, Carla (2002) 'Moral Constructivism: A Phenomenological Argument', *Topoi,* 21, pp. 125-38.

Barbuto, Gennaro Maria (2007) *Nichilismo e Stato totalitario. Libertà e autorità nel pensiero politico di Giovanni Gentile e Giuseppe Rensi,* Naples: Guida.

Bellamy, Richard (1987) *Modern Italian Social Theory: Ideology and Politics from Pareto to the Present,* Stanford, CA: Stanford University Press.

Berlin, Isaiah (2002) 'Two Concepts of Liberty', in Henry Hardy (ed.) *Liberty,* Oxford: Oxford University Press, pp. 166-217 (essay originally 1958).

Berti, Enrico (1988) 'La dialettica e le sue riforme', in Pierro di Giovanni (ed.) *Il neoidealismo italiano,* Bari: Laterza, pp. 45–69.

Besch, Thomas M. (2008) 'Constructing Practical Reason: O'Neill on the Grounds of Kantian Constructivism', *Journal of Value Inquiry,* 42, pp. 55–76.

Bird-Pollan, Stefan (2011) 'Some Normative Implications of Korsgaard's Theory of the Intersubjectivity of Reason', *Metaphilosophy,* 42 (4), pp. 376–80.

Blackburn, Simon (1999) 'Am I Right?' (Review of T.M. Scanlon's *What We Owe to Each Other*), in *New York Times,* 21/02/1999, [Online], http://www.nytimes.com/books/99/02/21/reviews/990221.21blact.html.

Bosanquet, Bernard (1922) 'A Word About Coherence', *Mind,* 31 (123), pp. 335–6.

Bradley, F.H. (1909) 'On Truth and Coherence', *Mind,* 18 (71), pp. 329–42.

Bradley, F.H. (1909) 'Coherence and Contradiction', *Mind,* 18 (72), pp. 489–508.

Buss, Sarah (2005) 'Valuing Autonomy and Respecting Persons: Manipulation, Seduction and the Basis of Moral Constraints', *Ethics,* 115 (2), pp. 195–235.

Calandra, Giuseppe (1987) *Gentile e il fascismo,* Bari: Laterza.

Callan, Eamonn (1997) *Creating Citizens,* Oxford: Clarendon Press.

Caponigri, A. Robert (1963) 'The Status of the Person in the Humanism of Giovanni Gentile', *Journal of the History of Philosophy,* 2 (1), pp. 61–9.

Caponigri, A. Robert (1977) 'Person, Society and Art in the Actual Idealism of Giovanni Gentile', in Simonetta Betti, Franca Rovigatti and Gianni Eugenio Viola (eds.) *Enciclopedia 76-77: il pensiero di Giovanni Gentile* (Volume 1), Florence: Istituto della Enciclopedia Italiana, pp. 171–83.

Carioti, Antonio (2004) 'Sanguinetti venne a dirmi che Gentile doveva morire', *Corriere della sera,* 06/08/2004, p. 29, [Online], http://archiviostorico.corriere.it/2004/agosto/06/Sanguinetti_venne_dirmi_che_Gentile_co_9_040806079.shtml

Cavallera, Hervé A. (1994) *Immagine e costruzione del reale nel pensiero di Giovanni Gentile,* Rome: Fondazione Ugo Spirito.

Cavallera, Hervé A. (1995) 'Gentile e Spinoza', *Idee,* 28–9, pp. 185–212.

Chiarini, Roberto (ed.) (2004) *Stato etico e manganello: Giovanni Gentile a sessant'anni dalla morte,* Venice: Marsilio.

Clayton, Thomas (2009) 'Introducing Giovanni Gentile, "the Philosopher of Fascism"', *Educational Philosophy and Theory,* 41 (6), pp. 640–60.

Cohen, L. Jonathan (1978) 'The Coherence Theory of Truth', *Philosophical Studies: an International Journal for Philosophy in the Analytic Tradition,* 34 (4), pp. 351-60.

Coli, Daniela (2004) *Giovanni Gentile: la filosofia come educazione nazionale,* Bologna: Mulino.

Coli, Daniela (2006) 'La concezione politica di Giovanni Gentile', in *Logoi,* Castelvetrano: Edizioni Mazzotta, pp. 37-57.

Croce, Benedetto (1946) 'In commemorazione di un amico inglese, compagno di pensiero e di fede', *La Critica,* 4, pp. 60-73.

Dauer, Francis W. (1974) 'In Defense of the Coherence Theory of Truth', *Journal of Philosophy,* 71 (21), pp. 791-811.

Davidson, Donald (1984) 'On the Very Idea of a Conceptual Scheme', in *Inquiries into Truth and Interpretation,* Oxford: Oxford University Press, pp. 183-98.

Davidson, Donald (1995) 'The Problem of Objectivity', in *Problems of Rationality,* Oxford: Oxford University Press, pp. 3-18.

Davidson, Donald (2004a) 'The Emergence of Thought', in *Subjective, Intersubjective, Objective,* Oxford: Oxford University Press, pp. 123-34.

Davidson, Donald (2004b) 'The Second Person', in *Subjective, Intersubjective, Objective,* Oxford: Oxford University Press, pp. 107-21.

de Burgh, W.G. (1929) 'Gentile's Philosophy of Spirit', *Journal of Philosophical Studies,* 4 (13), pp. 3-22.

de Ruggiero, Guido (1926) 'Main Currents of Philosophy in Italy', *Journal of Philosophical Studies,* 1 (3), pp. 320-32 (translated by Constance M. Allen).

de Santillana, George (1938) 'The Idealism of Giovanni Gentile', *Isis,* 29 (2), pp. 366-76.

Defoe, Daniel (1987) *Robinson Crusoe,* Leicester: Galley (originally 1719).

Del Noce, Augusto (1990) *Giovanni Gentile: per una interpretazione filosofica della storia contemporanea,* Bologna: Il Mulino.

Descartes, René (1984) *The Philosophical Writings of Descartes* (2 volumes), Cambridge: Cambridge University Press (edited and translated by John Cottingham, Robert Stoothoff and Dugald Murdoch).

Di Lalla, Manlio (1975) *Vita di Giovanni Gentile,* Florence: Sansoni.

Evans, Valmai Burwood (1929) 'The Ethics of Giovanni Gentile', *International Journal of Ethics,* 39 (2), pp. 205-16.

Evola, Julius (1955) 'Gentile non è il nostro filosofo', *Ordine Nuovo,* 1 (4-5), pp. 25-30.

Germino, Dante (1961) '*The Social Philosophy of Giovanni Gentile,* by H.S. Harris; and *Genesis and Structure of Society,* by Giovanni Gentile, translated by H.S. Harris' (review), *Journal of Philosophy*, 23 (3), pp. 584-7.

Giesinger, Johannes (2010) 'Free Will and Autonomy', *Journal of the Philosophy of Education*, 44 (4), pp. 515-28.

Gorani, Fabio (1995) 'Logo concreto e logo astratto nel pensiero di Giovanni Gentile', *Idee*, 28-9, pp. 139-60.

Gowans, Christopher W. (2002) 'Practical Identities and Autonomy: Korsgaard's Reformation of Kant's Moral Philosophy', *Philosophy and Phenomenological Research*, 64 (3), pp. 546-70.

Green, Thomas F. (1972) 'Indoctrination and Beliefs', in I.A. Snook (ed.) *Concepts of Indoctrination: Philosophical Essays*, London: Routledge and Kegan Paul, pp. 20-36.

Gregor, A. James (1969) *The Ideology of Fascism*, Toronto: The Free Press.

Gregor, A. James (1977) 'Giovanni Gentile, Contemporary Analytic Philosophy, and the Concept of Political Obligation', in Simonetta Betti, Franca Rovigatti and Gianni Eugenio Viola (eds.) *Enciclopedia 76-77: il pensiero di Giovanni Gentile* (Volume 1), Florence: Istituto della Enciclopedia Italiana, pp. 445-55.

Gregor, A. James (2001) *Giovanni Gentile: Philosopher of Fascism*, New Brunswick, NJ: Transaction.

Griffin, Roger (1993) *The Nature of Fascism*, Abingdon: Routledge (originally 1991).

Gross, Ronald (1961) '*The Social Philosophy of Giovanni Gentile*, by H.S. Harris; and *Genesis and Structure of Society*, by Giovanni Gentile, translated by H.S. Harris' (review), *Annals of the American Academy of Political and Social Science*, 336, pp. 222-3.

Haddock, Bruce (2005) *A History of Political Thought: 1789 to the Present*, Oxford: Polity.

Haddock, Bruce (1994) 'Hegel's Critique of the Theory of Social Contract', in David Boucher and Paul Kelly (eds.) *The Social Contract from Hobbes to Rawls*, London: Routledge, pp. 147-63.

Hare, R.M. (1978) 'Moral Conflicts', *Tanner Lectures in Human Value*, pp. 171-93, [Online], www.utilitarian.net/singer/by/tanner.pdf.

Harris, H.S. (1960) *The Social Philosophy of Giovanni Gentile*,. Urbana, IL: University of Illinois Press.

Harris, H.S. (1977) 'Gentile's Reform of the Hegelian Dialectic', in Simonetta Betti, Franca Rovigatti and Gianni Eugenio Viola (eds.) *Enciclopedia 76-77: il pensiero di Giovanni Gentile* (Volume 1), Florence: Istituto della Enciclopedia Italiana, pp. 473-80.

Hebb, D.O. (1974) 'What Psychology is About', *American Psychologist*, 29 (2), pp. 71-9.

Hegel, G.W.F. (1945) *Philosophy of Right*, Oxford: Oxford University Press (translated by T.M. Knox. Original German publication 1820-21; this translation originally 1942).

Hegel, G.W.F. (1955) *Lectures on the History of Philosophy*, New York: The Humanities Press (translated by E.S. Haldane and Frances H. Simson).

Hegel, G.W.F. (1977) *Hegel's Phenomenology of Spirit*, Oxford: Oxford University Press (translated by A.V. Miller).

Heidegger, Martin (2002) *Gesamtausgabe II, Vorlesungen 1919-1944. Band 8: Grundbegriffe der aristotelischen Philosophie*, Frankfurt am Main: Vittorio Klostermann.

Herbart, J.F. (1913) *Outlines of Educational Doctrine*, London: Macmillan (translated by Alexis F. Lange and annotated by Charles de Garmo. Original German publication 1835; this translation originally 1901).

Hill Jr., Thomas E. (2001) 'Hypothetical Consent in Kantian Constructivism', *Social Philosophy and Policy*, 18, pp. 300-29.

Hill Jr., Thomas E. (2008) 'Moral Construction as a Task: Sources and Limits', *Social Philosophy and Policy*, 25 (1), pp. 214-36.

Holmes, Roger W. (1937a) 'Gentile's *Sistema di Logica*', *Philosophical Review*, 46 (4), pp. 393-401.

Holmes, Roger W. (1937b) *The Idealism of Giovanni Gentile*, New York: Macmillan.

Hume, David (1978) *A Treatise of Human Nature*, Oxford: Oxford University Press (edited by L.A. Selby-Bigge and P.H. Nidditch).

Hume, David (2003) *Enquiries Concerning Human Understanding and Concerning the Principles of Morals*, Oxford: Oxford University Press (edited by L.A. Selby-Bigge and P.H. Nidditch).

Inwood, Michael (1992) *A Hegel Dictionary*, London: Blackwell.

Joachim, Harold H. (1906) *The Nature of Truth*, Oxford: Clarendon Press.

Kant, Immanuel (1929) *Critique of Pure Reason*, London: Palgrave Macmillan (translated by Norman Kemp Smith).

Kant, Immanuel (1948) *The Moral Law: Kant's Groundwork of the Metaphysics of Morals*, London: Hutchinson (translated by H.J. Paton).

Kant, Immanuel (1997) *Critique of Practical Reason*, Cambridge: Cambridge University Press (translated by Mary Gregor).

Kant, Immanuel (1998) *The Metaphysics of Morals*, Cambridge: Cambridge University Press (edited and translated by Mary Gregor).

Kirkham, Richard (1997) *Theories of Truth: A Critical Introduction*, Cambridge, MA: MIT Press.

Korsgaard, Christine M. (1989) 'Personal Identity and the Unity of Agency: a Kantian Response to Parfit', *Philosophy and Public Affairs*, 18 (2), pp. 101-32.

Korsgaard, Christine M. (1996a) *The Sources of Normativity,* Cambridge: Cambridge University Press (edited by Onora O'Neill).
Korsgaard, Christine M. (1996b) *Creating the Kingdom of Ends,* Cambridge: Cambridge University Press.
Korsgaard, Christine M. (1997) 'The Normativity of Instrumental Reason', in Garrett Cullity and Berys Gaut (eds.) *Ethics and Practical Reason,* Oxford: Oxford University Press, pp. 215-54.
Korsgaard, Christine M. (2003) 'Realism and Constructivism in Twentieth-Century Moral Philosophy', *Philosophy in America at the Turn of the Century* (APA Centennial Supplement to *Journal of Philosophical Research*), pp. 99-122.
Krasnoff, Larry (1999) 'How Kantian is Constructivism?', *Kant-Studien,* 90, pp. 385-409.
Künne, Wolfgang (2005) *Conceptions of Truth,* Oxford: Clarendon Press (originally 2003).
Lenman, James (1999) 'Michael Smith and the Daleks: Reason, Morality and Contingency', *Utilitas,* 11 (2), pp. 164-77.
Lenman, James (2013) 'Ethics Without Errors', *Ratio,* 26 (4), pp. 391-409.
Lenman, James and Yonatan Shemmer (eds.) (2012) *Constructivism in Practical Philosophy,* Oxford: Oxford University Press.
Lyttelton, Adrian (2004) *The Seizure of Power: Italian Fascism in Power, 1919-1945* (revised edition), New York: Routledge.
Marcuse, Herbert (1955) *Reason and Revolution: Hegel and the Rise of Social Theory,* London: Routledge & Kegan Paul (second edition; originally 1941).
Mautner, Thomas (ed.) (2005) *Dictionary of Philosophy,* London: Penguin.
Milo, Ronald (1995) 'Contractarian Constructivism', *Journal of Philosophy,* 92 (4), pp. 181-204.
Moss, M.E. (2004) *Mussolini's Fascist Philosopher: Giovanni Gentile Reconsidered,* New York: Peter Lang.
Mure, G.R.G. (1950) '*Genesi e struttura della società,* by Giovanni Gentile' (review), *Philosophical Quarterly,* 1 (1), pp. 83-4.
Neurath, Otto (1983) 'Protocol Statements', in R.S. Cohen and M. Neurath (eds.) *Philosophical Papers 1913-1946,* Dordrecht: Reidel, pp. 91-9 (this essay first published 1932).
O'Doherty, E.F. (1963) 'Brainwashing', *Studies: An Irish Quarterly Review,* 52 (205), pp. 1-15.
O'Neill, Onora (1989) *Constructions of Reason: Explorations of Kant's Practical Philosophy,* Cambridge: Cambridge University Press.
O'Neill, Onora (1992) 'Vindicating Reason', in Paul Guyer (ed.) *The Cambridge Companion to Kant,* Cambridge: Cambridge University Press, pp. 280-308.

O'Neill, Onora (1996) *Towards Justice and Virtue: A Constructive Account of Practical Reasoning*, Cambridge: Cambridge University Press.

O'Neill, Onora (2003a) 'Constructivism in Rawls and Kant', in *The Cambridge Companion to Rawls*, Cambridge: Cambridge University Press, pp. 347-67 (edited by Samuel Freeman).

O'Neill, Onora (2003b) 'Constructivism vs. Contractualism', *Ratio*, 15, pp. 319-31.

Paley, William (1881) *Natural Theology*, New York: American Tract Society (originally 1802).

Parfit, Derek (2002) 'What We Could Rationally Will', *Tanner Lectures on Human Value* (Volume 24), pp. 287-369, [Online], http://tannerlectures.utah.edu/lectures/documents/volume24/parfit_2002.pdf/

Parfit, Derek (2010) *On What Matters* (Volume 1), Oxford: Oxford University Press (edited by Samuel Scheffler).

Payne, Stanley G. (1995) *A History of Fascism, 1914-1945*, Abingdon: Routledge.

Pedrizzi, Riccardo (ed.) (2006) *Giovanni Gentile: il filosofo della nazione*, Rome: Pantheon.

Pesce, Antonio G. (2011) 'La fenomenologia della coscienza in Giovanni Gentile', *Quaderni Leif*, 5 (6), pp. 39–54.

Pesce, Antonio G. (2012) *L'interiorità intersoggettiva dell'attualismo: il personalismo di Giovanni Gentile*, Rome: Aracne.

Peters, Rik (1998a) *The Living Past: Philosophy, History and Action in the Thought of Croce, Gentile, de Ruggiero and Collingwood*, Nijmegen: Katholieke Universiteit Nijmegen.

Peters, Rik (1998b) 'Talking to Ourselves or Talking to Others: H.S. Harris on Gentile's Transcendental Dialogue', *Clio*, 27 (4), pp. 501-14.

Plato (1921) *Plato in Twelve Volumes* (Vol. 12), Cambridge, MA: Harvard University Press (translated by Harold N. Fowler).

Rawls, John (1971) *A Theory of Justice* (original edition), London: Harvard University Press.

Rawls, John (1980) 'Kantian Constructivism in Moral Theory', *Journal of Philosophy*, 77 (9), pp. 515-72.

Rawls, John (1985) 'Justice as Fairness: Political, not Metaphysical', *Philosophy and Public Affairs*, 14 (3), pp. 223-51.

Rawls, John (1988) 'The Priority of Right and Ideas of the Good', *Philosophy and Public Affairs*, 17 (4), pp. 251-76.

Rawls, John (1993) *Political Liberalism*, New York: Columbia University Press.

Rawls, John (2000) *Lectures on the History of Moral Philosophy*, Cambridge, MA: Harvard University Press (edited by Barbara Herman).

Redner, Harry (1997) *Malign Masters: Gentile, Heidegger, Lukács, Wittgenstein*, Basingstoke: Macmillan.

Rescher, Nicholas (1973) *The Coherence Theory of Truth*, Oxford: Clarendon Press.

Rickman, H.P. (1962) '*Genesis and Structure of Society* by Giovanni Gentile and H.S. Harris; *The Social Philosophy of Giovanni Gentile* by H.S. Harris' (review), *International Review of Education*, 8 (3/4), p. 498.

Rinaldi, Giacomo (1994) 'Italian Idealism and After: Gentile, Croce and Others', in Richard Kearney (ed.) *Continental Philosophy in the 20th Century*, London: Routledge, pp. 350–89.

Roberts, David D. (2002) 'Maggi's Croce, Sasso's Gentile and the Riddles of Italian Intellectual History', *Journal of Modern Italian Studies*, 7 (1), pp. 116–44.

Roberts, Peri (2007) *Political Constructivism*, London: Routledge.

Romano, Sergio (1984) *Giovanni Gentile: la filosofia al potere*, Milan: Bompiani.

Ronzoni, Miriam (2010) 'Constructivism and Practical Reason: On Intersubjectivity, Abstraction, and Judgment', *Journal of Moral Philosophy*, 7, pp. 74–107.

Rossi, Mario M. (1950) '*Genesi e struttura della società*, by Giovanni Gentile' (review), *Journal of Philosophy*, 47 (8), pp. 217–22.

Ryle, Gilbert (1990) *The Concept of Mind*, London: Penguin (originally 1949).

Sabine, George H. (1961) *A History of Political Theory*, London: George G. Harrap.

Sasso, Gennaro (1998) *Le due Italie di Giovanni Gentile*, Bologna: Mulino.

Scanlon, T.M. (1998) *What We Owe to Each Other*, Cambridge, MA: Belknap Press.

Schneewind, J.B. (1992) 'Autonomy, Obligation and Virtue: an Overview of Kant's Moral Philosophy', in Paul Guyer (ed.) *The Cambridge Companion to Kant*, Cambridge: Cambridge University Press, pp. 309–41.

Schneider, Herbert W. (1968) *Making the Fascist State*, New York: Howard Fertig (originally 1928).

Sciaky, Isacco (1956) 'L'io e i molti io e il significato dello spirito come atto', *Giornale critico della filosofia italiana*, 3, pp. 332–54.

Shklar, Judith N. (1973) 'Hegel's *Phenomenology* and the Moral Failures of Asocial Man', *Political Theory*, 1 (3), pp. 259–86.

Shklar, Judith N. (1976) *Freedom and Independence,* Cambridge: Cambridge University Press.
Sneddon, Andrew (2011) 'A New Kantian Response to Maxim-Fiddling', in *Kantian Review,* 16 (1), pp. 67–88.
Spinoza, Benedict de (1996) *Ethics,* Oxford: Oxford University Press (edited and translated by Edwin Curley).
Street, Sharon (2008) 'Constructivism about Reasons', in Russ Shafer-Landau (ed.) *Oxford Studies in Metaethics* (Volume 3), Oxford: Oxford University Press, pp. 207–46.
Street, Sharon (2012) 'Coming to Terms with Contingency', in James Lenman and Yonatan Shemmer (eds.) *Constructivism in Practical Philosophy,* Oxford: Oxford University Press, pp. 40–59.
Tarquini, Alessandra (2005) 'The Anti-Gentilians During the Fascist Regime', *Journal of Contemporary History,* 40, pp. 637–62.
Taylor, Charles (1989) *Sources of the Self: The Making of Modern Identity,* Cambridge: Cambridge University Press.
Turi, Gabriele (1998a) *Giovanni Gentile: una biografia,* Milan: Giunto.
Turi, Gabriele (1998b) 'Giovanni Gentile: Oblivion, Remembrance, and Criticism', *Journal of Modern History,* 70 (4), pp, 913–33 (translated by Lydia P. Cochrane).
Underhill, Evelyn, R.G. Collingwood and W.R. Inge (1923) 'Can the New Idealism Dispense with Mysticism?', *Proceedings of the Aristotelian Society, Supplementary Volumes,* 3, pp. 148–84.
Vincent, Andrew (1991) *Theories of the State,* Oxford: Blackwell (originally 1987).
Vincent, Andrew (1995) *Modern Political Ideologies,* Malden: Wiley-Blackwell (second edition; originally 1992).
Wakefield, James (2012) 'Alessandro Amato, *L'etica oltre lo Stato*' (review), *Intellectual History Review,* 22 (4), pp. 548–51.
Walker, Ralph C. (1989) *The Coherence Theory of Truth: Realism, Anti-Realism, Idealism,* London: Routledge.
Walker, Ralph C. (2001) 'The Coherence Theory', in Michael Patrick Lynch (ed.) *The Nature of Truth: Classic and Contemporary Perspectives,* Cambridge, MA: MIT Press, pp. 123–58.[1]
Westphal, Merold (2003) 'Hegel between Spinoza and Derrida', in David A. Duquette (ed.) *Hegel's History of Philosophy: New Interpretations,* Albany, NY: New York University Press, pp. 143–63.
Williams, Bernard (1978) *Descartes: the Project of Pure Enquiry,* Harmondsworth: Pelican.

---

[1] Note that this article consists of extracts from Walker (1989), above, plus additional material. Where the two overlap I have cited the earlier version.

Williams, Garrath (2009) 'Kant's Account of Reason', in Edward N. Zalta (ed.) *The Stanford Encyclopaedia of Philosophy*, [Online], http://plato.stanford.edu/entries/kant-reason/ [Accessed 28/03/2012] (originally 2008).

Wolf, Susan (1982) 'Moral Saints', *Journal of Philosophy*, 79 (8), pp. 419–439.

Wringe, Colin (1984) *Democracy, Schooling and Political Education*, London: George Allen & Unwin.

1iii. Useful further reading not directly cited

Croce, Benedetto (1909) *Logica come scienza del concetto puro*, Bari: Laterza.

[Croce, Benedetto (1917) *Logic as the Science of the Pure Concept*, London: Macmillan (translated by Douglas Ainslie).[2]]

Croce, Benedetto (1926) *La filosofia della pratica: economica e etica*, Bari: Laterza (originally 1909).

[Croce, Benedetto (1913) *Philosophy of the Practical: Economic and Ethic*, London: Macmillan (translated by Douglas Ainslie).]

de Ruggiero, Guido (1925) *Storia del liberalismo europeo*, Bari: Laterza.

[de Ruggiero, Guido (1959) *The History of European Liberalism*, Boston, MA: Beacon Press (originally 1927; translated by R.G. Collingwood).[3]]

Gentile, Giovanni (1899) *Rosmini e Gioberti*, Bari: Laterza.[4]

---

[2] I include two out of the three books in constituting Croce's *Filosofia dello Spirito*, excluding his works about aesthetics. Although I have tried to avoid the already much-discussed issue of the link between Gentile and Croce, the latter's works are instructive for understanding what Gentile set out to deny. Throughout his close collaboration with and subsequent estrangement from Croce, he believed that the older philosopher replicated the same problems that had existed in the works of previous idealists in Italy and Germany alike. Note that Douglas Ainslie's translations are conspicuously dated and sometimes less clear than Croce's original Italian. Colin Lyas produced a clearer translation of the *Estetica* in 1992, but regrettably this has not been followed by those of the two books listed above.

[3] De Ruggiero is one of the most interesting of Gentile's critics because he was for a time (at least philosophically) very close to him. He does not discuss Gentile's philosophy in this book, but it is nevertheless useful for its insights into the context from which Gentile's thought arose, and as an illustration of how someone who rejected Fascism responded to the turbulent historical currents prevailing in early twentieth-century Italy. Many of de Ruggiero's direct criticisms of Gentile can be found in articles available in English.

[4] This is one of Gentile's earliest published works, and demonstrates his debt — or what he perceived to be his debt — to the nineteenth-century Italian philosophers Antonio Rosmini and Vincenzo Gioberti.

Gentile, Giovanni (1981) 'The Reform of the Hegelian Dialectic', *Idealistic Studies,* 11 (3), pp. 189-214 (translated by A. MacC. Armstrong).[5]

Gentile, Giovanni (1995) 'Fascism as a Total Conception of Life', in *Fascism: A Reader,* Oxford: Oxford University Press, pp. 53-4 (edited and translated by Roger Griffin).

2. Appendix: abbreviations for Gentile's works

Many of Gentile's works have unwieldy titles. For the sake of brevity, and given the need for me to refer repeatedly to some of these works, I have referred to them by the abbreviated titles listed in the table below. Note that the 'Year' column specifies in which year each work was first published, not the edition(s) referred to when writing this book. See the bibliography for details of the editions I have used.

Original title	Year	English title	Abbreviation
Scuola e filosofia	1908	*School and Philosophy*	*Scuola*
L'atto del pensare come atto puro	1912	*The Act of Thinking as Pure Act*	*'Pensare'*
Il metodo dell' immanenza	1912	*The Method of Immanence*	*'Immanenza'*
Sommario di pedagogia (2 volumes)	1913-14	*Summary of Pedagogy: General Pedagogy (vol. 1)/Didactics (vol. 2)*	*Sommario 1/2*
La riforma della dialettica Hegeliana	1913	*Reform of the Hegelian Dialectic*	*Hegeliana*
Teoria generale dello Spirito come atto puro	1916	*General Theory of Spirit as Pure Act*	*Atto puro*
I fondamenti della filosofia del diritto	1916	*Foundations of the Philosophy of Right*	*Diritto*
Discorsi di religione	1920	*Lectures on Religion*	*Religione*
Sistema di logica come teoria del conoscere (2 volumes)	1917-22	*System of Logic as Theory of Knowing*	*Logica 1/2*

---

5 This is a translation of the essay 'La riforma della dialettica hegeliana', which appears in Gentile's book of the same name. It is listed separately because the book contains several other essays as well.

La riforma dell'educazione	1922	Reform of Education	Educazione[6]
Origini e dottrina del fascismo	1927	Origins and Doctrine of Fascism	Origini
Introduzione alla filosofia	1933	Introduction to Philosophy	Introduzione
La filosofia dell'arte	1931	The Philosophy of Art	Arte
Genesi e struttura della società: saggio di filosofia pratica	1946	Genesis and Structure of Society: an essay on practical philosophy	Genesi

---

[6] Note that Gentile re-wrote the first chapter of *La riforma dell'educazione* for Dino Bigongiari's English translation. Rather than assigning the English version a separate abbreviated title, I refer simply to 'Bigongiari translation' wherever I distinguish one from the other.

Index

abstract/concrete distinction, 40–3, 103, 114
  criticism of, 49–50
  and education, 164, 167, 170
  and judgement, 125–30, 141–5, 150, 208, 213
  and the self, 64n1, 70, 70n20, 71–3
  and the state, *see* state, the
  and the will, 44–6, 49–50, 154–5
abstraction vs. idealisation, 11, 136–7, 207, 207n34, 212
abstractionism, vicious, 19
actual idealism, *passim*
actualism, *see* actual idealism
affirmation
  and coherence theory, 53–8
  and reasons, 83–4, 120–5, 181, 183
  and the IDP, 194–206, 209–13, 222–6
  role of in actual idealism, 35, 43–51, 57–8, 59–60, 59n76, 66, 70, 83–4, 120–3, 129–30, 141–2, 160–3
agency, 49–50, 64, 77, 97–8, 139, 145–6, 145n66, 183–8, 225–6
agreement
  actual, 69n17, 81–2, 97–8
  hypothetical, 179n47, 181n53, 206–11
  and the IDP, 124–5, 192–226
  in Kant's theory, 138–49
  in Rawls's theory, 6–11
  in social contract theory, 97–8, 205–6
  see also disagreement
alter-ego, *see* socius
Alexander the Great, 21n51
Amato, Alessandro, 231–2
anarchism, 98
anti-realism, 4, 7–8, 120–1, 140–2, 159–62, 192–7

Aquinas, Thomas, 99n27
Aristotle, 14n25, 21n51, 33, 54, 129, 155
Augustine, 33
autarchy, 128n19, 149–53, 156, 237
autoctisi, 35, 36n24
authority
  moral/normative, 5, 8, 8n17, 26, 75, 79, 83–91, 108–10, 114, 121, 124–30, 132, 136, 139–44, 146–7, 149–54, 159–62, 166, 167–71, 177n43, 180–1, 187–9, 209, 216, 231–4, 236
  political, 19n14, 93, 94n4, 100n28, 102–3, 105, 113–4, 116, 166–7, 172–3, 181–3, 224–5
autonomy
  and autarchy, *see* autarchy
  in GG's theory, 149–53
  in Kant's theory, 144–57
  strong vs. weak, 151–2
Autonomy Formula, 144–53

Being There Problem, 46–50
belief, *see* affirmation
Berlin, Isaiah, *see* freedom, positive and negative
Bird-Pollan, Stefan, 151–2
Book Hypothesis, 56–7
brainwashing, 183

Caesar Hypothesis, 56–8
Cartesianism, *see* Descartes, René
categorical imperative, 119–57, 218–21, 232
Catholicism, *see* religion
certainty, 34–8, 45, 52, 55–61, 120–3, 130, 150n80, 151, 159, 193–4, 197, 210, 212, 219–20, 233
Charity Principle, 203–4, 219, 221

children, 106, 167, 176–7, 177n43, 180, 182–4
Church, the, *see* religion
civil society, 96, 100, 102–4, 112
Coercion Objection, 179–81
cogito ergo sum, 34–6
Cogito Justification, 37–9
coherence, 50–62
  and comprehensiveness, 61–2
  and construction, 79, 89, 119–23, 129, 142–6, 161–5, 174, 181, 188–9, 204–5, 209–13, 215–6, 219, 224
  pure, implausibility of as theory of truth, 55n70
  as test of compatibility, 51, 54n68, 57
communitarianism, 139, 220, 226
community, 72n28, 74n34, 78, 81, 87–8, 115, 173–6, 171n53, 220
conscience, 73–8, 73n31, 81, 84–5, 87–9, 95–6, 96n11, 138n65, 194n6, 231
constructivism
  all-the-way-down, 9–11, 149, 160, 218n50, 236
  defined, 1–11
  Gentilean, 11–4, 63–91, 119–226
  Humean, 3n3, 5n10
  institutional, 158
  Kantian, 1–3, 5n, 8–11, 24, 119–57, 192–4, 207n32, 215–22, 236–8
  procedural vs. epistemological, 8, 12, 43, 46, 84, 116
  Rawls's definition of, 3
  Ronzoni's definition of, 5
  social, 75, 84, 161–2
  Street's definition of, 5n9, 116n66
correspondence theory, 31–3, 53–9
crossword puzzles, example of, 179n11
Crusoe, Robinson, 73–4, 81–2, 93, 108, 124–5, 165n18

Davidson, Donald, 197–204, 212, 221
deliberative perspective, *see* standpoints
Del Noce, Augusto, 20–1, 20n46
democracy, 9, 19, 171–2, 176n62, 180, 216, 225
Descartes, René, 34–40, 58–9, 141–2, 165n18, 198

desires, 45–6, 49–50, 73, 79, 83, 129, 134–5, 145n67, 147, 150n81, 151–2, 155, 171–2
dialogue
  external vs. internal, 85–7
  as model for reasoning, *see* Internal Dialogue Procedure
disagreement, 6, 8, 31, 160, 172, 186–8, 189–90, 201–4, 206–9, 225–6
disvalue (*disvalore*), 45n44, 217
dreams, 58–9, 60n78
dualism, 37–40, 119, 130, 143–6, 156, 198
  see also transcendence
duty
  to do one's duty, 150n81, 153–4
  to think, 51, 51n58, 84n56

education, 158–90
  moral function of, 76, 89, 95–6, 156–7, 162–72, 183–90
  and the state, 95–6, 113–4, 185–8
egoism, 66, 76
empirical reality, existence of, 3–4, 33, 35, 45–6, 64, 235–6
enemies, internal vs. external, 76–7, 76n36, 84
equality, 6–10, 140–1, 160, 170, 184, 208, 235–7
Equality Principle, 203–4, 208, 219–26
error, 30–1, 45–6, 120–1, 192, 196n9, 218–9, 219n51, 230, 234
ethical state, 92–116
  GG's conception of, 93–6, 104–8, 114–5
  Hegel's conception of, 96–103
Etica, GG's, 19n42
evil, 45, 45n44, 76, 218–20, 234
Evola, Julius, 48–9
external alter-ego, 85–90

facts
  as abstractions in GG's theory, 41–2, 45, 48–9, 48n52, 97, 153
  and values, distinction between, 84n56, 116, 163–4
  moral, 3–5, 10, 203, 217, 236–7
Falsity Objection, 173–6
Faith
  in Christian philosophy, 33–4, 59

in thinking, 51–2, 60, 122, 203, 219
in truth, 51–2, *see also* affirmation
falsificationism, analogy between Internal Dialogue Procedure and, 211–3
family, 102–8, 112
Fascism
  GG's relation to, 13–22, 17n33, 25, 104n38, 111, 240
  other authors' responses to, 17–22, 93n3, 109, 111n59, 166–7, 231–2
'Fascist' as pejorative term, 19n41
formalism
  Kant's, 142, 144n63, 145, 145n63, 153–6
  actual idealism and, 159–62, 186–90, 218–23
freedom, 19, 26, 44, 97–8, 100, 108, 110, 135n37, 139–41, 145–6, 155, 160, 164–6, 169–72, 172n36, 180, 189, 225, 240
  positive and negative, 170, 183n56
  and thinking, 49, 71, 114, 141, 168–9, 175–85, 187

Gentile, Giovanni, *passim*
God, 5, 33–4, 50, 54, 59, 79, 82, 82n53, 88n65, 99–102, 109, 141, 184
Golden Rule, 146n67, 204, 221n59, 222
goodness, 6–9, 44–5, 45n44, 51n58, 66, 68n16, 76n36, 90, 90n69, 153–5, 163–4, 180, 196n10, 211, 22n58, 215–9, 219n52
Gowans, Christopher, 161
Gregor, A. James, 17n34, 22n54, 111n59, 166, 185–6

Haddock, Bruce, 111
Harris, H.S. 18–9, 19n
  interpretation of GG 48–48n, 52n, 66n, 73n, 77n, 89n, 93n, 107n, 108, 109n, 122n, 124n, 166n, 183n, 184, 184n
  reviews of 20n, 22–3
Hegel, G.W.F., 23n56, 71n24, 96–109, 112, 145n64, 156, 163, 167, 170, 207n34, 234
  GG's relation to, 17, 23n56, 92, 93n2, 105–9, 145, 145n64, 152, 155, 170
Heraclitus, 31

heroic examples in practical reasoning, 196n10
Hill Jr., Thomas E., 207–8, 207n34
Hobbes, Thomas
  on Descartes, 37–8
  as example of hypothetical interlocutor, 165–6
  GG's interpretation of, 68n15
Holmes, Roger W., 30n3, 47–8, 52, 65n3–4, 66–7, 70n20, 73n29, 235
human nature, 71, 75, 77–8, 77n41, 106, 164, 225
Hume, David, 3, 70n20

Idealisation Objection, 136–7
identity
  practical, 66–79, 81–3, 88–90, 92, 98–103, 106–8, 109n54, 147–9, 158n1, 160–4, 171, 174–9, 196n10, 220, 226, 237
  national, 14, 72n27, 81, 89, 95, 100–1, 103, 115, 174–6, 178–9, 186–8, 226
IDP, *see* Internal Dialogue Procedure
imagination, 49–50, 65n4, 69, 71–3, 108, 125–7, 130, 133n31, 195–7
immanence, 30–52, 102, 109, 120–21, 125, 152, 156, 208, 217–8, 238
impartial spectator, 124, 128
individual, status of the, 40, 65n3, 71–9, 77n41, 87–9, 96–8
Indoctrination Objection, 172–81
  replies to, 181–4
innate ideas, 59
intention vs. action, 44–6
Internal Dialogue Procedure
  design of, 123–31, 131n27, 133n31, 140–2, 149–57, 188–90, 192–226
  as means to objectivity, 125–30, 135, 142, 150–52, 156, 129–95, 202–5, 211–7, 223–4
  selection of interlocutors for, 80–90, 194–7, 222–3
  'stacking', 213–7
internal society
  emergence of in GG's work, 73–5, 74n34, 123–215
  see also Internal Dialogue Procedure
inter-subjectivity, 5, 122, 126, 160, 193, 193n3, 198–201, 213–5
Italian Social Republic, 14

'I think' 37, 39–40, 43

James/Crispin example, *see* names, significance of
Jesus Christ, 196n10
Jigsaw Analogy, 61–2

Kant, Immanuel
  on autonomy, 132, 135n37, 144–9, 145n65, 152–3
  categorical imperative, *see* categorical imperative
  GG's relation to, 84, 155–6, 232–3
  residual dualism of, 40, 42, 135–6, 135n37, 142–3, 232–3
Kantian constructivism, *see* constructivism
Kingdom of Ends Formula, 142–4
  see also categorical imperative
knowledge, 29–40, 43–6, 52–62
Korsgaard, Christine M., 3, 5, 9–10, 10n21, 45n45, 97, 133, 142, 145n66, 147–9, 151–2, 156, 160–2, 218n50
Künne, Wolfgang, 55

language
  Davidson on, 199–201
  in GG's theory, 69n17, 71–4, 74n34, 163, 173–9, 201–2
Lenman, James, 3, 8n17
liberalism, 9, 13n24, 98, 172, 180, 187, 236–7
liberty, *see* freedom
Linguistic Objection, 136–7
Locke, John, 206
Logical Priority Justification, 39–40, 64
logos, 31–3, 42, 46, 64n2, 103, 106, 127–9, 204
love, 76, 78–9, 78n44, 106–7, 106n47, 169–70, 170n31, 221–2
Louis XIV of France, 99–100
Lyttelton, Adrian, 182

man, nature of, *see* human nature
Manipulation Objection, 176–9, 181–2
Marcuse, Herbert, 17, 144
master/slave dialectic, 170
moral reality, 67–9, 120n1
Moss, M.E., 113–4
Mussolini, Benito, 14–5, 17n35, 77n42, 104n38, 112–3, 166, 232

mysticism, 32, 32n8–10, 53, 63

names, significance of, 148–9
nation, concept of, 76n35, 95, 107
  see also identity, national
National Socialism, 14, 93
natural law theory, 96–8, 146
Nazism, *see* National Socialism
noumenon, *see* Kant, residual dualism of

objectivity
  means of achieving, 4–5, 8–10, 125–31, 135 *see also* Internal Dialogue Procedure as means to objectivity
  not perfectly attainable, 5, 10, 12, 51, 74, 116, 125–7 *see also* transcendence
O'Neill, Onora, 4n7, 5, 118, 137–42
original position, *see* Rawls, John

Parfit, Derek, 24
particularity vs. universality, 41–4, 49–51, 73–85, 115, 125–8, 150, 155–6, 161, 192, 192n1, 208–10
Particularity Objection, 80–4, 126
Partito Nazionale Fascista, *see* Fascism
Passé Castaway example, 81
perfection
  absolute, 32–3
  Aristotelian vs. Gentilean conceptions of, 155
personalism, 69–70
Peters, Rik, 19n40, 52n57, 111, 111n60
phenomenon, 32, 42–3, 122–3, 135n37, 146, 155–6
phenomenology
  of education, GG's, 162–6
  and actual idealism, 1, 11, 30
philosophy
  GG. on man as 'philosophical animal', 225
  universality of, 51n57
Plato, 21n51, 31–3, 66, 98–9, 129, 184n59, 202
pluralism, 7–8, 78–9, 180–1, 187–8, 237
police states, 109, 179
'positivity' of actual idealism, 39–40, 58–62
Practical Application Objection, 134, 136

propaganda, 89, 113–4, 167, 179
Protagoras, 67

Rawls, John, 2–11, 24, 24n59, 85n57, 134, 150n80, 205–6, 207n32, 214n46, 215–6, 236–7, 237n8
realism, 42, 48, 138n44, 155, 235–6
  moral, 3–4, 9–12, 26, 116, 148, 151, 206, 238
  'simple-minded', Lenman's example of, 3, 8n17
reasons
  authority of, 8n17, 26, 68, 74–5, 79–80, 84–91, 108–9, 114, 121, 124, 127, 136, 139–41, 144, 147, 159–62, 181, 189, 209–10, 216, 231, 234
  and the heart, 128–30
Recognition Problem, 86–9
Rescher, Nicholas, 52
reflective equilibrium, 7, 84n57, 210n41, 214n46
reflectivity, 211
Regress Problem, 86, 89
relativism, 4, 4n7, 181n53, 201, 232
religion, 22, 32n10, 33, 71, 102, 106
  analogy with pupil-teacher relationship, 169–70, 183–4
  Catholicism, 33–4, 82n53, 99n27, 115n65, 183–4
  GG's, 82n53, 99n27
  'Love thy neighbour', see Golden Rule
Rickman, H.P., 22–3
  see also Harris, H.S., reviews of
rights, 93n1, 97, 220, 237
Roberts, Peri, 137
Romano, Sergio, 16
Ronzoni, Miriam, 4–5
Rousseau, Jean-Jacques, 164–5

Salò Republic, see Italian Social Republic
Sasso, Gennaro, 110–2, 232
Scanlon, T.M., 210n41, 212
scepticism, 4, 30, 58–61
Scholasticism, 33–4, 33n12, 38
  see also, Aquinas, Thomas
sense
  individual, limits of, 110n
  experience, 69
  and intellect, 128, 129

shopping lists example, 196n9
social contract, see agreement
socius, 71–91, 92, 96, 103, 110n57, 114–6, 119–31, 197–217, 131–2
  see also Internal Dialogue Procedure, selection of interlocutors for
solipsism, 12, 25–6, 64–7, 71–2
Solipsist Objection, 64–7
soulcraft, 185, 185n
Spaventa, Bertrando, 35
Spinoza, Benedict de, 35–6, 99
spirit, GG's conception of, 32n10, 44, 46n48, 65–7, 67n14, 71–2
stacking, see Internal Dialogue Procedure
standpoints, 5n9, 8, 8n18, 69, 100, 111, 115–6, 122, 135, 142, 146, 146n69, 152, 159–60, 192n1, 193n2, 213, 216–7, 221, 224, 231, 240
state, political vs. spiritual conceptions of, 94–5, 100–3, 108–9, 114, 185–6
statolatry, 109, 109n54
Street, Sharon, see constructivism, Street's definition of

teacher/pupil relationship, 158, 158n1, 160–72, 173–84, 188
thing-in-itself, see noumenon
thinking
  inescapability of, 12, 34–40
  prior to reason, 127
  pure act of, 12, 22, 35–6, 26n24
  self-correcting nature of, 81–2, 123, 126–7
thought, as distinct from thinking, 34–7
time, 36–7, 40–2
Torturer example, 47–9, 141
totalitarianism, 14–5, 17, 20n44, 93, 93n3, 95–6, 102, 104–5, 108, 112, 162n7, 172n35–36, 229n1, 238
transcendence, absurdity of, 12, 30–5, 43–4
transcendental society, see internal society
triangulation, 198–203
truth, 43–62
  and belief, see affirmation

relation to will, 44–52
   and value, 52–8
Turi, Gabriele, 15n29, 17n35, 21

universality, *see* particularity and universality
universal will, 73–85, 73n34, 88, 102, 110, 112, 115, 152
unknown, the, 58–62
utilitarianism, 106, 106n

value, *see* facts and values, distinction between
verificationism, analogy between Internal Dialogue Procedure and, 209–11
violinist example, 171

Walker, Ralph, 53, 55n70
war, GG's view of, 104n34, 107–8
will
   good, 45n44, 76n36, 146n64
   role in GG's theory, 35–6, 44–50
   see also abstract/concrete distinction and the will; truth, relation to the will

Yafee, Gideon, 177-179